Jerry

This book provides an
excellent insight into productivity
improvement management.

D Hahn 8/22

Productivity, People, & Profits

Productivity, People, & Profits

JOEL E. ROSS

Professor of Management
Florida State University

RESTON PUBLISHING COMPANY
A Prentice-Hall Company
Reston, Virginia 22090

ISBN: C 0-8359-5626-1
ISBN: P 0-8359-5625-3

Copyright © 1981 by Reston Publishing Company
A Prentice-Hall Company
Reston, Virginia 22090

10 9 8 7 6 5 4 3 2 1

PRINTED IN THE UNITED STATES OF AMERICA

Contents

CHAPTER 2
Productivity Means Results   21

CHAPTER 3
Measuring Productivity   42

CHAPTER 8
Supervisory Skills: Communication & Appraisal   167

CHAPTER 9
Your Leadership Style   193

CHAPTER 10
Problem Definition & Analysis   214

CHAPTER 11
Tools for Improving Work Methods   237

CHAPTER 12
Decision Making   273

Preface

The need to improve productivity in organizations today is evident to everyone; national leaders, chief executives, and individual managers alike. Better management practice at all levels in the organization is the method increasingly accepted as the single best way to improve productivity. The means by which individual managers can achieve productivity through improved management are not as obvious.

As a management practitioner, author, teacher, and consultant, my growing concern is that the way we teach management is correlated with the shortcomings of current management practices. This book discusses solutions to three of these basic shortcomings.

First, there is the growing proliferation of topics, techniques, and theories. These range from time management to decision making, from communications to basic supervision, from managing conflict to leadership styles, and so on. All of these topics are important but there has been no integrating framework that relates one topic to the other and to the whole. Hence it is difficult for a manager or a student of management to build a logical, integrated body of knowledge and practice. I think this book helps to deal with that shortcoming by integrating the most important and basic management techniques around a system of *results management* with a central theme of *productivity*.

A second problem has been the lack of an applied approach that tells the user how this or that topic can be applied on the job. I have tried to guide the reader so the idea or technique can be put to work for immediate improvement in productivity on the job.

A third and final shortcoming in teaching applied management has been that they stop short of converting the idea into action. After you have learned "decision making" what do you then do with the decision? After you have learned "management by objectives" what do you do with your objective, once established? I have tried to *operationalize* the topics of this book by relating them to the necessary implementing procedure of *action planning* and the related disciplines of problem solving and decision making. Finally, all the topics of management are related to the central theme of productivity.

My thanks go to the thousands of university students who increasingly demand reality in management education and to the thousands of supervisors and managers in seminars who have found these ideas and methods to be valuable in improving their own productivity.

Joel Ross

PRODUCTIVITY IN THE UNITED STATES

CHAPTER 1

"The United States is the fastest "underdeveloping" country in the world."

Arthur Laffler, *Economist*

Just a few years ago the economic power of the United States was unquestioned around the globe. Our technology was the world's best, and our dollar was as "good as gold." The productivity of the American worker was unsurpassed because the workforce reflected our historical Protestant work ethic. Any product stamped MADE IN USA had unqualified acceptance anywhere. All this has changed.

DECLINE OF PRODUCTIVITY

Rank of U.S. among Industrialized Nations

Why Reverse the Trend?

NATIONAL LEVEL

COMPANY LEVEL

INDIVIDUAL LEVEL

RANK OF U.S. AMONG INDUSTRALIZED NATIONS

By almost any measure the productivity record in the United States can only be described as dismal. Although America remains slightly ahead in absolute output per worker, the gap is closing rapidly as the rest of the industrial world accelerates productivity growth. The Japanese automobile worker makes 50 cars per year compared with 25 for the U.S. worker; the steelworker produces 421 tons in Japan to 250 in the United States.

The capital-intensive United States, home of industrial engineering and the assembly line, production planning and the computer, has recently witnessed the first significant productivity decline in output per working hour in three decades. Japan and the leading nations of Western Europe bettered us in rate of growth as we fell to ninth place—*last place* among industrial nations of the world. (See Table 1–1.)[1] As we entered the decade of the 1980s, our relative lack of growth has become a critical national issue.

TABLE 1–1. Annual productivity growth
among industrialized nations

(1960–78) Output/Manhour	Percent
JAPAN	8.8
SWEDEN	6.0
FRANCE	5.7
W. GERMANY	5.5
CANADA	4.0
UNITED KINGDOM	3.4
UNITED STATES	2.5

Source: Bureau of Labor Statistics

REVERSING THE TREND

Reversing this trend is of substantial concern to each of us. At the *national* level it is the best way to stop inflation and improve real income. Indeed, economic growth and possibly our national survival may depend on reversing this trend. At the *company* level it is the

[1] The decline in productivity would be significantly worse if it were not for the *gains* in agriculture. In 1950 Americans spent 22.2 percent of their disposable personal income for food. This has gone down to 16.6 percent.

only way to reduce costs and improve profits. Increased productivity allows organizations to give customers more product value per dollar; compete more effectively in the marketplace; utilize resources more effectively; and increase sales volume, profits, and return on investment. And for the *individual manager,* improving personal productivity is central to his or her job. Finally, for all of us, *worker and manager* alike, productive work is rewarding work, both psychologically and financially. It provides more personal satisfaction while at the same time giving us more opportunity for personal growth and advancement.

CONSEQUENCES OF THE DECLINE
National Economy
Standard of Living
Inflation

The reaction to the decline in American productivity is typified by this comment from the president of Chase Manhattan Bank: "My fear is that if this trend continues, our standard of living will steadily sink and our nation will become a second-rate industrial power before this century ends." Although the productivity decline pervades all aspects of our lives, the three areas of most concern are the national economy, our standard of living, and the continuing inflation that we are experiencing.

THE NATIONAL ECONOMY

The impact on the national economy was summarized by the Joint Economic Committee of the U.S. Congress when it concluded: "Productivity is the economic linchpin of the 1980s." The significance of this conclusion can be better appreciated by recalling that a linchpin is the pin that goes through the end of an axle outside the wheel to keep the wheel from coming off. Aside from the internal consequence of the problem, our external situation is adversely affected, as is evidenced by the declining trade balance. This deterioration can be traced directly to the reduction of our relative standing among industrialized nations with respect to productivity growth.

THE STANDARD OF LIVING

The impact on our standard of living is both personal and dramatic. The average American household is now earning about $4,000 *less* than it would have earned had our nation maintained its 3 percent productivity growth of the 1950s and 1960s. We now have a *real income gap*—the difference between what we are earning and what we could earn. In 1980, Federal Reserve Chairman Paul Volcker summarized the problem: "When productivity is declining, there isn't any way you can increase your standard of living in the nation as a whole just by asking for higher wages or prices."

INFLATION

Double-digit inflation, accompanied by the debilitating fall of the dollar, can be traced directly to the slow growth in productivity. This *decline* in the rate of growth, accompanied by *increases* in wages and compensation, gives us the "productivity gap," a reliable measure of inflation pressures. Table 1-2 shows the dramatic decline of the rate of productivity growth for selected periods in the United States. When these figures are matched with wage increases for the same period, we get the approximate inflation rate. Although this is certainly not the whole story of inflation, it is a significant part of the explanation. The arithmetic is fairly simple and the consequences are evident.[2] The decline in manufacturing productivity for selected periods is shown in Table 1-3. The amount of decline in the rate of change in the United States is exceeded only by Canada.

TABLE 1–2. Productivity growth in the United States
Selected periods (1950–1979)

Period	Percent
1950–60	2.6%
1965–73	2.0%
1973–78	1.0%
1979	−0.9%

Source: Bureau of Labor Statistics

[2]Nobel Laureate economist Milton Friedman says that higher wages and the price-wage spiral are an *effect* of inflation, not a *cause*. See *Free to Choose: A Personal Statement,* by Milton and Rose Friedman (New York: Harcourt Brace Jovanovich, Inc., 1980).

TABLE 1–3. Manufacturing productivity in seven
countries: Average annual rates of change

	Output per hour	
Country	1977–78	1978–79
United States	.5	1.5
Canada	4.7	.8
Japan	7.9	8.3
France	4.9	5.4
Germany	3.4	5.2
Italy	3.0	8.7
United Kingdom	1.2	2.2

Source: Bureau of Labor Statistics

Figure 1-1 shows the accelerating "spread" among productivity,
compensation, and unit labor costs. This is nowhere more evident
than in the steel industry. Between 1973 and 1979, steel's total hourly
labor costs shot up from $7.68 to $16.80, a 119 percent boost, while
the consumer price index rose 63 percent. Yet in 1980, the industry
granted the United Steel Workers a three-year pact that raises labor
costs by 34.5 percent, assuming a 10 percent annual inflation rate.
These wages and the increases have historically been greater than
productivity increases in the industry. It appears that some costs of
employing union labor have become uncontrollable.

WHY HAS PRODUCTIVITY DECLINED?

Management Inattention
Government Regulations
Capital Investment
SAVINGS RATE
SOCIAL CHANGES
SERVICE ECONOMY
Research and Development
Inflation
Energy Cost
Lack of Programs
Lack of Goals
REASONS IN THE NATIONAL ECONOMY

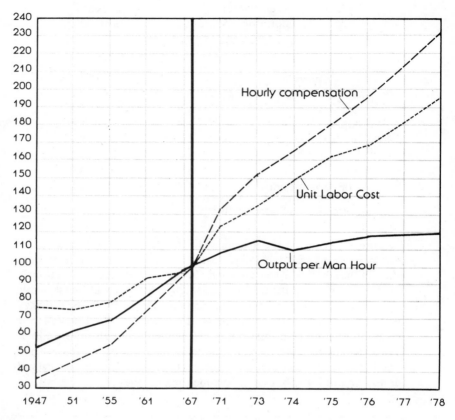

Figure 1–1. *Output per man hour; hourly compensation; and unit labor cost trends, private economy, 1947–1978 (1967 = 100). (* Basic data: *U.S. Bureau of Labor Statistics)*

DECLINING PRODUCTIVITY: REASONS IN THE NATIONAL ECONOMY

What's the problem? Why the decline? Whatever your personal view, you can probably find support for your opinion. Hearings have been held, grants awarded, and research conducted. Commentators have commented and experts have expounded. On any given day, the business press will contain dozens of references to the causes and cures of the productivity decline. The general public has heard so frequently that productivity growth is the main cause of the country's relative economic decline that they have started to take the subject seriously.

Interest and pressure groups continue to suggest remedies that are self-serving and promise to do most to feather their own nests. Wall Street argues for the elimination of "phantom" capital gains and the "double tax" on dividends, arguing that this cure will provide more risk capital to industry. Corporations lobby for relaxed government regulations so that more funds can be diverted to capital investment and plant improvement. Unions maintain that corporations export work to foreign countries with low labor rates rather than modernize the U.S. plant. And so it goes. Everyone has a pet reason.

Despite the debate over the several causes that are advanced for the productivity decline, the underlying reasons are still somewhat puzzling. The answer seems to lie in a number of influences that combine to explain the pattern of retardation. Some of these are examined below.

MANAGEMENT INATTENTION

C. Jackson Grayson, founder of the Houston-based American Productivity Center, believes that one of the biggest impediments to productivity gains lies in the corporate boardroom. He says that management has neglected productivity in favor of concentrating on such things as market share, mergers, acquisitions, and so on. They've tried to play the earnings game while ignoring the supply side of their operations. A related managerial shortcoming is suggested by Jerome Rosow, president of the Work in America Institute. He believes that the traditional "authoritarian fix" and military type of hierarchical organization structure of American industry gets in the way of worker productivity. He explains, "We really have two societies. We have a world of work in the fine institutions like IBM, General Foods, and Exxon. And then we have a world of companies that are on the margin, that meet their economic survival by paying the lowest that they can and giving the least benefits."

Productivity is somewhat like the weather; many managers are talking about it but few are doing anything. If you asked the question: "Who's in charge of productivity?" the typical answer in most firms would be, "Nobody!"

Some industries are particularly lax in efficiency. This appears to be higher than average in service industries, which make up about 50 percent of our gross national product. When you combine this with the "service" or overhead departments of other types of business you have an enormous sector that is not being gauged by any value-added measure. A senior executive in a large insurance company says, "The service industries cannot answer some of the basic questions relating to their operations. We spent three years installing our information system but we can't tell how much it cost since we don't have a cost accounting system to tell us. However, as slow as the insurance industry is, it appears that the banking industry is still behind us."

Government agencies and industries regulated by the government come in for their share of criticism. Twenty years ago the railroads guaranteed delivery of a head of lettuce from California to the East in six days. Today it takes eleven days. It is estimated that a rail car is moving under load only 7 percent of the time. Productivity varies by as much as 1,000 percent in some government operations.

During the most recent period for which data are available, productivity in Japan increased at five times the rate of the United States. Japanese government expenditures on productivity improvement are over six times the amount spent by the U.S. government, despite the fact that our federal budget is five times larger than Japan's.

GOVERNMENT REGULATIONS

There is no question but that government regulations are responsible for slower productivity growth. Although no accurate measures are available, some estimates suggest that the cost in lost productivity could add up to as much as 2 percent of the gross national product. And how can you put a value on the diversion of executive attention from matters of business to matters concerned with the firm's interaction with government? Some executives say that attention has turned from the concerns of competitors, customers, suppliers, and internal operations to activities that center on outwitting the government bureaucrat. Former Secretary of the Treasury Michael Blumenthal represents perhaps the prevailing view with the comment, "Economic equity rarely comes out of the barrel of a regulatory gun."

It is generally agreed in most industries that new regulations are putting a significant drag on productivity by diverting capital to nonproductive uses, by slowing research and development, and by prohibiting use of efficient production processes. General Motors, for instance, employs about 24,000 people who report to various regulators. Consider the chemical industry, in which nearly one-quarter of capital investment has been diverted to the purchase of pollution abatement and other unproductive assets.

The expenditures by regulatory agencies continue to grow. The net effect of the Environmental Protection Agency (EPA), the Food and Drug Administration (FDA), and the Occupational Safety and Health Administration (OSHA), to name a few, appears to significantly throttle the productive energy of the country. The growth of expenditures on federal regulatory activities alone is illustrated by these figures:

Fiscal Year	$ Millions
1974	2,240
1975	2,683
1976	3,064
1977	3,714
1978	4,543
1979	4,823

It is estimated that the paperwork necessary to meet the requirements of the federal government alone cost the American business community more than $40 billion per year.

CAPITAL INVESTMENT

According to the Council of Economic Advisors, a major reason for the productivity decline is the weakness of business fixed investment over the past several years. In support of this contention, the Council offers statistics to show the decline of capital stock per unit of labor from an annual rate of 3 percent to 1.75 percent.

There is no doubt that capital investment and productivity are directly related. Figure 1-2 demonstrates this graphically and shows the poor record of the United States relative to other nations. And the lack of capital investment is not the whole story. The average age of a U.S. plant is twenty years—eight years older than the equivalent German plant and more than ten years older than the equivalent Japanese facility.

The Declining Savings Rate

Several reasons (e.g., slack in existing capacity, diversion of funds to social services and environment, energy costs, inflation, uncertain climate for risk capital) have been advanced to explain this shortfall in capital investment. Not the least of these reasons is the declining savings rate and hence a lessened availability of savings for investment. While the Japanese rate of savings as a share of after-tax personal income is 25 percent, and West Germany saves at the rate of 17 percent, the U.S. rate has declined from 7.7 percent in 1975 to less than 4 percent in 1980.

Social Changes: "People Don't Want to Work Anymore"

The above comment, like the related one that "young people don't work like we did at their age," is probably the most *popular* explanation for low productivity. No less a person than Arthur Burns, then Chairman of the Board of Governors for the Federal Reserve System, stated, "My own judgment is that we have been undergoing a change

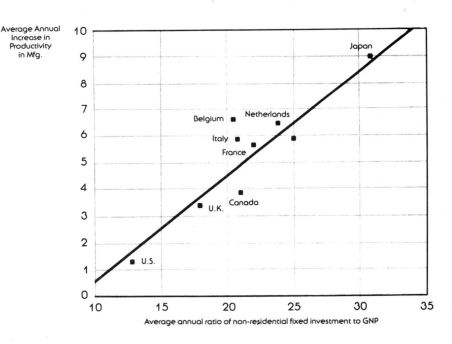

Figure 1-2. The nation with the highest ratio of investment to GNP had the highest rate of productivity growth: investment and productivity in the U.S. and other industrial nations, 1960–1976. (Basic data: U.S. Bureau of Labor Statistics and the Organization for Economic Cooperation and Development)

in our social values and attitudes that has contributed significantly to poorer job performance in recent years."

Many executives think that militant *labor unions* restrict improvement in productivity. No doubt this feeling has some validity. In some companies it appears that an imbalance of power between management and labor has occurred. In some extreme cases unions may have as much to say about day-to-day operations as management. One frustrated executive remarked, "Workers believe that since they come to the plant forty hours per week they can't be expected to work, too!"

Although the significant change in the labor force (i.e., more women, younger workers with less experience and training, shift to service workers) may account for a part of our productivity decline, there is no demonstration or clear evidence that a decline in the work ethic is at fault. Even if it were true, the challenge represents an opportunity for managers everywhere.

Shift to Service Economy

Service industries (e.g., retailing, health, travel, banking, education, insurance, government, etc.) are clearly outpacing manufacturing in growth. Already services employ more than twice as many people as do goods producers. And when you consider the large numbers of workers in "service" jobs (e.g., accounting, data processing, personnel, design, market research) within goods-producing firms, it becomes evident that this sector is enormous.

So the service sector is growing. What does this mean? It is frequently asserted that the opportunity for raising productivity is less for service workers than for production workers. This assertion appears to be doubtful on two counts: First, there is no statistical evidence to support a lesser productivity growth rate in services than in manufacturing. The exception to this may be office work, where costs are expected to double over the next six years. Second, the opportunity for improvement seems to be at least as great in services as in any other sector of the economy. Again, this represents a challenge for the management process and for managers in the service sector.

Some other reasons, not as frequently advanced as those above, may nevertheless demonstrate a causal relationship with the decline of productivity.

DECLINE OF RESEARCH AND DEVELOPMENT

Many studies have suggested that the apparent decline in Yankee ingenuity and innovation, as reflected in R&D expenditures, is a reason for declining productivity. The conclusion of a two-day meeting held by the American Association for the Advancement of Science was that "The United States is losing its competitive edge in technology because American industry is spending less on research and because the federal government withdrew much of its support for industrial research at the ends of the Apollo space program and the Vietnam War."

Other researchers conclude that this relationship between R&D and productivity does exist but the "lag" between expenditures and application payoff is too long to explain the fairly recent precipitous drop in productivity. Moreover, the decline of R&D has been largely in federal government programs for defense and space, whose connections with productivity advances are slight at best. There is also evidence that R&D financed by individual companies is turning more to short-term projects designed to meet regulatory requirements, rather than long-term projects with impact on future productivity.

In summary, lagging R&D is probably not responsible for much of the *recent* retardation in productivity. This is not to say, of course, that continued and expanded R&D efforts should not be undertaken for future productivity and for projects designed to improve output per unit of input rather than adding little or nothing to real output.

INFLATION

Is the productivity decline caused partly by inflation or is it the other way around? We can be certain that *lower* results in productivity combined with *higher* wages can only result in inflation. Perhaps there is a "vicious circle" effect in operation.

To the extent that inflation results in increased *relative* cost of plant and equipment as compared to labor and the relative cost of operating capital, there can be little doubt that these investment *disincentives* are bad news. Inflation and uncertainty about the future also tend to become self-fulfilling; if we think it will happen, it will happen. This expectation is another disincentive for investment. The entire process has a tendency to substitute labor for capital.

ENERGY COST

The rise in energy costs has provided a major shock to the world economy and to each of us as individual investors and consumers. The impact of this price rise on productivity, however, is not clear.

Aside from the inflationary effects noted above, arising from the *cost* of energy, the mere rise in cost alone has little effect on productivity (output/input). The "productivity" of my car's engine is 18 mpg (output/input) and remains at this *ratio* despite the price rise of gasoline. The cost of driving the car may rise, but the productivity of the engine does not change. The relationship is not so simple, however.

Some economists argue that the rise in energy costs does have a negative effect that results from the tendency to economize on energy by substituting the use of other resources, including labor. This substitution of labor for energy causes a reduction in the firm's capital/labor ratio, which in turn results in lower labor productivity. Other researchers say that this effect is minimal, and they cite statistics showing that energy used per unit of output has increased only about 4 percent over the amount normally expected *without* the price rise.

LACK OF PROGRAMS

Few programs have been developed or implemented at the federal level to deal specifically with the problem of productivity decline. Aside from the usual sporadic efforts at reforming monetary and fiscal policy, what can be done?

Federal government efforts could include those policies and/or programs designed to increase incentives for improving labor skills, increasing the quantity and quality of plant, equipment, research and development, and to produce and utilize energy resources efficiently. Second, Washington could make some effort to develop programs targeted for productivity. For example, the United States is the only major industrial power without substantial government sponsorship of *productivity centers.* Compare this with Japan, for example. During the most recent period for which data are available, productivity in Japan increased at five times the rate of the United States. Japanese government expenditures on productivity improvement and productivity centers are over six times the amount spent by the U.S. government, despite the fact that our federal budget is five times larger than Japan's. Many other industrialized nations have government-sponsored productivity centers for the express purpose of conducting research and promoting a variety of productivity programs.

LACK OF GOALS

It is an axiom of management that without a goal, no plan is possible; "If you don't know where you're going, there's no way to get there." What is the goal of productivity improvement in the United States? To "do something" or "improve productivity?" These platitudes are as elusive as the phrases "contain inflation" or "do something about unemployment."

Until goals and objectives are set for productivity and related to other components of the economy, few specific action plans can be devised on a national basis to deal with the problem . . . or to turn the problem into an opportunity. Fortunately, the individual organization, public and private, can more easily set objectives for productivity improvement and get on with the necessary action plans to reach these objectives.

WHY HAS PRODUCTIVITY DECLINED?

Focus on Short-Term Results
Lack of Programs
Crisis Management
Lack of Awareness
Use of Financial Ratios
Single-Factor Focus
Poor Measurement
Lack of Training
REASONS IN THE INDIVIDUAL FIRM

DECLINING PRODUCTIVITY: REASONS IN THE INDIVIDUAL FIRM

The shortcomings just described that relate to the national economy are of concern and interest to the individual company and to its manager. But there is little that we can do as individuals to influence change on a macro or *national basis.* However, on an individual firm basis, there is a great deal that can be done. A beginning can be made by listing the major causes of productivity decline that can be traced to individual firms.

FOCUS ON SHORT-TERM RESULTS

Because the individual manager and his or her managerial style is such a critical variable in influencing productivity in the firm, or department of the firm, it will be instructive to preface the discussion by examining a charge that is frequently leveled at the American approach to management. The charge is that we have "tunnel vision," that we focus on short-term *financial* results at the expense of achieving productivity over the near and long term.

Many experts suggest that the time horizon of the American manager seems to be several years nearer than the horizon of managers who are our competitors in other nations. While the American is concentrating on the "rational" measure of profit for this year, or this quarter's "bottom line," the foreign manager is thinking of corporate longevity and growth over the near and long term. The result of our short-term view is that the future, and the productivity of the corporation, gets lost in the shuffle.

This focus on the immediate bottom-line financial results, the "produce or else" philosophy, can lead to a variety of shenanigans, even "creative bookkeeping" that is detrimental to productivity. Maintenance is delayed, machinery and plant improvement is canceled, R&D is postponed and other decisions made that may make this quarter's profits look better but may decrease or delay productivity over the longer haul.

LACK OF PROGRAMS

Richard Gerstenberg, former chairman of General Motors, says he is astonished at how few major companies "even know what productivity is." In a survey of 6,000 business managers, the American Management Associations found serious worry over productivity, but two-thirds of the respondents in the survey reported that their companies were making no special effort to evaluate the problem. It has been estimated that fewer than one hundred major corporations have in place a comprehensive productivity improvement program.

Most managers will endorse productivity as a good thing but when pressed to describe what they are doing about it will say, "Yes, we have a cost reduction drive . . . or an MBO program . . . a suggestion box . . . cash awards . . . an incentive program . . ." and so on. These techniques are OK but do not comprise a planned program. Indeed, few managers can really define, measure, plan for, or even understand the topic. Too often any effort in this direction has short-run financial improvement as its objective rather than long-run, systematic, or comprehensive programs.

CRISIS MANAGEMENT

On dozens of occasions I have heard supervisors and middle-level managers complain: "I'm too busy fighting fires to think about productivity improvements," or "I'll get around to it as soon as my backlog is worked off." Statements such as these reflect short-run thinking, inability to get organized, and a style of management that concentrates on crisis and drives.

Most managers who complain of fire-fighting or crisis management will admit that the "fire" or "crisis" has happened many times before. Indeed, it seems that the same event occurs time after time, over and over again. Usually the "crisis" returns to the status quo after it is over. Except now, the economy drive that reduced design engineering has resulted in an inferior product, the training budget that was cut has resulted in an inferior sales force, the cost-reduction drive has high-salaried executives typing their own letters.

Peter Drucker's comments are instructive. He says, "In an organization which manages by drives people either neglect their job or get on with the current drive, or silently organize for collective sabotage of the drive in order to get their work done. In either event they become deaf to the cry of 'wolf.' And when the real crisis comes, when all hands should drop everything and pitch in, they treat it as just another case of management-created hysteria. Management by drive is an admission of incompetence."

LACK OF AWARENESS

Most managers and workers do not understand the concept of productivity. Managers believe it to be *more production,* which it is not, or *more profits,* which it is not. More production can result in more productivity *provided* the input per unit of output is less for the increased amount produced. This is not always the case. Nor is productivity necessarily the same as profits. Profit is measured in dollars ($), not units of production. Thus, profits can go up or down depending on such dollar variables as price ($), level of sales ($), or cost of sales ($) as represented by labor, materials, or other inputs. None of these changes alone reflects any change in productivity.

Lacking an understanding and awareness of productivity, many managers take the traditional view that it means speedups, cost cutting, overtime, tighter controls, and the other classical measures that result in running faster and working harder rather than working smarter. Employees, on the other hand, perceive productivity to mean layoffs, pressure, dehumanization, stop-watches, and exploitation, instead of new jobs and higher wages.

USE OF FINANCIAL RATIOS

Since Pacioli discovered double-entry bookkeeping in the fifteenth century the vocabulary of business has been accounting. Now this tradition has come under fire. To quote Drucker again: "The vocabulary of business—especially of accounting—in relation to productivity has become so obsolete as be misleading."

This charge against an old profession may be a bit harsh, but it serves to point out the danger of equating accounting ($) figures with productivity (output/input) figures. As I suggested previously, financial ratios are not productivity ratios.

This shortcoming of financial figures may be more easily understood by considering the remark of one executive in an industry where warehouse cost is a significant item. He says:

One of the toughest jobs our industry had to face was convincing operators of the distinction between cost ratios and performance ratios. Every business runs on the basis of cost ratios. For example, percent of warehouse labor to sales is a common accounting entry. It is sometimes mistakenly used as a productivity ratio. When labor percent to sales goes up, management feels concern. But it may, in fact, be totally unrelated to productivity. Cost ratios tell us whether gross margins cover costs, but they do not tell us whether an operation is as efficient as it could be.

Two of the vital determinants of productivity in the organization are *time* and *knowledge*. Time, our most perishable resource, is not measured by an accounting figure. And nothing is less productive than the idle time of expensive capital equipment or highly paid people. Regarding the most important worker in the organization, the knowledge worker, what is a measure of his or her productivity? The contribution of the design engineer, the systems analyst, the market researcher, or the personnel specialist cannot be equated with a financial ratio.

The way in which financial data and ratios are misleading can be demonstrated by considering the giant American Telephone and Telegraph Company. Reported 1979 net income was $5,674 million ($8.04 per share). However, when these figures are recast or adjusted for general inflation (constant dollars) they become $1,837 million and $2.45 per share.[3] One wonders what the results would have been if the company had not maintained productivity improvement growth during the 1970s at a rate more than three times that of the private domestic economy.

SINGLE-FACTOR FOCUS

In some companies, due to organizational misalignment or the particular functional interests of top executives, one or two resources or functions may be emphasized while others are overlooked. Sales may be emphasized to the detriment of manufacturing; return on investment to the exclusion of cash flow; direct labor to the exclusion of general and administrative expense. Overemphasis of direct labor is particularly common in manufacturing. Such an emphasis tends to hide the tradeoffs between other inputs. Sometimes, mechanization of a production line can cost more than it's worth.

Every business, every organization, needs productivity objectives, measures, and plans for each of its major resources—land, labor, capital, material, and energy—and with respect to *overall* productivity itself. We will see how this is accomplished in a later chapter.

[3]Traditionally, financial statements have been prepared on the basis of historical costs—i.e., the actual number of dollars exchanged at the time each transaction took place. However, it is recognized that general inflation has caused the purchasing power of dollars to decline, the result of which is the presentation of financial statement elements in dollars of varying purchasing power. To eliminate this disparity, such elements may be restated in "constant" dollars, each of which then has equal purchasing power. To reflect the effects of inflation and thus express operating results in dollars of comparable purchasing power, Statement No. 33 of the Financial Accounting Standards Board (FASB), "Financial Reporting and Changing Prices," requires companies to show what the FASB characterizes as "income from continuing operations," as if depreciation of assets had been based on asset amounts expressed in dollars of constant purchasing power.

POOR MEASUREMENT

Productivity improvements, *results and achievements*, are difficult unless measured against some specific, clearly defined target. Unfortunately, most companies rely primarily on financial measures for planning and control. Aside from the shortcomings of financial measures previously mentioned, the popular financial plan and its accompanying *budgets* do not provide the measures that are needed to plan and improve productivity.

Manufacturing has its measures of direct labor, material standards, and overhead. These measures are necessary for financial planning and reporting but do not meet the requirements of a *productivity measurement system*. Outside of manufacturing, the measures are usually contained in a "budget" or "allocation" that is tied to "what they are doing" rather than "what they should get done." Thus, results and performance are not really measured except in financial or accounting terms that have the inherent weakness previously discussed. Budgets usually misdirect because there isn't an adequate measure of output. Hence, meeting the budget frequently becomes the goal.

LACK OF TRAINING

Training and management development is a multibillion-dollar industry. Every possible topic from forklift maintenance to organization development is available and promoted as the answer to improving results. Despite this abundance of topics, very few programs exist with the specific objective of developing *skills* in productivity improvement.

The recent interest in the topic of productivity and the recognition of the need for training have resulted in a variety of training/ development efforts. Most of these take the form of either a "briefing" or a "survey" of what productivity is all about, or they take a traditional training topic (e.g., basic supervision, communications, MBO, team building, problem solving, methods analysis) and relate it to the emerging demand for productivity training. Few, if any, programs synthesize the necessary subjects into an integrated approach designed for *skill* training and development where the bottom line is *productivity improvement. To do that is a primary objective of this book.*

PRODUCTIVITY MEANS RESULTS

"Nothing is more important for the long-run economic welfare of a country than improving productivity."
—Milton Friedman, *Economist*

Management consultant John Patton, who has been studying the subject for thirty years, says, "Declining productivity is not entirely the fault of organized labor ... it is not entirely the fault of our partronizing, interfering government ... it is not entirely the fault of the shifting attitudes of our younger generation. ... The real fault lies squarely at the feet of management, for not seizing the initiative to take remedial action."

THE LEVERAGE OF PRODUCTIVITY IMPROVEMENT
Productivity and the Bottom Line
The 10 Percent Result

PRODUCTIVITY AND THE BOTTOM LINE

If Patton is right, why do so many managers overlook the leverage potential of productivity improvement? It may be because they never get around to estimating the bottom-line impact, or they are unaware of the techniques and methods at their disposal.

The payoff from relatively small increases in productivity can have a disproportionate and positive effect on both operating margins and net profits—the bottom line. Consider that by eliminating one nonproductive hour in a day for each worker you can increase workforce productivity by 20 percent. Gains of up to 25 percent as a result of using employees as an intelligent resource are not uncommon. With payroll costs running on the average at about eight times net profit, the potential is great.

At Texas Instruments, where productivity improvement is a way of life, productivity growth has averaged 15 percent per year for the last ten years. This has resulted in a unit labor output more than three times as great as previously.

In one U.S. Navy West Coast shipyard, serious problems were encountered with too high costs, low productivity, leave abuse, and high turnover. Following an incentive productivity improvement program, productivity improved by 18 percent, overtime and backlog were eliminated.

Consider a hypothetical case of a firm that makes an operating profit of 4 percent—$4 per $100 of sales. In order to increase profits by $1, to $5, it is necessary to increase sales to $125, *a sales increase of 25 percent.* However, if the company could cut costs by only *1 percent,* it would make the same increased profit of $1—*the same as increasing sales by 25 percent.* Now ask yourself which alternative is easier and more logical—*increasing sales by 25 percent or improving productivity by 1 percent?* Most managers continue to think that increased sales is the primary route to the bottom line.

THE 10 PERCENT RESULT

In seminars and conversations with over a thousand supervisors I have asked these questions: "Do you think that you could achieve an improvement of *10 percent* in the cost or output of your job? Are you willing to commit yourself to this improvement?"

In well over 90 percent of the cases I have found that the supervisor or worker involved will reply: "No problem," or "Sure, I can do it," or a similar answer followed by a commitment to achieve the *10 percent* improvement. Many will "sign up" for 20 percent, some for 30 percent.

What would happen if everyone in the company improved productivity by 10 percent? To demonstrate the *leverage* of such improvement, I have taken the financial income statement (P&L) of General Electric for the year 1979. (See Table 2-1.) The bottom line (net earnings after income tax) was 6.3 percent of sales, which is slightly higher than the average of 1,200 companies for that year. (The all-industry composite of 1,200 companies was 5.1 percent, ranging from 1.1 percent for 25 companies in the automotive industry to 10.4 percent for 27 companies in the office equipment and computer industry.)

Column 1 of Table 2-1 shows the actual financial results of General Electric for the full year 1979. Column 2 calculates what the results would be if *operating* costs were reduced by 10 percent while sales remained the same. Column 3 calculates the results if sales were to increase 5 percent while costs were reduced by 5 percent. The results are impressive. In each example both operating margins and net earnings would increase almost *100 percent*!

Abbott Laboratories, the drug firm, is proud of its productivity record. The chairman comments:

One vital statistic measuring Abbott performance never appears as a separate item in our earnings statement. This is the company's continuing outstanding record for increased productivity. Number of employees increased 2 percent but sales in constant dollars per employee increased 10 percent.

Potential gains in the public sector are equally impressive. If, for example, overall productivity could be increased by only 1 percent in the federal government, 29,000 fewer workers would be needed, to say nothing of related savings.

THE CONCEPT OF PRODUCTIVITY

Organization System: Input/Activity/Output

$$\text{Productivity} = \frac{\text{Output}}{\text{Input}}$$

Results = Value Added

Input Focus is Wrong

Activity Focus is Wrong

Output Alone is Wrong

$$\text{Repeat: Productivity} = \frac{\text{Output}}{\text{Input}}$$

TABLE 2-1 General Electric Corporation—1979
Estimated Results of Productivity Improvements

	(1) Actual		(2) Cost down 10%		(3) Sales Up 5% Cost Down 5%	
	$Millions	Percent	$Millions	Percent	$Millions	Percent
SALES	22,460	100	22,460	100	23,583	100
OPERATING COSTS						
Cost of Goods Sold	15,990	71.1	14,391	64.1	15,190	64.4
Selling, G&A Expense	3,716	16.5	3,345	14.9	3,530	14.9
Depreciation, Depletion, Amortization	624	2.8	624	2.8	624	2.6
Total	20,330	90.4	18,360	81.8	19,344	81.9
OPERATING MARGIN	2,130	9.6	4,100	18.2	4,239	18.0
EARNINGS BEFORE TAX¹	2,391	10.6	4,619	20.6	4,758	20.2
Income Tax	(982)		(1,898)		(1,955)	
NET EARNINGS AFTER TAX	1,409	6.3	2,721	12.1	2,803	11.9

	Operating Margin	Net Earnings After Tax
Column (2), where costs are reduced by 10%	Up 92.6%	Up 93.1%
Column (3), where sales are up by 5% and costs are reduced by 5%	Up 99.1%	Up 98.9%

¹Earnings Before Tax includes other income that is not shown in order to reflect only operating profit.

There is now almost universal agreement that the primary job of a manager is to create a whole that is larger that the sum of its parts, an organizational entity that *turns out more than the sum of the resources put into it*. In business this is termed *profit*. In the public sector it may be called *surplus*. All organizations must add some value to the inputs they receive. Likewise, individual managers must add value to the resources that are placed into their custody for processing into outputs.

THE ORGANIZATION SYSTEM

Consider the concept of an organizational *system*, shown in Figure 2-1. The system (organization or company) is comprised of three components:

☐ *Inputs*. These are money, human resources, materials, machines and other fixed assets, technology, and information.

☐ *Activities*. These are the normal functions of design, manufacturing, selling, servicing, etc.

☐ *Output. A result.*

The organization (or subsystem, department, individual) receives inputs, *adds value* to get an output—a result.

Let me repeat. The organization (subsystem, department, individual) receives inputs and adds value to get an output—a result!

The ratio of $\dfrac{OUTPUT}{INPUT}$ *is productivity!*

Let me repeat. The ratio $\dfrac{OUTPUT}{INPUT}$ *is productivity!*

Needless to say, if the ratio $\dfrac{Output}{Input}$ is not a positive number, the organization or department is in trouble, they are not "earning their way."

THE CONCEPT OF ADDED VALUE: RESULTS

Added value, in the case of the entire company, the division, or the profit center, includes all the costs of all the efforts of the organizational entity and the entire reward received for these efforts. It accounts for all the resources the business itself contributes to the final product and the appraisal of the efforts of the business by the market. Hence, in many aspects, the added value can be called a result.

In the example of General Electric (Table 2-1), the company took inputs of 90.4 cents per sales dollar and *added value* of 9.6 cents (operating margin) to get an after-tax net profit of 6.3 cents on each sales dollar. Thus the productivity ratio $\frac{\text{Output}}{\text{Input}}$ was $\frac{\$100}{\$90.4}$. Although the company as a whole achieved this *added value* of 9.6 cents (6.3 cents after tax), *there is no assurance that the departments and individuals within the company achieved the same result.* Therein lies much of the difficulty in improving productivity—the inability of departments and individuals to *define and measure* their contribution, added value, or results.

While it is easy to compute the result of the entire organization with such ratios or measures of $\frac{\text{Output}}{\text{Input}}$ as $\frac{\text{Return}}{\text{Investment}}$ (return on investment) or $\frac{\text{Profit}}{\text{Sales}}$ (profit on sales), it is not easy for the single department or individual to define the *result* of the department or individual effort. A worker may perform to a standard (result) of 2.1 units per man-hour but what is the result, standard, or productivity ratio for market research, computer programming, design engineering, or training?

The difficulty of defining and measuring the productivity ratio $\frac{\text{Output}}{\text{Input}}$, which we shall call *result*, is evident and lies at the bottom of much of the difficulty of measuring and improving productivity. You can't very well plan to improve something you can't measure or define. And yet the overwhelming majority of people in an organization *cannot define the result expected from their job* in terms of value added. They insist on thinking of their job in terms of *input* or *activity* rather than results. Despite the simplicity of the INPUT/ACTIVITY/OUTPUT concept of productivity, many managers continue to focus on input or activity, sometimes with total disregard for results!

INPUT IS THE WRONG FOCUS

People characterized as *input* managers, or employees, are recognizable by their dedication to organization input. They delight in

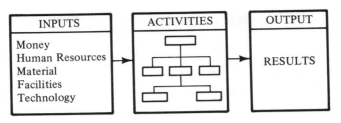

Figure 2–1. The organizational system

collecting voluminous data for variance reports or closely examining the details of your expense account. Their emphasis is on paperwork and the maintenance of records. They are the guardians of company rules and procedures, but are unconcerned about or unaware of any relationship between their own input and results expected. The *means become the end.* They emphasize form and administration (doing things right) rather than process and management (doing the right things).

The input person also confuses *efficiency* with *effectiveness*. Efficiency is working harder, putting out more effort. Effectiveness is getting *results*; improving the $\dfrac{\text{Output}}{\text{Input}}$ ratio. The design department can be very efficient at designing the wrong product, or the sales department can be very efficient at calling on the wrong customers or selling the wrong products. In staff jobs we can measure the output per staff-hour (e.g., people trained or programs written), but these measures do not indicate value of this output—*the result*.

The input type of manager is most frequently found in staff services. Such people have three strikes against them when it comes to improving productivity. First, their output or result can't be defined in terms of customer value because the dissatisfied or disinterested customer is inside the organization and doesn't have to pay. Hence the computer specialist, the budget analyst, the organization planner will argue that the customer, the operating manager, must be convinced of the value of the service, and this requires more resources and a larger budget.

Second, because the output or service of the input-type manager is normally funded by a budget allocation, his or her efforts are misdirected to *activity* rather than results. This is because he is being paid for the effort involved in the activity, not for the performance.

Finally, this manager (or department, or individual) has a tendency to focus on form, not substance; to think procedure, not productivity; in short, to manage "by the book." This tendency is illustrated by a true story concerning British artillery crews during World War II. It was found that the soldiers still jumped to attention and raised their arms in a salute just before their field pieces were fired—all in accordance with the Manual of Arms. It was discovered that the Manual of Arms had not been revised since the days of the horse-drawn caisson, when the soldier was required to hold his horse's reins during firing.

ACTIVITY IS THE WRONG FOCUS

The *activity* manager is perhaps the one most frequently in evidence in the typical company; most of us are guilty of focusing on activity and ignoring results. The accountant focuses on preparation of the cost report rather than on reduction of overhead costs. The sales representative thinks of calling on customers, not on optimizing the profitability of the product/customer mix. The engineer is concerned only with the technical specifications of design without regard to cost, value analysis, or competitive consideration.

Few managers see their responsibilities in terms of results expected. When asked to define their results they will reply with such platitudes as "improve the operations," "supervise the assembly unit," "meet the needs of the customer," "keep maintenance costs down," "stay within the budget," "have the right person at the right place at the right time," and so on.

All of us have witnessed cases in such operations as the retail store or the hospital where results are being impeded by "activity focus." All too frequently the salesperson in the store is bent on complying with company policy and carrying on busywork related to paper procedures rather than getting results through the real job of selling and servicing the customer. In the typical hospital the nurse is bound to her desk by a surfeit of paper, to the detriment of the real job of patient care. And did you ever try to get admitted to the hospital?

Other examples abound. A federal government study on computer usage found substantial waste and misdirection. The data-processing center's concept of productivity was *throughput*—the number of pages of output printed and the operating time of the computer. This view, of course, has little to do with the *effectiveness* of computer usage by the ultimate user—the customer. Moreover, it overlooks the systems design effort, which accounts for about one-half of the costs. Other government examples of activity focus include the police force in which getting the little old lady's cat out of a tree or stopping the noise of a party because the next-door neighbor can't sleep are activities that are scored as high as a crime prevention. And how about government "programs"? The U.S. Employment Service is suspected of *perpetuating* unemployment! Is that the result expected?

It can be said of bureaucracy that focus on activity seems perfectly logical to those who are trapped within it. The activity may seem logical to the individual, but to an outsider it is obviously wasteful.

There is an old story that tells of three bricklayers on a construction job who were asked by their foreman what they were doing. The first replied, "I am making a living." The second bricklayer said simply, "I am laying bricks." The third announced proudly, "I am building the best office building in town." The third bricklayer, of course, was the one who focused on results.[1]

OUTPUT ALONE IS THE WRONG FOCUS

The managers who thinks only of output (not of the $\dfrac{\text{Output}}{\text{Input}}$ ratio) are easy to spot. They are the Marine Corps drill sergeants. They demand results in such terms as: "We've got to get on the ball around here," or "Let's sharpen up the operations," or "Sell more," or "Do a better job." Some managers even shout "Bottom line!" or "What did you do for the 'bottom line' today?" Doing something for the bottom line is a very fine goal, but unless subordinates understand their "piece" of the bottom line in terms of results expected, they become frustrated and demotivated. They may work harder but not smarter. They may run faster—in circles!

$$CONCLUSION: Productivity\ is$$
$$making\ the\ \frac{Output}{Input}\ ratio$$
$$BIGGER!$$

[1] For a different twist on this story, consider the reply of the foreman to the third bricklayer: "You are fired because you don't know the objective. We are building a warehouse."

FIVE WAYS TO IMPROVE PRODUCTIVITY

(Making the Ratio $\frac{O}{I}$ Get Bigger)

Reduce Costs
Manage Growth
Work Smarter
Pare Down
Work Effectively

At this point it should be rather clear that productivity is a *ratio* concept and that improvement means making the ratio bigger—the ratio of the output of goods and services produced divided by the input used to produce them. Hence, the ratio can be made bigger either by increasing the output, reducing the input, or both.

Historically, productivity improvement has focused on technology and capital to reduce the input of *labor* cost of production. Output was generally thought to be subject to improvement by getting more production through the application of industrial engineering techniques such as methods analysis, workflow, and so on.

Both of these approaches are still appropriate, but to a much lesser degree. The movement today is toward better utilization of the potential available through human resources. Each worker can be his or her own industrial engineer—a mini-manager, so to speak. This potential can be tapped by allowing and encouraging people to innovate in one or more of the five ways described below.

REDUCE COSTS

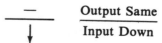

Without a doubt, cost reduction is the traditional and most widely used approach to productivity improvement. This item from an American Standard Company newsletter is typical of this type of program:

In this inflationary environment we have no alternative but to increase our productivity—in other words, to reduce out costs per unit of output. Only by doing so can we maintain the profitability that enables us to provide products for our customers, dividends for our stockholders, and jobs for our employees.

Cost reduction is, of course, a very appropriate route to improving productivity. However, many companies maintain a somewhat outdated "across-the-board" mentality that results in mandates for everyone to "cut expenses by 10 percent." Frequently, staff services are slashed. Training is reduced, and the result is an inefficient salesforce, reduced advertising, loss of market share, reduced R&D. The result is a noncompetitive product; maintenance is delayed and machine downtime is increased, secretarial help is cut, and highly paid executives type their own letters.

Under this "management by drive" approach people are perceived as a direct expense, and the immediate route to cost reduction is seen as cutting this expense as much as possible. Almost always, this policy leads to employee resentment. This in turn leads to resistance, slowdown, and in some cases sabotage. The "rate-buster" is universally resented because everyone, worker and union alike, is concerned about spreading the work. Naturally, management's efforts to cut back are resisted.

This "panic" or "crisis" approach to cost reduction is frequently counterproductive. It may result in trading today's headache for tomorrow's upset stomach.

The chairperson of International Harvester, a disciple of cost cutting, saved $460 million in two years and cut 11,000 jobs from the company payroll. Earnings were boosted by 98 percent. But when he chose to engage the powerful United Auto Workers in his cost-cutting crusade, the result was a strike that idled 36 percent of the workforce. Neither he nor the union would yield on union work rules concerning overtime. The impact was devastating. At last report, market share was down, dealers were unhappy due to parts shortages, capital expansion was delayed, product innovation was put off, earnings were reduced, and the customer base was eroding.

For a more positive approach to cost reduction, consider these examples:

Hughes Aircraft Company is in an industry that spends huge sums on R&D, most frequently to produce technical specifications without adequate consideration of manufacturing costs. The company's present policy is to encourage cost reduction by designing for ease of manufacturing, an approach to productivity that is overlooked by many design engineers.

At Aluminum Company of America (Alcoa), where management approaches productivity with almost a religious fervor, improvements are attributed to a 50/50 split between better workforce utilization and capital investment. In the Mill Products Division, a centralized material-handling group in a major plant was decentralized. Resulting job combinations and practice changes reduced numbers of employees needed by 20 percent, or 55 people. No capital was expended.

MANAGE GROWTH

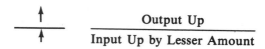

Growth without productivity improvement is FAT!

In this approach to improvement, an investment or *cost addition* is made that will return more than the cost of the investment, thus making the *ratio bigger*. Capital and technological improvements, systems design, training, organization design, and development are among the many ways to manage growth. These are particularly important to organizations whose sales and production are increasing. Once again some examples:

Many firms have achieved excellent results by applying electronics technology in process control, information systems, and related applications. The big movement of computer activity in manufacturing is through materials requirement planning (MRP), the growing component of an overall computerized manufacturing control system. Its purpose is to improve productivity by enabling a shop to react on a weekly or daily basis to changes in the master schedule, bill of materials, and labor costs, or to permit greater productivity levels with existing inputs.

At Burger King, computer readout terminals were installed in kitchens. Incoming orders entered into the computerized cash register out front are flashed on the screen in proper order. The cooks make fewer mistakes and don't waste so much food. Equally important, according to one manager: "The demand at peak hours is so great that if we can produce more we can sell more. We have to do it in a very tight time frame. Nobody cares how many hamburgers we can make between 11:00 P.M. and 6 A.M."

In 1790, a census clerk with a pencil could process about 30 items a minute. *In the 1980 census the computers handled about 45 million items of information in the same time.*

This approach does not necessarily mean additional investment in capital or methods improvement. It can also mean reducing the amount of input per unit of output during growth periods. This may be termed "cost avoidance."

At Corning Glass, energy is a substantial part of product cost. At the company's Glass Works, energy costs were $18 million in 1972. Between 1972 and 1979 volume grew, but so did the price of energy, so if operations had been the same as in 1972 the energy bill would have been $80 million. Instead, the company ended up paying only $56 million for energy.

WORK SMARTER

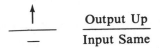

Working smarter means more output from the same input, thus allowing increases in sales or production at the same gross input and lower unit cost. We witness cases of this in attempts to "freeze" employment or budgets while expecting a higher level of activity. This mentality or approach is a short-run stopgap measure; it is hardly a rational course of action to improve productivity over the longer haul.

Better ways of making this ratio *bigger* might be getting more output by reducing manufacturing cost through product design, or getting more production from the same level of raw materials—increasing raw-materials turnover.

In one IBM plant, most employees were trained in methods analysis and improvement. The results were outstanding. Suggestions for improvements accepted by the company went from 500 to 2,600. Three out of four employees turned in suggestions and improvements over $1 million were clearly identified.

At Burger King, "the company that is run by 50,000 teenagers," a Drive-Through Task Force computed that it took 11 seconds to react after a car drove over the bell hose that announced the car's arrival at the drive-in window. The "productivity experts" moved the hose back 10 feet, so that by the time a car had braked, the order taker was waiting to scribble down the customer's order.

PARE DOWN

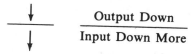

$$\frac{\text{Output Down}}{\text{Input Down More}}$$

Paring down is similar to cost reduction, except that in this case sales or production is off but input should be reduced by a larger amount, thus making *ratio bigger*.

This productivity improvement can frequently be achieved through "sloughing off." Marginal or unproductive facilities, employees, customers, products, or activities are candidates to be "sloughed off." In most organizations, there are many more opportunities than are generally realized. To quote Peter Drucker, "Most plans concern themselves only with the new and additional things that have to be done—new products, new processes, new markets, and so on. But the key to doing something different tomorrow is getting rid of the no-longer-productive, the obsolescent, the obsolete."

In an article entitled "Getting By Without a Tin Cup," Fortune magazine reports that U.S. Steel chairman David M. Roderick has announced that he is prepared to take a hard line on rising labor costs and falling productivity. Just before Christmas, Roderick announced the closing of sixteen plants and other facilities in several states. The action was a calculated move to weed out uneconomic facilities.

WORK EFFECTIVELY

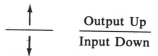

$$\frac{\text{Output Up}}{\text{Input Down}}$$

In this, the most effective of all approaches to productivity improvement, we can get more for less.

Crompton Company is a New York–based manufacturer of corduroy and velveteen in the highly competitive textile industry, where it is not unusual for 10 percent of finished cloth to be defective and sold for 30¢ on the dollar. Crompton knows that the overriding ingredient in this business is people, and through people involvement has managed to hold rejects to under 4 percent while sales are increasing.

Visual Graphics, a Fort Lauderdale company that manufactures high-quality industrial cameras, has been experiencing rapid growth accompanied by new and modified products. The company was able to reduce unit cost in the face of rising raw-material cost by value analysis, product design, and production scheduling.

SUMMARY

The examples given above have been taken mostly from manufacturing firms. Admittedly, it is perhaps easier to identify opportunities in manufacturing than in service organizations. That is the challenge—and the opportunity. The principles of productivity improvement are applicable in any work environment—public or private, manufacturing or service. Moreover, these principles are applicable to each department, manager, and worker regardless of the job or the type of work involved.

SETTING PRODUCTIVITY IMPROVEMENT OBJECTIVES

Objectives Are Action Commitments
Objectives Are Results Expected
How to Express Productivity Improvement Objectives
(Results Expected)

The general inclination to state responsibilities and improvement goals in such vague terms as "generate more business," or "reduce costs," or "do a better job of design" is not acceptable in the *results management* approach to productivity. Objectives are not abstractions. They are the action commitments by which an individual's contribution to the next higher level of goals is measured. As such, they must be capable of being converted into specific targets and specific assignments. They must be *measurable* and *quantifiable* wherever possible.

HOW TO EXPRESS PRODUCTIVITY IMPROVEMENT OBJECTIVES

Objectives can be expressed and results measured in terms of one or more of these basic yardsticks: quantity, quality, time, or dollar value. These are illustrated:

Yardstick	Illustration
Quantity	Set a sales quota of 600 Produce two units per direct labor hour
Quality	Improve the technical specifications Reduce errors
Time	Complete the project in six months Reduce overhead by May 15
Dollar Value	Develop a training program at a cost of $250 per person Achieve a return on investment of 20 percent

A popular style for expressing objectives is illustrated in Table 2-2. It permits any combination of yardsticks illustrated above. Note particularly that each statement should be specific in terms of (1) *results expected*, (2) *time of completion*, and (3) *cost*.

It is essential that objectives be expressed in *specific* terms, not platitudes or generalities. To illustrate this requirement and the improvements that can be achieved by simply thinking *specifics*, see the list following for some actual *before* and *after* statements made by seminar participants who committed themselves to productivity improvements. The *before* statements were written prior to a discussion of setting specific objectives and in response to the question: "What are the results of your job?" The *after* statements clearly reflect an understanding of productivity improvement and a statement of *results expected*—a statement that can be converted into an *action plan*.

Function	Statement of Results Expected	
	Before	After
Service	Keep the customers happy	Reduce justified complaints to zero while maintaining 10 percent annual growth rate in service calls with same number of employees
Operations	Maintain efficient territory operations	Maintain an average response time of 4

TABLE 2-2. Expressing productivity-improvement objectives

Action Verb	Results	Time	$
To complete	redesign of plant layout	by November 30	at a cost not to exceed $1,000.
To reduce	direct labor cost on assembly line #1	by the end of the quarter	to a per unit cost of $2.36.
To introduce	the new product in the western territory	during the next six months	without exceeding the sales budget.
To achieve	an accounts-receivable level of forty-five days	by July 1	and improve cash flow by 10 percent.
To establish	a "chargeback" system in data processing	this fiscal year	in which costs will not exceed commercial rates.

| Function | Statement of Results Expected (cont.) | |
	Before	After
		hours to a call; increase net customer base by selling four service agreements per month
Aircraft Engine Test	Stay within operating budget	Reduce test cost and man-hours per test-run hour by 10 percent from average existing level by December 31
Material Control	Control the equipment	Reduce by 25 percent man-hours required to move and locate equipment; reduce waiting time to zero and complete within existing budget.
Controller	Provide information for management	Reduce interest expense by $250,000; improve cash flow by 10 percent during next fiscal year
Sales	Meet the sales plan	Increase sales of products 4, 16, and 20 by 30 percent in 1980 and market share by same amount while maintaining sales and promotional costs at existing level; retain price parity with competition.
Data Processing	Maintain order-processing system	Improve order processing to reduce administrative time by 80 percent by the end of 1980 at a

Statement of Results Expected (cont.)

Function	Before	After
		development cost of $100,000 (this will provide a cost saving of $1 million per year and reduce customer backlog by ten days)
Raw-Materials Inventory Control	Keep sufficient raw materials to meet production schedule	Improve inventory turn from four to six times per year; reduce average cost of inventory by $600,000 while maintaining the same stockout rate

Many managers are unwilling or reluctant to allow subordinates the freedom to set their own productivity improvement objectives. This unwillingness derives either from inability to delegate or from a fear that employees will "sandbag" or "put chestnuts away" by setting lower standards or goals. This fear is almost universally unjustified.

A. Ray McCord, executive vice president at Texas Instruments, a company with a worldwide reputation for productivity, says: "We have continually built productivity enhancement techniques into our corporate culture. We have found that the employees will set tougher goals for themselves than any manager would dare to set alone. The employees are in the best position to judge their own performance and invariably come up with excellent suggestions for improving productivity."

Pat Donahue, a supervisor in the Microsystems Division of ITT, reduced the labor content of thick film to less than one-fourth the previous amount and built up manufacturing capacity by a factor of five. Frank Tyrrell, also a supervisor in the same division, reduced production stoppages due to parts shortages to zero while improving the performance related to inventory levels, shortages, vendor sources, and parts cost. In both cases the improvements were the result of a team operation.

Sil Ruffolo, manager of receiving at Motorola, designed a double-decking system for storage and improved productivity 100 percent for two years running. The system also provides for moving "hot" items in order to maintain high productivity in the factory.

Tim Burke, warehouse supervisor at Western Electric, designed a relocation system to optimize "walk time" and thereby saved the company $298,000.

Joseph Fabian, design-to-cost engineer in the Avionics Division of Bendix, designed and modified a flow solder machine that increased throughput in the printed circuit assembly area five fold.

MEASURING PRODUCTIVITY

"Without productivity objectives, a business does not have direction. Without productivity measurements, it does not have control."
                          —Peter Drucker

It is a prerequisite to any productivity improvement effort to establish a system of measurements through which an organization can determine its level of productivity and compare it against past performance, the experience of similar firms, and industry average. Measures form the basis upon which strengths and weaknesses can be analyzed and against which action plans for improvement can be made.

Despite the importance of measures, useful techniques for establishing them are not widely available and are frequently misunderstood and misdirected. This chapter is not and cannot be an exhaustive treatment of the topic. Sophisticated approaches involving complicated weighting systems, price deflators, and surrogate measures will be avoided. These are not required for the typical firm, particularly in the early stages of organizing for productivity improvement. The advantages of complexity are few; the advantages

CHAPTER 3

of simplicity are many. The cardinal rule in measurements is *Keep it simple*!

WHY HAVE PRODUCTIVITY MEASURES?

Managing Work

MANAGEMENT PROCESS	INDUSTRY COMPARISON
ESTABLISH GOALS	BASELINE FOR IMPROVEMENT
MAKE DECISIONS	AWARENESS
JUSTIFY EXPENDITURES	TRACK TRENDS
ESTABLISH WORK PRIORITIES	PLANNING TOOL
COMMUNICATE	EARLY WARNING

Managing Workers

RESULTS VS. ACTIVITY	NEW BREED OF EMPLOYEE
DELEGATION	KNOWLEDGE WORKER

RECOGNITION AND COMPENSATION

Managing Yourself

FOCUS ON OBJECTIVES

80/20 RULE

ASSIGN PRIORITIES TO WORK

The reasons for having productivity measures can be summarized simply: *They make possible better management—of work, of workers, of yourself.* The job of a manager is to *make work productive* and *to make workers achieve.* Additionally, you must manage yourself. The three dimensions of this management triad are shown in Figure 3-1. The central idea is to achieve better productivity through *results management.* In order to practice better management, measures of results—*of productivity*— are necessary.

MANAGING WORK

□ The *management process* is facilitated. Planning, organizing, and controlling are difficult to practice without targets, goals, and measures.

□ Measures allow the *establishment of goals.* Without a measurement system, goals become broad generalities or platitudes.

□ *Making decisions*, making a rational choice among alternatives to achieve an objective, cannot be practiced without some target by which to weigh alternative courses of action.

□ Measures of productivity (e.g., return on investment) provide a means to *justify projects and expenditures* and to allocate limited funds and resources among competing uses.

□ *Priorities can be established for work* according to those actions and projects that have higher productivity payoffs.

□ *Communication* and dialogue between departments, managers, and between superiors and subordinates is improved when there is mutual agreement on specifics such as, "Reduce reject rate to 2 percent," rather than, "Let's do a better job on rejects."

□ *Competitive* action and industry comparison can be done when there are some yardsticks against which you can compare your record.

□ *Improvement is promoted* when there is a baseline, a benchmark, a beginning point from which actions to improve can begin.

□ *Awareness* is achieved through a measuring system. The mere fact that productivity is being measured brings an awareness and interest to all concerned.

□ *Trends can be tracked* and comparisons can be made. Trends should be measured over time, against management targets, and against the competition.

□ Measures provide a *planning tool.* Plans become generalities unless there is a yardstick from which to begin and another to provide a target. A plan allows you to determine where you are and where you want to go.

□ Measures that are tracked and controlled through performance evaluation provide an *early warning device* that will encourage the avoidance of variance.

MANAGING WORKERS

□ *Awareness of results vs. activity* (see discussion in Chapter 2) is essential if we are to avoid the activity focus that is so prevalent. It is important to divert attention from job descriptions, or "What are you doing?", to results expected, or "What are you going to get done?"

□ Measures facilitate *delegation*, as well as effective means of supervision and development of subordinates. It's difficult to delegate an activity or generality such as "I'm holding you responsible for maintenance costs." But a result that is stated in specific

Figure 3–1. The management triad

terms and is well understood enhances the delegative process. It is better in this case to delegate by asking, "Are we agreed that you can maintain line #1 at one labor-hour per one hundred machine-hours with no increases in downtime?"

☐ We are told that there is a *new breed of employee* in America, one who wants involvement, participation, recognition, and a source of achievement in the job. If this is true (and it is), it becomes important to involve employees, to let them participate in goal setting and improvement techniques.

☐ The *service/knowledge workers*, a rapidly growing group, are characterized by self-motivation and self-direction. It is difficult to define, let alone measure, productivity for most of them. It is essential, therefore, that they become involved in developing self-imposed targets and results. Because most of them are at least as knowledgeable as their superiors, the traditional carrot and stick accompanied by imposed standards will not work.

☐ *Recognition and compensation* are essential for human productivity. We should evaluate the continuance of a system of recognition and compensation based on standard job descriptions, trait appraisals, and paternalistic management styles against the alternative of results management based on self-imposed measures of output.

MANAGING YOURSELF

☐ Measures of performance and productivity allow you *focus on objectives rather than activities*. Put another way, measures allow you to organize the appropriate activities that will achieve your objective of productivity improvement.

☐ According to the *80/20 rule*, known more formally as Pareto's Law, in any group of activities, a vital few account for the bulk of the benefits. In other words, a few of your activities (10 to 20 percent) are more important in achieving results than all the others combined. Yet many of us spend up to 80 percent of our time trying to achieve some result that accounts for only 20 percent of our "productivity."

☐ An understanding of targets expressed in terms of productivity improvement allows us to practice the 80/20 rule, and to assign *priorities to our work* for greater effectiveness. By assigning priorities to what needs to be done and setting deadlines, we are working smarter, not harder.

A WORD ABOUT ACCOUNTING AND FINANCIAL MEASURES

Measurement systems built around the financial accounting structure constitute a special area of study too complex to discuss within this book; also, the accounting system is not appropriate for the needs of the majority of managers.[1] To be effective, our system of productivity evaluation should be readily understood, simple to implement, easy to administer, and cost-effective. In many organizations the accounting system may not meet these criteria. Moreover, work should be evaluated at the point where the work is done. The further away from this point the evaluation takes place, the more obscure and less meaningful the results become. In short, the accounting system serves the main purpose of historical dollar cost

[1]For a comprehensive treatment of accounting measurement systems, see Hiram S. Davis, *Productivity Accounting* (University of Pennsylvania Press, 1978). Also, you may want to contact the American Productivity Center in Houston, Texas. That organization has developed a sophisticated accounting model and periodically conducts three-day seminars on the topic of measurement. Also, during 1979–1980, the Subcommittee on Productivity of the National Association of Accountants developed a series of position papers that were published in *Management Accounting*, beginning in May 1980.

recording, but is not generally applicable to planning and control of productivity improvement at the front-line level. This is not to say that specific productivity measurement techniques (e.g., price deflation) are not available for integration with proven accounting principles. This would be particularly true at the *total factor* level (see below).

There is also a tendency for accounting figures to focus on direct-labor or blue-collar operations. This is not good because, as we will see, there is a decreasing and sometimes minor portion of expenditures earmarked for this type of expenditure.

In times past, P/E ratios, earnings growth rate, or earnings per share were considered adequate measures of a company's vigor and potential. Today we look for more specific measures. We analyze corporate productivity. It's the bottom line.—First Chicago Bank, The Productivity Bankers

---

MEASURES OF PRODUCTIVITY

Overall Measures

TOTAL FACTOR PRODUCTIVITY

PARTIAL PRODUCTIVITY

Functional Measures
Departmental Measures
Individual Measures
Industry Measures

OVERALL MEASURES

To repeat, productivity is the efficiency with which resources are used to produce goods and services. It is generally expressed as a ratio of outputs to inputs.

Overall measures, those that measure the total output of an organization or one of the major inputs, are usually classified as:

Total Factor Productivity and *Partial Productivity Measures*

Total Factor Productivity

This is the broadest measure of output to input and can be expressed thus:

Total Productivity

$$= \frac{\text{Total Output}}{\text{Total Input}}$$

$$= \frac{\text{Total Output}}{\text{Labor} + \text{Materials} + \text{Energy} + \text{Capital}}$$

It is significant to the state of productivity measurement that the government doesn't even compile total productivity figures, since the measurement problems are immense. A variety of public sources, such as the Bureau of Labor Statistics' *Output per Employee and Output per Employee-Hour*, are available for macro-economic measures. However, these ratios only consider the efficiency of using human resources and thus are partial productivity measures. Total factor productivity is not only concerned with how many units are produced or how many letters are typed but also considers all aspects of producing goods and services. Hence, this measure is concerned with the efficiency of the entire plant or company.

One innovative approach to measuring total factor productivity has been designed by the Texas Hospital Association for measuring the performance of hospitals of varying sizes and complexity. Output *is defined as the* synthesized case, *covering the time from patient admission to discharge.* Inputs comprise labor (*wages, benefits, etc.*) *and* nonlabor *costs. This system of total factor productivity allows the hospital administrator to perform productivity and cost analysis over time and against other hospitals of like size.*

Partial Productivity

Partial productivity measures are established by developing ratios of total output to one or more input categories, and can be expressed thus:

$$\text{Partial Productivity} = \frac{\text{Total Output}}{\text{Partial Input}}$$

$$\text{Labor Productivity} = \frac{\text{Total Output}}{\text{Labor Input}}$$

$$\text{Material Productivity} = \frac{\text{Total Output}}{\text{Material Input}}$$

TABLE 3–1. Measurement Methodology—An Illustration

Automobile Products Company

Products: Alternators and crankshafts
Labor: Electricians and machinists

PRODUCTION DATA

	Period 1			Period 2		
Total Output	Value (V)	Quantity (Q)	Price (P)	Value (V)	Quantity (Q)	Price (P)
Alternators	$50,000	1,000	$ 50	$66,000	1,200	$ 55
Crankshafts	40,000	200	200	33,600	160	210
Total	$90,000			$99,600		
Labor Input						
Electrician	$24,000	4,000	$ 6.00	$30,400	3,800	$ 8.00
Machinist	8,000	1,000	8.00	8,320	800	10.40
Total	$32,000			$38,720		

$$\text{Capital Productivity} = \frac{\text{Total Output}}{\text{Capital Input}}$$

$$\text{Energy Productivity} = \frac{\text{Total Output}}{\text{Energy Input}}$$

TABLE 3–2. Performance Measures—Labor

$$\text{Index A (current data)} = \frac{\left(\dfrac{\text{Sales}}{\text{Man-Hour}}\right)_2}{\left(\dfrac{\text{Sales}}{\text{Man-Hour}}\right)_1} \times 100$$

$$= \frac{\left(\dfrac{99,600}{4,600}\right)_2}{\left(\dfrac{90,000}{5,000}\right)_1} \times 100$$

$$= 120.3 \text{ (A 20.3\% increase)}$$

Inflation effect not removed—sales are expressed in current dollars.
Differences in skill level of labor input not accounted for.

All measures are ratios of $\dfrac{\text{Output}}{\text{Input}}$ *quantities.* Although some ratios can be expressed in quantitative terms such as "units produced per man-hour," others must combine unlike *quantities:* tons and gallons of products; employee-hours; pounds, kwhs, etc. of inputs. To solve this problem, a set of weights representative of the relative importance of the various items can be used to combine unlike quantities. Base-period prices are the recommended weights to be used for total productivity calculation, although other weighting systems such as "man-hour equivalents" can be used. You can determine the relative change in quantities from the base period to the current period by summing the current quantities and multiplying this figure by their respective weights, then dividing the same weights by the sum of the base-period quantities. This calculation is performed separately for the outputs and the inputs. The output/input ratio of these results in the relative change in productivity from the base to the current period.

When base-period prices are used as the weighting system, the product of the current quantity times the base price yields the deflated value (in base-period dollars) of the current quantity. In situations in which relevant quantity and unit-price data are not available (such as capital costs), the same results can be obtained by deflating the current value by an appropriate price index. While individual company or plant-price indexes are preferable, the detailed price indexes published by the Bureau of Labor Statistics can be used. (The

TABLE 3–3. Performance Measures—Labor

$$\textit{Index B} \text{ (financial)} = \frac{\left(\dfrac{\text{Sales}}{\text{Compensation}}\right)_2}{\left(\dfrac{\text{Sales}}{\text{Compensation}}\right)_1} \times 100$$

$$= \frac{\left(\dfrac{99{,}600}{38{,}720}\right)_2}{\left(\dfrac{90{,}000}{32{,}000}\right)_1} \times 100$$

$$= 91.5 \text{ (An 8.5\% decrease)}$$

Important financial measure.

Assumes ratio is self-deflating—but if both sales prices and wage rates move at different rates, ratio is not a valid measure of productivity.

TABLE 3–4. Performance Measures—Labor

$$\textit{Index C} \text{ (unit cost)} = \frac{\text{Standard Cost} - \text{Actual Cost}}{\text{Standard Cost}} \times 100$$

$$= \frac{\left(\dfrac{\text{Labor Cost}}{\text{Units Produced}}\right)_1 - \left(\dfrac{\text{Labor Cost}}{\text{Units Produced}}\right)_2}{\left(\dfrac{\text{Labor Cost}}{\text{Units Produced}}\right)_1} \times 100$$

$$= \frac{\left(\dfrac{\$32,000}{1,200}\right)_1 - \left(\dfrac{\$38,720}{1,360}\right)_2}{\left(\dfrac{\$32,000}{1,200}\right)_1} \times 100$$

$$= \frac{\$26.67/\text{unit} - \$28.47/\text{unit}}{\$26.67/\text{unit}} \times 100$$

$$= -6.8 \text{ (6.8\% above standard)}$$

Distorted by change in output mix.

Distorted by change in labor mix.

Must remove changes in wage rates to use as productivity measure.

problems related to the selection and weighting of these measures are illustrated in Tables 3-1 through 3-6.)

Table 3-1 contains the basic data of an automobile products company with two products—alternators and crankshafts—and two types of labor input—electricians and machinists. The problem is to

TABLE 3–5. Performance Measures—Labor

$$\textit{Index D} \text{ (unweighted)} = \frac{\left(\dfrac{\text{Items Produced}}{\text{Man-Hours Used}}\right)_2}{\left(\dfrac{\text{Items Produced}}{\text{Man-Hours Used}}\right)_1} \times 100$$

$$= \frac{\left(\dfrac{1,360}{4,600}\right)}{\left(\dfrac{1,200}{5,000}\right)} \times 100$$

$$= 123.2 \text{ (A 23.2\% increase)}$$

Fails to account for quality differences in output—alternators different from crankshafts.

Fails to account for quality differences in input—electrician skills are different from machinist skills.

TABLE 3–6. Performance Measures—Labor

$$\text{Index } E \text{ (base-period price weighted)} = \frac{\left(\dfrac{\text{Price-Weighted Output}}{\text{Price-Weighted Input}}\right)_2}{\left(\dfrac{\text{Price-Weighted Output}}{\text{Price-Weighted Input}}\right)_1}$$

$$= \frac{\left(\dfrac{1,200\,(50) + 160\,(200)}{3,800\,(6) + 800\,(8)}\right)}{\left(\dfrac{1,000\,(50) + 200\,(200)}{4,000\,(6) + 1,000\,(8)}\right)} \times 100$$

$$= 112.0 \text{ (A 12.0\% increase)}$$

Adjusts for quality and mix changes in both output and input.

Employs base-period price weighting, which facilitates trend analysis in future periods.

establish a performance measure of productivity for *labor input.* Below is a summary of the measures and indexes in Tables 3-2 through 3-6:

Index	Description	Change
A	Sales/Man-Hour	+20.3
B	Sales/Compensation	− 8.5
C	Unit Cost	− 6.8
D	Items/Man-Hour	+23.2
E	Weighted Output/Weighted Input	+12.0

The best measure of resource utilization is Index E, because it shows how well you used labor.[2]

Labor, broadly defined as the contribution of all organizational members, is usually a pivotal input to measure. This is logical. The labor input is not only a substantial cost of producing output, but it is through the *people* input that we achieve optimum use of the other inputs of capital, material, and energy.

At Texas Instruments, a company that successfully uses productivity measurement principles, a People Effectiveness Index (PEI) *has been devised. It is calculated by dividing net sales billed by total payroll plus payroll-related benefits. This index gives a measurement of productivity improvement, takes into account decreases in prices and*

---

[2]The foregoing discussion of measures and the following examples are adapted, by permission, from material furnished by the American Productivity Center.

increases in wages and benefits, and is easily calculated using two figures that appear in each annual report. Return on assets (ROA) is the conventional performance measurement derived by dividing net after-tax income by the average assets employed during the year. Combining the PEI with the ROA yields the profit-sharing percentage, an excellent measure of over-all productivity growth.

FUNCTIONAL AND DEPARTMENTAL MEASURES

The productivity coordinator of a major electrical manufacturer had this to say: "A company is much more likely to benefit from the detailed monitoring of key departments and activities than from an effort to apply comprehensive, companywide coverage."

Most firms rely largely on budgetary dollar accounting data to analyze their operations, even though these data include the effects of inflation, tax, depreciation, and somewhat arbitrary accounting-cost allocations. Frequently these data are not significantly related to the process under study. It is desirable, therefore, to develop measures that reflect output and input in more realistic terms. Where financial measures are used, it is appropriate to deflate them as described above.

It is impractical here to list the many functions and departments of the typical company and the several measures that could be devised for each. The sampling listed below should be sufficiently detailed to encourage individuals to develop their own functional or departmental measure(s).

Function	Measure
Customer Support	Cost per field technician, cost per warranty callback, service cost per unit shipped
Data Processing	Computer instructions per program, computer operations employees per systems design employees, data processing-expense to company expense, data-processing expense per CPU hour
Quality Assurance	Units returned for warranty repair as a percentage of units shipped

Function	Measure
Design	Drafting time per original drawing, drawing error rate
Materials Storage	Parts picking time, storage per square foot, stockout rate
Order Processing*	Orders processed per employee, sales per order-processing employee
Personnel	Rate of offers accepted, hires per recruiter, department expense to total company expense
Production Control	Inventory turnover rate, items in inventory to items not moved in 12 months, order cycle time, machine utilization, total production to production schedule
Plant Engineering	Drawings produced to number of draftsmen, drawings produced to design engineering staff
Receiving	Volume handled to unloading man-hours, receipts per workday
Shipping	Orders shipped on time, demurrage charges to total nonlabor expense, packing expense to total shipping expenses
Testing	Man-hours per run-hour, test-equipment calibration time, test expense to rework expense

---

*One company computed that it cost $5 to process an order. Since profit on sales was 5 percent and half the orders were under $100, a new pricing policy became evident: "No orders under $75."

INDIVIDUAL MEASURES

Productivity measures, just like standards of performance, offer the individual manager and worker alike guidelines for responsible action, and open the way to increased productivity.

To the fullest extent possible, a measure should always be designed to be specific and quantitative. It should be as clear as *par* on the golf course. A golfer can go out on the course alone or with a foursome, but when the eighteenth hole is reached, the player knows just how good a golfer he or she is and how much improvement is needed. Indeed, the golfer is aware of achievement as the game unfolds—it is not necessary to await the finish.

Perhaps the easiest and most effective way to set standards is to list the responsibilities of the job on a piece of paper, then list the measures (results expected) that would indicate that the job is being performed satisfactorily. For example:

Responsibility	Measure
Maintenance	Maintain an uptime machine rate of 94 percent.
Assembly	Maintain production schedule to actual production at 90 percent.
Accounts Receivable	Maintain an accounts-receivable level at 42 days.
Computer Programming	Write computer programs on time and to customer specifications.

Having established these measures, or standards, the individual can then write a *productivity improvement objective* (results expected). Following the format suggested in Table 2-2, these measures could be written:

My productivity improvement objective is

Action Verb	Results Expected	Time	Cost
To Improve	machine uptime from 94 percent to 97 percent	by June 30	at no increase in manpower or preventive maintenance costs
To Increase	actual production from 90 percent of schedule to 95 percent	in the remainder of year	at the same cost of manufacture and product quality.
To Improve	cash flow by 10 percent and	by May 31	within existing budget, personnel,

	reduce A/R level to 36 days		and equipment.
To Avoid	program and system retrofit expense by debugging program	prior to second system test	in no additional time or reduction in programs written.

A final note on individual measures is the caution to pay careful attention to employee perceptions of their evaluation. If the measure is "laid on" or it is perceived as a formal and critical evaluation, the person may "play it safe" by working on sure things or focusing only on the activities that are being measured.

The obvious answer is to encourage people to develop their own measures. This is especially appropriate in staff or white-collar jobs, in which measuring productivity is so difficult.

Occidental Life Insurance Company in California installed a productivity improvement program which set up flexible working hours, shortened summer workweeks to 4½ days, and let employees establish their own output goals. "Take a person who's been running a family—planning, organizing, and controlling—and it doesn't make sense to suppress those capabilities during the working day," commented the vice president of personnel. "It's hard to measure productivity in an insurance company. That's why it's important to get employees involved in setting their own objectives."

INDUSTRY MEASURES

A productivity measurement is not only the best yardstick for comparing different divisions, units, and profit centers within the same multidivisional company, it also provides an excellent way to compare the management of different companies within the same industry. All businesses have access to pretty much the same resources. The only thing that differentiates one business from another in the same industry is the quality of their management. We measure this quality by the degree to which resources (inputs) are utilized.

Comparing your firm with others in the same industry:

☐ Provides a benchmark so you can gauge your productivity change in relation to the industry.

☐ Provides the trigger for an analysis of different ways to implement productivity change.

☐ Can be an aid in forecasting trends and patterns.

☐ Indicates specific improvement potentials in major productivity inputs.

Availability of Industry Measures

The two major sources of measures for interfirm comparison are the federal government and industry or trade assocations.

The Bureau of Labor Statistics (BLS) has pioneered in industry measures and is known worldwide. A wealth of information is published by BLS, including *News* (monthly), *Handbook of Labor Statistics*, and *Productivity Indexes for Selected Industries*. See also its comprehensive list, *BLS Publications on Productivity and Technology*.

In addition to the BLS effort, the Department of Commerce has been actively promoting productivity measurement at the firm and plant level. Also, the National Science Foundation has accelerated its efforts in this direction.

Trade associations have not been particularly active in promoting interfirm measures. The gap results either from ignorance or a lack of interest. A few progressive associations are inhibited in such efforts by members who fear that the sharing of cost and revenue data may be interpreted by the federal watchdogs as collusion or price fixing.

One Canadian manufacturing association developed industry measures for its members that compared production, sales and administrative costs, productivity and asset utilization. The results were quite useful and striking. The value added per man-hour, as between comparable firms in each industry, varied by 17 to 112 percent as between the median and best performers, and by 75 to 314 percent as between the lowest and best performers.

The National–American Wholesale Grocers' Association developed a warehousing productivity measurement program that compares a company's productivity performance with its own experience in a prior period and with that of other wholesaler groups in the industry. The pertinent data, with tons handled per man-hour as the unit of measurement, are very specific—for example, man-hours required to unload cars, truck loading, record handling, and maintenance.

SERVICE ORGANIZATIONS AND WHITE COLLAR JOBS

The Service Worker
The Public Sector
Measuring the Unmeasurable

Fifty or perhaps as much as 60 percent of the GNP (gross national product) in the United States today does not go to the business sector but to, or through, public-service institutions such as governments, schools, health facilities, and nonprofit activities. Add to this the service/staff jobs in industry and the service industries themselves, such as banking, retailing, and insurance, and we find that most of the workforce are working in service jobs. Most of them produce little except information—or paperwork.

In the manufacturing sector, productivity is easy to measure by comparison. If a worker at a machine bores three holes for bolts in the time it formerly took to bore two holes, and his working hours remain the same, his output has increased 50 percent. But in the service job productivity is more difficult to determine. How many audits should an accountant handle or how many students should a teacher teach? Since these activities are of different types and are judged on the basis of quality, a quantitative measure of productivity is not so easy to attain. Moreover, there has been a tendency in the past for professional and service workers to obfuscate their real output.

The task of measuring productivity in these jobs reflects the following characteristics of the typical "service" worker (managers, professionals, administrators, secretaries, clerical workers, researchers, and so on):

☐ Their work is generally more costly than that of the manual worker.

☐ Aside from the automation of some paperwork, technology has not made a big impact on productivity.

☐ Work is difficult to describe and define, so service workers are not accustomed to thinking in terms of results and cost-benefit analysis.

☐ They are generally resistant to change in the ways of performing their work.

The costs of running offices constitute an especially knotty problem. It is estimated that during the last ten-year period office productivity grew only 4 percent, while factory-worker productivity grew 85 percent. Office costs are rising at about 15 percent per year and there is no slowdown in sight. These expenses are taking an increasing share of the expense dollar.

MEASURING THE SERVICE WORKER

It should be clear by now that this is a problem of great magnitude. However, it is not unsolvable. Some principles for improving the measurement and hence the productivity of service or "knowledge" or "information" workers might include these:

Think Output, Not Activity

The best example I know is education. We always think of it as an *activity* called *teaching*, when we consider the workers in the industry. This is false and misleading. Ask, "What is the end product?" The answer then becomes "*Learning*." What value is added to the student input to achieve an output? Consider these examples:

Job	Activity	Output
Systems Analyst	Design computer systems	Improve inventory turn from 4 to 6 and reduce stock level by $500,000.
Product Development	Product design	Develop new product X that is marketable at a return on investment of 24 percent over a life cycle of ten years.
Hospital Lab Technician	Conducts lab tests as required	Conduct an average of 14 tests in 4 categories per workday.
Typist in Word Processing	Type insurance policies	Type an average of 16 policies per day with a production point value of 1.00 and of acceptable quality.

Hughes Aircraft Company conducted an exhaustive study surrounding productivity in an R&D environment. Some "productivity indicators" (measures) of the R&D function that were developed included:

Dollar volume of production generated per R&D dollar spent

Work completed and cost incurred versus work scheduled to be completed and cost budgeted

Drawing change rate

Value of won proposals versus cost of bidding

Overhead burden on direct charge labor

Use Industrial Engineering Techniques to Set Standards

Work analysis and related techniques have been used for decades in production activities to measure the output of manual workers. The same approaches, principles, and methods apply to most clerical work and many staff jobs as well. Order processing, billing, keypunching, turning out paperwork of all kinds, and most accounting work are essentially production work. This systematic approach can also be applied to so-called "knowledge" workers—the market researcher, the systems designer, the sales manager.

The College of American Pathologists has developed a methodology for measuring workload in a hospital laboratory. The ratio is:

$$Productivity = \frac{Total\ Workload\ in\ Units}{Man\text{-}Hours}$$

The divisor includes all total paid man-hours including vacation, sick time, and overtime. The dividend (total workload) is comprised of a unit-value time *(technical, clerical, aide) to perform one or more of eight standard laboratory tests. Unit-value* time *was determined from standardized time and motion studies.*

Get a Plan to Improve Productivity

It won't happen without a planned approach to productivity improvement. The plan is developed in accordance with planning principles outlined elsewhere in this book.

Robert V. Head, a respected expert in the field of managing computer systems resources, has summarized productivity problems in terms of three tiers or phases as shown on page 60.

At the bottom level are the well-established tools for measuring equipment performance in a computer center. This level is the starting point for beginning a productivity improvement program in a computer center. The intermediate level indicates approaches for

```
RESOURCE PLANNING

SYSTEM DEVELOPMENT
Life-Cycle Management
Software Engineering
Structured Programming

COMPUTER PERFORMANCE EVALUATION
Hardware
Software
```

the more difficult "knowledge worker" area of systems development. At the top level of the pyramid lie the actions necessary for longer-run productivity—the long-range productivity plan, so to speak.

Let People Set Their Own Measures

A basic theme throughout this book is *participation/involvement*. Productivity can only be achieved through people. Self-measurement and self-control, within the proper management environment, can get results.

THE PUBLIC SECTOR

The public sector is large and growing. Today's cost of government accounts for about 30 percent of the United States' gross national product. Inflation, coupled with an increasing gap between citizen demands for services on the one hand and resources available on the other, are providing increased pressure to improve public-sector productivity.

The problems of improvement in the public sector are very similar to but perhaps greater than those in the service firm and service work discussed above. In the government there is no market mechanism to measure effectiveness. Many government units (and service units in business) are not workload-driven, but rather are oriented toward research, development, and evaluation. Additionally, many activities produce outputs that are consumed within the organization. The personnel function is a case in point. It represents administrative support which, though measurable, is difficult to allocate among final outputs.

There can be little doubt that productivity in government programs and agencies is low and that this reflects the fact that there are few accepted ways of measuring results and diverting resources from low productivity and failing operations. This in spite of the fact that in 1979 alone over a quarter of a billion dollars was spent for evaluations of effectiveness.

Peter Drucker tells us that making service institutions (including government) perform requires a system of management. Such a system would include these steps: (1) Formulate a definition of *mission and purpose* ("What is our business and what should it be?"); (2) Derive clear *objectives and goals* from the purpose and mission; (3) Think through *priorities* of concentrations; and (4) Define *measures of productivity and performance*.

The need is to measure results—develop the public equivalents of the business bottom line. Then each unit and employee of the organization can relate individual, functional, and departmental outputs to the whole.

MEASURING THE UNMEASURABLE

Some departments and individuals seem to defy measurement. This problem is in itself a discovery worth nothing. What are these people doing, how well, how much, how often? Maybe if you can't define it or measure it, the job should be redefined in measurable terms or eliminated. People who can't measure their jobs can't really know what's expected of them.

One of the most frequent problems is reflected in the comment: "The nature of my job defies measurement. How do you measure creativity?" This attitude is most likely to be expressed by the design engineer, the market researcher, the planner, or any one of the many staff employees of "service" departments. The complaint is commonly found in banks, insurance companies, government and public-service organizations, and the staff departments of other business firms.

Managers of these activites traditionally have attempted to measure the efficiency of the operation by devising some method of cost control or budgetary allocation that is largely unrelated to the volume or *output* or the *results expected*. This is not enough. Far more important is a measure of effectiveness. The latter measure will place the emphasis on the result.

Many of these activities and people are providing some service to an internal customer within the organization. If this is the case, it can be measured in terms of its effectiveness; for the computer specialist by turnaround time, for the personnel analyst in terms of how long it takes to fill an opening, for the supervisor in maintenance by a ratio relating his service to the user (e.g., cost per machine-hour). Sometimes, the effectiveness of a service department can be measured by asking the question: "What would it cost to buy the service from an outside source?"

On dozens of occasions I have been asked this question by design engineers: "How do you measure creativity?" This is a valid question and not easy one to answer. I usually reply with the suggestion that creativity in design can be measured by asking yourself two questions: "What have I contributed to the knowledge and the results in my department and to the company in the last year?", and "How many answers to design problems have I come up with during the past year?" The answers to these questions may prove embarrassing. On the other hand, if the questions were phrased in terms of next year, the answers might be helpful in measuring "creativity," despite the qualitative nature of the expected result. By asking these same questions the supervisor of design engineers and other "creative" persons involved in "intangible" work will be able to distinguish between the most creative and the least creative employee in a department.

A top executive in a major insurance company, tired of hearing the "intangibility" argument and other excuses, has organized a Productivity and Performance Measurement Program. Innovative methods include activity analysis (measuring performance in field offices around fifteen activities performed), business planning (establishing standards for staff time by function within major product lines), cost-effectiveness analysis (definition of marketing/ effectiveness ratios), and the allowable expense concept. These methods represent an attempt to depart from the fixed budget and focus on cost-control methods of the past. It is an attempt to measure effectiveness *and* productivity *rather than the illusion of efficiency provided by the traditional budget.*

AN ORGANIZATION SYSTEM THAT RELATES ACTIVITIES
TO OUTPUT INDICATORS[3]

---

[3]The approach described here is adapted from a system in use at IBM called the "Common Staffing Study," or "CSS."

For an organizationwide system of measurement it is desirable to relate the many *activities* and the *functions* that they comprise to some form of *output indicator*. In other words, we want to know what "drives" the activities. By relating the "drivers" or "indicators" to the activities we can not only obtain a better estimate of whether the supporting activities are justified but we can also judge productivity trends over time as well as against like units in the organization.

Although the manufacturing worker (one who physically alters the product) has been measured for decades by time standards, time studies, and work sampling, it is not so easy to set standards for the nonmanufacturing employee or the service activity. I have pointed out the difficulty of measuring the productivity of the "service" or "indirect" or "white-collar" or "knowledge" workers, whether in manufacturing or service firms. Indeed, there is probably no feasible or economical way to achieve measurement in the sense of determining a time standard such as we have for the manufacturing worker. This difficulty notwithstanding, we can devise a system that will describe the productivity of an *activity* at a point in time and then provide a baseline for judging continuous improvement over time. The system is particularly appropriate for multiplant or multidivisional companies with like products or services and for individual companies that comprise an industry.

The first step in designing the system is to start with the organization chart (Figure 3-2 is an example) and determine the input activities that comprise the basic organizational functions. For example, the *activity* of recruiting would be assigned to the

Figure 3-2. Organization chart

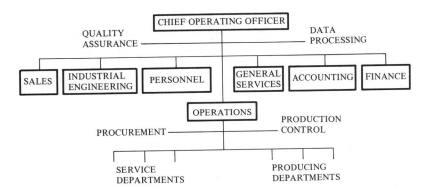

personnel *function*, the *activity* of computer programming to the data-processing *function*, the *activity* of accounts receivable to the accounting *function*, and so on. The typical organization may identify a hundred or more activities that are grouped into ten or more traditional functions. This is nothing more than good organization practice whereby labor specialization is grouped homogeneously into like activities and thence into functions or departments.

The next step is to identify the *output indicators* that "drive" the activities or cause work in the activities. In other words, if it were not for the work caused by or resulting from the *indicators*, there would be little need for the *activities*. If, for example, there were no manpower there would be no need for employee relations. If there were no purchasing there would be no need for vendor invoicing, and the resources utilized in the activity of vendor invoicing are therefore a dependent variable of the purchasing function. To put it another way, if activities are the "input" in the productivity ratio $\dfrac{\text{Output}}{\text{Input}}$, then the indicators are the "output." The concept is shown in Figure 3-3.

After the activities, functions, and indicators have been determined and grouped, an *organizational matrix* can be constructed similar to the one shown in Table 3-7. Note that the matrix can and should coincide with the organization chart of Figure 3-2. The organizational functions and activities should be assigned to the same managers who have the responsibility for improving productivity. In short, the system coincides with the organizational structure.

You can readily see the possibilities of this system in both manufacturing and service organizations for measuring and tracking the "indirect" employee. The "direct" employee is the one who has "hands-on" contact with the product or service. In manufacturing it is the person who physically alters the product. Everyone else (secretaries, personnel people, purchasing people, engineers, programmers, accountants, clerks, managers, guards, etc.) is indirect. In

Figure 3-3. Relating output indicators to input activities

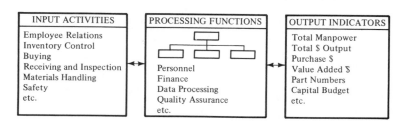

INPUT ACTIVITIES	PROCESSING FUNCTIONS	OUTPUT INDICATORS
Employee Relations		Total Manpower
Inventory Control		Total $ Output
Buying		Purchase $
Receiving and Inspection	Personnel	Value Added $
Materials Handling	Finance	Part Numbers
Safety	Data Processing	Capital Budget
etc.	Quality Assurance	etc.
	etc.	

TABLE 3–7. Organization Matrix

Processing Function	Input Activities	Total Manpower	Regular Manpower	Indirect Regular Manpower	Part Numbers	Total $ Output	Purchase $	Administrative Workload	Value Added $	etc.
Personnel	Employee Relations	X								
	Benefits		X							
	Training		X							
General Services	Cafeteria	X								
	Legal		X							
Finance	Financial Planning					X				
	Inventory Control				X					
	Vendor Invoicing						X			
Data-Processing	Information Systems							X		
Production Control	Parts Analyzing				X					
Procurement	Buying						X			
	Purchase Planning & Control						X			
Quality Assurance	Receiving & Inspection								X	
	Technical Support								X	
	Test								X	
Industrial Engineering	Cost Engineering					X			X	
	Procurement Cost Estimating						X			
	Material Handling			X						
Facilities & Services	Safety	X								
	Mail Service									X
etc.	etc.									

Output Indicators

a university it is the teacher—everyone else is indirect; in an airline it is the pilot, flight attendant, and ticket agent—everyone else is indirect; in a hospital it is the nurse, therapist, and physician— everyone else is indirect. In each case the workload and hence productivity of the *direct worker* is more easily measured because it is directly related to organization output (i.e., product, student, passenger, patient). The workload and hence the productivity of the *indirect* worker, on the other hand, is a function of the output indicators that "drive" the activities involved in support services. Thus the system, when combined with existing measures for direct workers, is a fairly reliable approach for integrating productivity measures for the entire organization. Taken together, the system can give a good indication of *how and where to improve productivity.*

PRODUCTIVITY MEASUREMENT: GETTING STARTED

Top Management Support
Select Personnel
What to Measure
Target Groups
Cost-Benefit Analysis
Concepts and Units of Measurement
Data Requirements and Availability
Report Format
Implement and Follow Up

In this chapter we have provided a somewhat cursory review of productivity measures on an overall basis, for functional/departmental units, individual measures, and the special problems associated with service firms and workers. You should remember that in attempting to outline a "how to get started" approach, all of these cannot be treated in depth. A comprehensive, organizationwide system would naturally require a great deal more research and preparation. Here my purpose is to outline preliminary steps for those who wish to do preplanning or install a system on a less ambitious basis.

If a measurement system is to be effective, it should be simple in its implementation, easily understood and administered, and return more than its cost in benefits. With these criteria in mind, the steps below are suggested for inclusion in starting a productivity measuring system:

☐ *Get top management support.* Without this imprimateur and support the effort has failed before it has begun.

- ☐ *Select personnel.* Experience suggests that the effort should be headed by a team, rather than a "hotshot" operations researcher or industrial engineer. Productivity is a line function. Although the staff specialist may act as coordinator, the advantages of a team approach are overriding.

- ☐ *Determine elements of organization to measure.* It is unlikely that you can "blanket" the entire organization, so consider a one-step-at-a-time approach. Cover one division, department, or situation at a time.

- ☐ *Get commitment from target groups.* Get them involved and get their endorsement and participation in the early stages, otherwise the effort will be perceived as a "here it comes again" staff report.

- ☐ *Perform cost-benefit analysis.* Will the benefits outweigh the long-run costs of the measurement effort? If the answer is no, regroup or drop the effort. In this connection, you need to establish what *criteria to use for evaluation* of tradeoffs and doing the cost-benefit analysis.

- ☐ *Select concepts and units of measurement* for the output and input of the company as a whole and for essential divisions, functions, or departments.

- ☐ *Evaluate data requirements and availability.* Choose appropriate weights, deflators, index-number methods, etc.

- ☐ *Design the format for reporting the measurement data.* Provide for analysis and interpretation; design for the benefit of the *user*.

- ☐ *Implement and follow up* to determine the need for modification and redesign.

PRODUCTIVITY & THE MANAGEMENT PROCESS

CHAPTER 4

"Better productivity results from better management."
—Richard Gerstenberg,
Former Chairman, General Motors

Managers today are on the horns of a dilemma. On the one hand they are faced with the bad news that combines inflation and rising costs, increasing regulation, shrinking real profits, and declining return on investment. On the other hand, energy, technology, and capital investment, the traditional substitutes for labor, no longer appear to be valid as alternatives for improved productivity and profits. This means that productivity may be the main controllable variable left to improve bottom-line results. New gains will have to come from *better management*.

IMPROVING PRODUCTIVITY WITH BETTER
MANAGEMENT

Management vs. Technology
Is Technology Peaking?
The Answer: Human Resources and Management

In the previously mentioned survey of 6,000 managers by the American Management Associations, the overwhelming choice for improved productivity was *better management*. In light of this, why do so many people overlook the leverage available from improved management? Perhaps it is because the managers themselves so frequently do not perceive it as the answer to improvement. This is unfortunate because significant improvements are available—today!

MANAGEMENT VS. TECHNOLOGY

Since the time of Adam Smith's historic eighteenth-century book *The Wealth of Nations* we have been taught to believe that *labor specialization* accompanied by *mechanization* was the secret to economic growth and productivity. Hasn't the Industrial Revolution proven this to be so? Even today, the conventional wisdom of the economists tells us that the rate of productivity growth is largely a function of the changes in real capital relative to labor. The political rhetoric for decades has concerned capital investment accompanied by legislation to provide investment incentives. Indeed, a major portion of monetary and fiscal policy (e.g., tax, depreciation, interest rates) has been devoted to this topic. Each candidate for major office demands "more incentives for business investment."

The business press, trade journals, and much industry advertising would have us believe that salvation lies in more investment in capital equipment and technology. Consider these examples from one issue of a recent trade journal:

Personnel Department Automates . . . *saves up to $50,000 a year. The personnel department of the Pillsbury Company filed and maintained résumés and applications of 250 job applicants every week. The employment manager and the manager of microfilm services decided something had to be done to control the monster. Using the resources of computer output microfilm (COM), a microfilm jacket, and internal computer timesharing, the paper tiger was laid to rest.*

Security Department Improves Productivity . . . *A plant security guard walks an average of 15 miles per day and spends about 132 hours per month walking. If he can cover the same distance in 44 hours per month with a powered personnel vehicle, 88 hours per month can be transferred to more productive tasks.*

Robots, the ultimate extension of the computer, *will perform dreary, dirty, dangerous tasks without complaint. They don't take coffee breaks, they don't take vacations, and most times they don't get sick.*

The big auto-makers seem to be leading the way with computer-controlled robots. At Ford Motor Company there are 236 robots doing such routine jobs as die casting, stamping, spray painting, and other tasks that cause worker discontent.

My purpose is not to downgrade technology and mechanization but to place them in their proper perspective vis-à-vis the potential to be achieved by the process of management and the better utilization of human resources. Two points need to be made. First, for the majority of managers, investing in further technology, except on a very small scale, is not a viable course of action either because the money is not available or because their activities do not lend themselves to the application of technology. Second, the potential for *managerial improvements* is more important in terms of payoff and is immediately and easily available at no cost.

To illustrate, consider the incredible technological advances that have been made in computers. The cost per function has *decreased* 100,000 times, while the speed of computation has *increased* 10,000 times. Yet we frequently fail, for managerial and "people" reasons, to take advantage of this tool.

The key element in a job manufacturing plant is the flow of work in process. Yet the actual manufacturing processes consume only 10 percent of the time involved—the 10 percent that gets most of management attention. Managers are spending all their time trying to improve efficiency in the narrow span of 10 percent and failing to concentrate efforts on the other 90 percent, which is waiting time. The potential here for improvement is obvious.

In Seattle, where Boeing is tripling its output of 747s, the company can cut its need for skilled labor by using a computer controller mechanism that selects wiring and assembles it for installation in the fuselage. But the bottleneck is the availability of skilled programmers.

The plants of the computer-makers are clean and quiet. "Stuffing" components onto a printed circuit board, a labor-intensive process, can be done by computer-controlled machines, but the worst bottleneck is writing computer software—and there is a shortage of skilled programmers.

The basic factor in the profitable growth of an individual firm or the development of the national economy is not so much technology and hardware as it is "brainware" and the application of managerial know-how. In 1900 a manufacturing company spent $5 on managerial, technical, and professional personnel for each $100 in direct labor. The substitution of mechanical leverage for the muscle leverage of labor was overriding at that time. Today in manufacturing companies, the two items of expenditure of direct and indirect labor are equal even though direct labor wages have risen much faster. Outside of manufacturing, productivity improvement has resulted from the replacement of labor with improved methods.

The Cincinnati Division of National Distillers ships more than 8 million cases of liquor and wine every year. By integrating the physical system with the management system *(controls and procedures), labor costs of $500,000 and demurrage of $100,000 were saved. In addition, a reduction in fluctuations in production levels and improved customer service were achieved.*

IS TECHNOLOGY PEAKING?

The answer to this question must be no. Indeed, in some applications, technology has yet to achieve significant inroads. Consider office and information costs. The demand for information has mushroomed so wildly that clerks, secretaries, and typists cannot cope with it. The cost of paperwork has climbed so calamitously that a frantic search is underway to control it. Office costs have swelled to 40 or 50 percent of all costs in some companies, and some experts estimate that the expense of preparing a business letter can run as high as $14 to $18. Yet while the average factory worker is supported by about $25,000 worth of technology, the office worker, as one office machine company put it, "works with $500 or $1,000 worth of old typewriters and adding machines, and is probably among the least productive workers in the world."

Despite the potential of technology in some applications, there is evidence that some industries and firms have passed the marginal stage and must seek increases in productivity elsewhere. The prestigious Strategic Planning Institute of Cambridge, Massachusetts maintains an extensive data base on hundreds of firms related to a variety of performance measures. This organization has concluded that many firms invest in "bad" productivity—productivity that costs too much, i.e., improvement achieved at a cost greater than the benefits. Indeed, the evidence indicates that "the more mechanized or automated or investment-intensive a business is, the lower its return on investment, and sharply so." Moreover, concludes the Institute:

A business that increases its labor productivity without much increase in investment, i.e., by such devices as improved morale or improved employee training or improved work practices, will tend to move ... into the region of greater profitability. In the opposite case, a business that adds investment without substantially reducing labor intensity will tend to shift ... into the region of lower profitability. [Italics added.]

An example of this tendency is the paper industry, one of the most technologically advanced and capital-intensive in the world. Sales have enjoyed a boom for decades, yet few firms produce anything but marginal profits and a return on investment that is little more than the cost of capital. The industry represents a triumph of technology over management![1]

THE ANSWER: HUMAN RESOURCES AND MANAGEMENT

During a recent visit to India I was able to visit several cities and talk to many managing directors of Indian firms. I was constantly amazed at the low level of application of technology except in the very largest firms. From my hotel room in Bombay I observed with interest as construction of a modern ocean-front hotel proceeded into the thirty-sixth month, half-completed. Typical work methods could be illustrated by dozens of "carriers" who spent their working day stacking a load of eight bricks onto the top of their heads and walking a hundred yards to the construction site where they queued for unloading into a muscle-powered lift. It wouldn't take an industrial engineer to calculate that one wheelbarrow, a piece of capital-intensive equipment in India, would replace about ten human workers.

The potential for muscle leverage that can be achieved by technology such as the wheelbarrow is easily understood and applied by both worker and manager alike in the United States. During the twentieth century we have become the most capital-intensive nation in the world. Our capital resources have combined with innovative engineering to provide us with a technology base that is unsurpassed. We have traditionally depended upon technology to solve everything

[1]If you are interested in evaluating your firm's operating effectiveness and whether it is a good candidate for further automation and technology application, see Bradley T. Gale, "Can Capital Buy Higher Productivity?" *Harvard Business Review,* July/August 1980.

from defense needs and environmental problems to our improved standard of living. The remaining two components of increased productivity, labor and management, have played a secondary role.

This emphasis is changing fast. Some say we've gone about as far as we can go until the human element catches up with technology. The former 3M chief executive, Harry Heltzer, reflects this conclusion in his comment: "You can't press the button any harder and make the automated equipment run any faster. In a rising cost spiral you've just got to find ways of pressing it more intelligently." In other words, working harder is not the total answer; we've got to work "smarter" too.

A SYSTEM FOR MANAGING PRODUCTIVITY, I

General Functions of Management

PLAN

ORGANIZE

CONTROL

Synergism, n. 2. the simultaneous action of separate agencies which, together, have greater total effect than the sum of their individual effects.
      —Webster's Dictionary, Unabridged, 2nd ed.

There is an old comedy routine that has been successful for generations and still gets a laugh today. The audience roars with delight as the comedian opens his closet door while the contents pour forth and crash around him in utter disarray and confusion.

Many executives view their organizations in this way. As the door to the "problems" closet is opened, out tumbles a disorganized array of functional crises brought on by subordinates who can't, or won't, work together. The executive wonders how to make a "system" of the mess.

Somewhat less in disarray, but nevertheless confusing, is the state of the art in the "science" of organization and management. It is the intent of this chapter to bring these pieces together into a system. This integration is necessary because it is a fundamental premise of this book that the process of management must be clearly understood before major inroads can be made in productivity.

In this chapter I will argue that a logical approach to an understanding of the *practice* of management is to divide the topic into three major parts (subsystems). These are:

□ *The general functions of management* (plan, organize, control).

□ *Supervisory skills* (work skills and people skills).

□ *The technical (operational) skills* associated with a particular profession, discipline, or input to the firm (money, human resources, material, facilities, technology, information, etc.).

The model for the system is shown in Figure 4-1.

GENERAL FUNCTIONS OF MANAGEMENT

The most widespread approach to management is the so-called process or operational school, which defines what managers do in terms of the managerial functions they perform: planning, orga-

Figure 4-1. A system for managing productivity

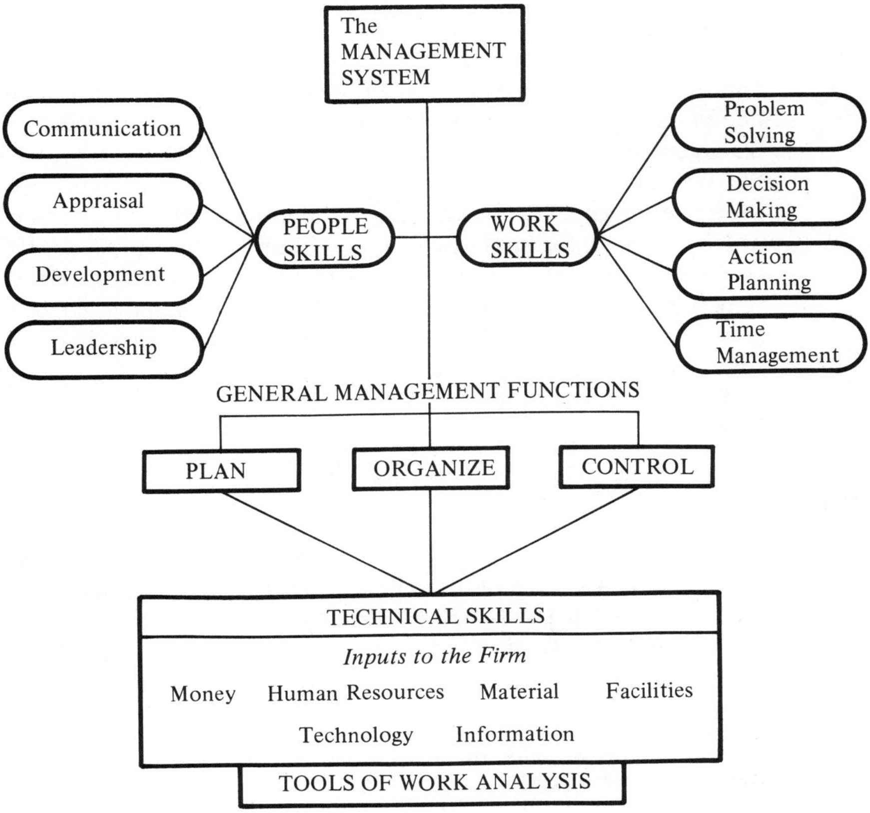

nizing, and controlling. These three functions also provide the central theme of our management system.

Each of these functions has its body of knowledge and techniques, and each utilizes knowledge from other fields of science. The process school does not deny the existence and validity of the other approaches to management. Indeed, the *functions of management* can absorb or utilize the methodology and techniques of all other disciplines, techniques, and approaches.

The overall job of a manager is to create within the enterprise the environment that will facilitate the accomplishment of its objectives. In doing this, the manager *plans* the work of his subordinates and his own activity, *organizes* the work and task relationships, and *controls* results by measuring performance against plan. These are the traditional functions of the manager.[1] As distinguished from *operational* functions (manufacturing, engineering, accounting, marketing, etc.), which differ among the various types of organizations, *managerial* functions are common to all.

This three-part or three-function approach to the job of the manager provides the basic action framework for the systems approach. Its continuing popularity and widespread use are probably due to its approach to the topic—the explanation of the process of management in terms of what managers do. Hence, it reflects the way the manager sees his job and is therefore most useful to him. Moreover, it appears that the functional approach to management will be with us for some time in the future. Although there will continue to be a need for managers with a high degree of *functional* skill, this skill must be accompanied by the essential *managerial* skills of planning, organizing, decision making, and measuring and controlling processes and operations.

The general nature by which management operates is shown in Figure 4-2.

Planning

The most basic and pervasive management function is planning. All managers at all levels plan, and the success of the performance of the other functions depends upon it. Planning is deciding in advance what has to be done, who has to do it, when it has to be done, and how it is to be done. It bridges the gap from where we are to where we want

---

[1] Two additional functions—*directing* and *staffing*—are also commonly considered to be managerial in nature. However, for our purposes of MIS, these are not considered to be overriding.

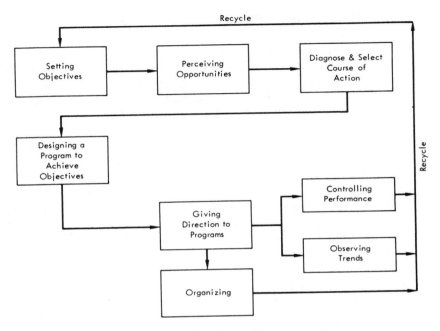

Figure 4-2. A concept of management

to go. Managers plan for the allocation of resources and the work of other people, in contrast to the nonmanager, who plans only his own activities.

The North American Society for Corporate Planning (the professional society for full-time planners) identifies a number of reasons for the tremendous upsurge in formal planning. These reasons include: the rapid rate of technological change, growing competition, the increasingly complex business environment, increased complexity of management, and the changing philosophy of management which admits that companies can influence their own future.

The steps in planning are basically the same as in decision making and problem solving: (a) definition of the problem or establishment of the objective, (b) collection and arrangement of facts surrounding the problem, and (c) reaching a decision or solving the problem. These basic concepts can be expanded to provide a logical sequence of steps for operations research and for systems design as well.

Most planning is conducted in an environment that lends itself to a certain basic approach. Expanding on the basic elementary steps of the preceding paragraph, this basic approach can be described in terms of a number of *iterative* steps. The process is shown in Figure 4-3.

☐ *Awareness of Opportunity.* A cardinal purpose of planning is to discover future opportunities and make plans to exploit them. Although strictly speaking, becoming aware of opportunities is not a step in the planning process, it must precede planning because the most profitable plans are those that identify and exploit opportunities.

☐ *Setting Objectives.* This step refers to establishing planning objectives as opposed to enterprise objectives, although if the latter have not been set, planning cannot proceed beyond this point.

☐ *Establishing Planning Premises.* Premises are those data, facts, and information that influence alternative courses of action to reach objectives. It should be evident that a *management information system* is an essential device for gathering, storing, and retrieving planning premises.

☐ *Determining Alternative Courses of Action.* This involves the search for and determination of alternative ways to achieve the objective of the plan. In formal planning, this process almost always involves the quantification and documentation of alternatives to permit analysis.

Figure 4-3. The planning process

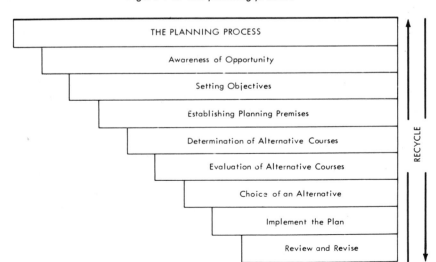

☐ *Evaluating Alternative Courses.* Evaluation of alternatives involves the weighing of the desirability of each alternative in light of planning premises and goals. Some choices are reduced to mathematical selection because all variables can be quantified. In these cases the new management science techniques are valuable. However, most planning problems are replete with intangibles and uncertainties; it is for this reason that a careful evaluation is so important. A properly designed *management information system* can be of great benefit in helping the decision-maker perform this evaluation.

Simulation and forecasting models hold great potential for evaluating alternatives. Fourth-generation MIS is developing to the point at which it is beginning to provide the necessary data to construct effective predictive models. The Pillsbury Corporation is using a model to support a cash-flow forecasting system of its chicken-raising business. The model is credited with enabling management to identify and solve problems that have a constraining effect on the profits of the business.

☐ *Choosing an Alternative.* This is the point at which a decision is made and a course of action is selected. It is taken after a consideration of premises, constraints, enterprise goals, and the factors of expediency, adaptability, and cost.

☐ *Implementing the Plan.* After selection of an alternative, the plan is translated into derivative plans, and its relation to all activities affected by it are worked out. This includes the details of where the action should be done, by whom, and in what order. We shall refer to this step later on as *action planning*, a vital step in improving productivity—it's not going to happen unless there is an *action plan*.

Westinghouse Electric Corporation is one of the major companies that has initiated a comprehensive corporatewide productivity program that is strongly supported by top management. The program is designed to get the commitment and support of personnel at all levels. Productivity improvement plans exist at three levels: strategic planning, business planning, and individual action planning. The company ensures that productivity planning pervades the organization.

Boise Cascade, an innovative company that is primarily in the paper industry, coordinates a corporatewide productivity program out of the chairman's office. The program is integrated with business and operational planning so that operational managers are required to "buy in" or "sign up" for productivity goals at the same time that operational and financial plans are developed.

Hershey Foods, the chocolate company, represents a growing number of corporations that have integrated productivity into strategic planning by making it a fundamental part of strategy. It is operationalized by the setting of specific goals and objectives for productivity as one of the key performance areas.

GK Technologies has established as one of the company's major objectives "contributing to the strength of the American economy through improved productivity."

Part of the strategy of International Paper is "to improve productivity in management as well as in resource, development and allocation, manufacturing, and distribution."

Organizing

The systems approach has as its second major dimension the integration of organizational subsystems (activities, functions, departments, etc.) in order to optimize the output of the whole organization. To say that most companies have something less than synergism is an understatement. As one frustrated chief executive remarked: "Sales is selling a product that Engineering can't design, that Manufacturing can't make, and to customers that Finance won't approve for credit!"

Lack of integration can best be illustrated by the traditional "confrontation" between Sales and Manufacturing. Sales wants to sell one of each color delivered this afternoon, and Manufacturing wants to ship one million unit lots, all black, when they are ready. There are constant problems regarding capacity, product mix, lead time, order backlogs, over- or underscheduling, over- or underbooking, and back schedules.

When this situation is at its worst, Manufacturing understates capacity and overstates lead times in self-defense. Sales will guard against Manufacturing conservatism by overbooking and accepting orders after the expiration of lead time. There is little effective communication about the status of items in process. Production planning becomes item expediting—a reflex spasm triggered by the latest complaint of the highest sales executive.

Much of the organizational inflexibility and antiproductive behavior can be traced to the way in which the typical company is organized. In most cases it has a traditional, classical organization structure. This continues to be the most common corporate structure in use today. *It inhibits productivity*!

ORGANIZE FOR RESULTS

The systems approach can increase productivity by modifying the restrictive characteristics of the bureaucracy. Part of the problem has been that we have always organized by activities and tasks—basic processes of labor specialization and classical organization theory— rather than by results. Just as the industrial engineer should question the final product before questioning the work process, the manager should question the results expected before designing the tasks and activities of the organization structure. Incidentally, this is a major reason for resistance to organizational analysts and industrial engineers; people can't identify with the output they are seeking.

In principle and in practice the systems approach helps to improve synergism. Instead of jockeying for position, or attempting to push special interests and arguing all the time, the crux of organizational disputes shifts from arguing about process (activities) to one of deciding on the best course of action to get results. They shift from quibbling about what is our present latitude and longitude to fruitful discussions about where we should head. Traditional organization theory is concerned with the organization of authority. The systems approach is concerned with organizing responsibility and getting on with the job.

Perhaps the best way to demonstrate how the systems approach (focus on results) can improve the classical structure is to compare the charges leveled at the bureaucracy against the advantages of a results management approach. This is done in Table 4-1.

The move to organizing around *results* rather than *activity* is reflected in the banking industry. Traditionally, most small and medium-sized banks have been organized around the two major functions—loans and deposits—with administration separated out as the bank grows. This structure was based on the outdated notion that the organization should focus on *internal activities*. Today, the innovative bank realizes that *results* are obtained by developing profitable deposits through the marketing of customer services. Hence, structure follows strategy and the organization focuses on results.

TABLE 4–1. Comparison of the Classical Organization and Results Management

Charges Leveled at the Classical Organization	*Advantages of Results Management*
Too mechanistic	Dynamic
Too structured to adapt to change	Permits flexibility as system adapts to change in output requirements
Formality hinders communications	Communications based on results, not procedure or directive
Inhibits innovation	Encourages innovation People seek innovative achievement goals
Pays the job and not the worker	Rewards based on appraisal by results
Relies on coercive control	Self-control
Job-defensive behavior encourages make-work	All work devoted to goal achievement based on results
Organization goals not compatible with goals of organization members	Individual and organization goals are the same: production
Out of date with human needs	Meets basic human need for self-actualization.

THE ICEBERG ANALOGY

We know that approximately 90 percent of an iceberg's volume is under water and hidden from the observer's view. Only a small portion is visible. To the uninformed traveler, only the visible portion seems to exist. However, a seasoned sailor seeks to account for the hidden part below the surface.

An organization is somewhat like an iceberg. The novice, or the seat-of-the-pants manager, sees only visible organizational potential and usually adopts a managerial style that is heavily dependent on tradition and personal experience. He likes to describe himself as "informal" and feels that popular management techniques are nothing more than common-sense descriptions of what he does

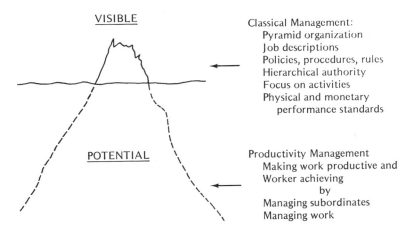

VISIBLE

Classical Management:
  Pyramid organization
  Job descriptions
  Policies, procedures, rules
  Hierarchical authority
  Focus on activities
  Physical and monetary
    performance standards

POTENTIAL

Productivity Management
  Making work productive and
  Worker achieving
      by
  Managing subordinates
  Managing work

Figure 4-4. The organization as an iceberg

instinctively. He runs things "by the book" and depends on formal authority and standard procedures. He is the classical manager.

What the classical manager frequently overlooks is the unreleased potential in the organization for improved productivity through more modern management methods. If he could visualize the potential for improved productivity, both he and the organization would benefit.

The potential for improved productivity is significant but is being suppressed by classical techniques of organization and management. The analogy between the iceberg and the organization is shown in Figure 4-4. The solution lies in the adoption of a systems approach to managing productivity.

TEAM ORGANIZATIONS

The real organizational problem, at least at the level of the front-line supervisor or middle manager, is to balance the existing functional structure with its skill specialization against the organization of people and tasks necessary to achieve results, to "break through" the pyramid, so to speak. The answer to this paradox appears to lie in the team approach to organization style. This approach complements the classical structure of functional grouping (the employee's "home") with a work team (the employee's "place of work"). Committees, expeditors, departmental meetings, and the like are not teams. The team organization is not a temporary expedient to solve a special short-run problem. It involves a design principle all its own.

The classical bureaucracy, which we have agreed cannot be abandoned, is traditionally based upon one of two design principles concerned with work. First, you can organize the work by project, stages, or some form of work breakdown such as the development of a product or the construction of a plant. Second, you can bring the work to where the skills and tools can be applied to it. An example of this is the assembly line where cutting, welding, assembly, and painting can take place.

In the team style of organization, you take the workers with different skills, tools, and competencies and move them to the job to be done. I have frequently experienced this style of organization when functioning as a lecturer in educational television productions. The team—the director, lecturer, the graphic artist, the camera operators, the set designer—work as a team although each does highly specialized work.

The team form of organization is not new. The task force and project manager have been around for years. IBM has always encouraged workers to form teams within the mass-production system. But the use of teams is growing. The automobile industry has been experimenting on the assembly line. The use of product managers and project managers is growing increasingly popular in industry. The venture team concept is a recent innovation developed to meet the demand for a breakthrough in product design and marketing. General Electric, always an innovator, has reorganized the entire firm around 63 "SBUs"—Strategic Business Units. At Texas Instruments, team management is a way of life and has been carried to a high degree of sophistication. Several hundred "TAPs"— tactical action programs—were organized to achieve company strategy and goals. Motorola has pushed decentralization down to the plant level where product managers develop their own strategy and product plans. Ralston Purina has local decision-making work groups right on the shop floor to innovate in work standards and methods. A few companies have organized "productivity teams."

The team approach to organization style offers the front-line supervisor and middle manager, whether line or staff, an alternative to the classical structure, or rather, a modification to it in order to achieve productivity. However, it is not a panacea nor does it apply in all situations. It is not generally appropriate by itself, but must be complementary to the existing structure.

It is a challenge for managers to determine for themselves how the team concept of organizational style can be applied to get results in a particular situation. Throughout this book I will argue that the team form of organization is the best for getting productivity where it counts—where the work is performed. I will suggest the device of the *Productivity Improvement Teams* (PITs).

Control

If the manager could depend upon the flawless execution of plans by a perfectly balanced organization, there would be no need for control; results would invariably be as expected. However, plans and operations rarely remain on course, and control is needed to obtain results. The real test of a manager's ability is the result he achieves.

Control is a definite process and is essentially the same regardless of the activity involved or the area of the organization. The fundamental process consists of three steps: (1) setting standards of performance, (2) measuring performance against these standards, and (3) correcting deviations from standards and plans. These three steps are discussed in the following paragraphs.

STANDARDS OF PERFORMANCE

Setting standards of performance involves defining for personnel in all levels of the organization what is expected of them in terms of job performance. Hence standards are criteria that results can be measured against. These criteria can be quantitative (e.g., 10 percent increase in sales) or qualitative (e.g., maintain high level of morale). A frequently used definition of standards of performance is a *statement of conditions existing when a job is performed satisfactorily.*

A discussion of standards can be better understood when related to actual examples. Table 4-2 illustrates the basic components of a very important operational plan—the financial plan. Note that a standard of performance is indicated for each of these major items.

The usual criteria for measuring performance against plan for an activity can be stated in terms of cost, time, quantity, or quality. For example, in Table 4-2 the unit *cost* of raw materials for manufacturing a product can be controlled in terms of cost per unit, and this standard would apply in the purchasing operation. *Time* is a standard for sales when performance is measured in terms of meeting sales quotas during established time periods (e.g., weeks, months). In manufacturing, the direct labor hours per unit of output in a process operation comprise common *quantity* measure. *Quality* is a common measure in judging the acceptability of such factors as product

TABLE 4–2. Standards of Performance for Controlling the Financial Plan

Financial Plan	Cost	Time	Quantity	Quality	Illustration of Standard
		Criteria			
Sales	x	x	x		Sales quota during time period at standard cost
Cost of Goods Sold:					
Raw Materials	x		x		Unit usage rate at standard cost
Direct Labor	x	x	x		Hours per unit of output
Manufacturing Expense	x	x	x		Maintenance cost per machine hour
Total					
Gross Margin on Sales	x		x		Percent of sales
Less:					
Distribution Expense	x				Percent of sales
Administrative Expense	x	x	x		Budgeted amount
Total					
Operating Income	x		x		Percent of sales
Federal Income Tax					
Net Income	x		x		Return on investment

specification, grades of products sold, and reject rates in quality control.

These are yardsticks and not areas of activity to be measured. Ideally, everyone in the organization should have some standard so that he understands what is expected of him in terms of job performance.

Other types of performance standards can be identified:

☐ *Physical.* Units per man-hour, raw-material usage rate.

☐ *Cost.* Overhead cost per unit of output, distribution costs.

☐ *Revenue.* Average sales per customer.

☐ *Program.* Time to complete events, technical specifications.

☐ *Intangible.* Employee morale, public relations.

In addition to operating standards, there are critical areas of *overall* company performance that are the concern of top management. Is the company achieving its objectives? Are its strategies paying off? By appraising overall company performance in these areas, the company will be evaluating its progress toward its basic purposes and objectives. Some of the areas for checking on overall performance include: profitability, market standing, productivity, innovation and product leadership, employee and managerial attitudes and development, public and social responsibility, use of resources, and the balance between short-range and long-range objectives.

It is extremely important for both the manager-user and the systems designer to be familar with the control process, because the majority of outputs from the management information system are *control reports.*

MEASURING PERFORMANCE

Once standards have been established, it is necessary to measure performance against the expectation of the standards. The statement of this measurement, and of any differences, is usually in the form of a personal observation or some form of report—oral or written.

The oldest and most prevalent means of measuring performance is by personal observation. The shop supervisor is on the scene and can personally check the time, cost, and quality of the work under his supervision. Sales managers visit sales offices or make calls with their salespeople to observe performance personally. Advantages include the benefits of immediacy, personal direct contact, and firsthand observation of intangibles such as morale, personnel development, or customer reaction. Disadvantages are those associated with the time-consuming nature of the method and the lack of precision in measurement.

Oral reports of performance may take the form of interviews, informal reports, or group and committee meetings. Measuring performance in this way has many of the advantages and drawbacks of the personal observation method. Additionally, the method of oral reporting does not usually result in any record-keeping of performance.

Control and performance reporting is increasingly being done in written form. This is due in part to the accelerating use of computer-based information systems and related reporting techniques. The written report has the advantage of providing a permanent record, subject to periodic review by the manager and subordinates. This method of measuring performance may take a variety of forms. Among the most common is the statistical report, which presents statistical analysis of performance versus standard, either in tabular or chart form. Special or one-time reports are frequently made in problem areas as they arise. A significant portion of written reports are operational in nature and concern performance rather than standards for the financial plan.

Hospital rates have risen more than five times as fast as the general consumer price index in the last ten years, but one-third of all hospital costs are related only indirectly to patient care. The potential for cost savings with computer-based control systems is great. Among the functions that can be automated and better controlled are admission and bed control, patient account reporting, personnel control, cost allocation, scheduling, operations control, and a variety of ancillary applications.

CORRECTING DEVIATIONS

It does little good to set standards of performance and measure deviations from standard unless corrections are made in order to get the plan back on course.

Summary

As the remainder of this book unfolds and we develop the necessary knowledge, skills, and actions to increase productivity, a fundamental theme will be *results management and self-control*—call it participative management, if you like. It means allowing—indeed, encouraging—those people in the organizational "iceberg" to develop individual and team productivity goals and to track their own performance. This concept, this philosophy of management, will not come easy. But it works! It is a prerequisite to productivity!

A SYSTEM FOR MANAGING PRODUCTIVITY, II
General vs. Technical Management
The Role of Industrial Engineering (I/E)
MIS: A Special Case

GENERAL VS. TECHNICAL MANAGEMENT

If you were to ask the manager-on-the-street his (or her) recipe for good management, he would likely reply, "Get a lot of experience." Until recent years this has been the commonly accepted route to becoming a manager. It has been assumed that good sales managers were experienced salespersons, good product managers were experienced product managers, and so on.

This method of managing, sometimes called the "experience" or "custom" approach, attempts to analyze management by an empirical study of experience. It is probable that a large proportion of practitioners and businesspeople belong to this school and hold the view that experience is the single greatest determinant of managerial success. Moreover, in their approach to the problems of management decision making and problem solving, there is a tendency to study the successes and mistakes made by other managers in similar cases. The hope is that by studying these cases, the manager may be able to come up with generalizations concerning similar problems or at least the answer to a specific problem. The subscriber to this school might ask, "How would my predecessor have solved such a problem?" It is more an approach to developing problem-solving skills than an attempt to develop a scientific approach.

The empirical approach, which attempts to transfer knowledge to the learner by a study of experience, is typified by the American Management Assocation. This group has its roots in the top management people of the nation and views its primary function as providing a forum where practicing managers can gather to trade experiences of other managers and other companies. In the academic world, this empirical approach is represented by schools of business that teach by the *case method*. The Harvard Graduate School of Business has been the forerunner in this movement.

While few may deny that the knowledge of successful management of yesterday's problems may be helpful in handling similar problems of today's management, there is the danger that yesterday's answer will not be good enough for today's problem, nor will it apply to tommorrow's. What fits one organization might not fit another at all, and comparing the past issues with those of present and future is hazardous for the novice. We are all familiar with the type of manager who brags of twenty years' experience; in reality he only has *one* year's experience *twenty* times.

All of this leads me to make a distinction between *general* management and *technical* management.

First, everyone must have some technical skill. Everone must be a salesperson, accountant, engineer, and so on, or must understand and practice the disciplines of advertising, data processing, inventory control, disbursing, and purchasing, among many others. Further, these disciplines are different depending on the particular industry in which they are practiced. Each has its body of knowledge, its industry and professional association, its textbooks and publications. Indeed, the Labor Department Dictionary of Occupational Titles lists over 20,000 job definitions, ranging from dog-bather to bomb-handler. All of these are *technical* skills requiring technical management knowledge and practice.

Sooner or later the *technician* is given the opportunity to supervise the work of other technicians. At this moment he or she becomes more than a technician; he or she becomes a manager, and this new job now takes on a new and much more important dimension requiring the new skills and knowledge of general management, as shown in Figure 4-5. It is here, in the arena of *general management*, that the potential for greater improvement lies.

Figure 4–5. General management vs. technical management

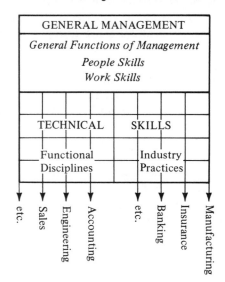

THE ROLE OF INDUSTRIAL ENGINEERING[2]

For the lack of a better label, I have grouped these techniques together under the convenient heading of industrial engineering. At the risk of too much abbreviation, it can be said that the basic fundamental I/E approach is to apply this problem-solving procedure to work—that is:

☐ Evaluate the function, comparing current performance against what it should be

☐ Analyze the improvement opportunities identified

☐ Improve the activities

Although not limited to manufacturing environments, I/E techniques have traditionally achieved the greatest payoff in these production-oriented activities:

☐ Receiving   ☐ Work Standards

☐ Stores   ☐ Plant Layout

☐ Product and Processes   ☐ Production Control

☐ Material Flow   ☐ Warehousing

☐ Material Handling   ☐ Shipping

☐ Work Methods   ☐ Maintenance

The industrial engineers, with their bagful of techniques (e.g., time and motion study, layout, process charting, methods analysis) face a paradox. At a time when we are demanding more output from "scientific methods," these methods appear to be on the decline. One reason may be the shift to a service economy and the resulting reduction in the number of jobs for which these techniques are appropriate. Perhaps it's the reluctance of the I/E to move from the factory floor into the service (office or white-collar) departments. Or perhaps in the era of the knowledge work the knowledge worker is in a better position than the work-study specialist to determine the best way to do a job. Moreoever, it just makes good "people" sense to harness the achievement drive and the desire for recognition by involving people in their work simplification, value analysis, group problem-solving, and other team efforts. The people in a department know more of what's wrong and how it can be corrected than anyone else in the company. Let the industrial engineer help them, not tell them what to do. Let the I/E be a trainer and consultant.

[2]See Chapter 11 for a discussion of tools of work analysis.

Sidney Harman, chairman of the Harman Company, says that the firm's methods engineers go out onto the factory floor and talk with the workers doing the job, asking what they would do to improve their work efficiency. This has produced much better results than simply sending the engineer out to time the duration of each task with a stop-watch.

Cole National Corporation of Cleveland, Ohio makes eyeglasses by the thousands. The firm had done everything right. All new equipment had been installed and the 80 or so jobs had been time-and-motion studied to death. Yet it was losing $1 million a year because deliveries couldn't be met. Rensis Likert, a recognized authority in behavioral science, coordinated a work-design program that included work teams, cross-training, and better coordination with sales. In less than five years, productivity has improved 92 percent, 98 percent of shipments are met, absenteesim and turnover have been substantially reduced.

MIS: A SPECIAL CASE

Why would a discussion of technical management and productivity include the topic of management information systems (MIS)?

It has been my experience with hundreds of managers in seminars and workshops involving productivity improvement that about 35 to 40 percent of their problems relate to the lack of information. "I can't schedule workload," or "I can't forecast my demand schedule," or "I don't have the information until it's too late." These are common complaints, and yet all too few managers know how to approach systems design. Instead, they are inclined to "leave it to the computer technician." That person cannot understand the needs of the user.

I believe that a minimum if cursory familiarity with the basic approach to *manager/user* design, not technical/analyst design, is very helpful. This cursory description below is just that. The purpose is to alert you to the need so that a more in-depth study can be made when the time comes, as it almost surely will.

The managerial contribution to systems design has these minimum steps:

☐ Set system objective(s)

☐ Determine information needs

☐ Determine information sources

☐ Detail the system concept

Set System Objective(s)

This first step in systems design is perhaps the most difficult, and is a step that must be stated and clearly understood before design can continue. Yet despite our clear understanding of the nature of and need for objectives in other areas of the company, it is frequently quite difficult to have them stated in the systems design context.

Unlike the *technician* who frequently turns to topics such as file structure and retrieval techniques, and who views the objectives of a subsystem only in terms of its input to a larger system, the *manager* must define system objectives in terms of legitimacy of information demands and not in terms of satisfaction of demands that are not related to an objective. Often the value of systems is measured in terms of transactions rather than of the benefit to the user. I have frequently heard systems analysts and computer salespeople state the objectives of systems design in terms of processing efficiency rather than of management effectiveness of the information processed. Several staff and functional supervisors have advised me that their objective was "to complete the required report on time for management use," without regard to the legitimacy of the report or its subsequent use for planning and control. I have witnessed the design of information systems in several government agencies in which the objective was the automation of hundreds of reports without regard to management of the many tasks related, or to functional or resource subsystems represented by the reports (e.g., training, employee relations, safety, recruitment, staffing, etc.). Such focus on the automation of records or the processing of existing data overlooks the real objectives of the operational organizational entity represented by the subsystem.

Yet is is no easier to determine the real objectives of an information system than to determine the objectives of the operational system served by it. A common fallacy in stating objectives is emphasis on the obvious or stating the objectives in vague terms: "Reduce costs"; "Improve efficiency"; "Keep accurate records"; "Meet the production schedule." A university president may say, "Provide quality education," and the government bureaucrat may say, "Provide more jobs for the unemployed," when asked to state their objectives. Yet in neither case is the objective stated in terms that are specific enough to provide a measure of performance of the system or to design an information system to help achieve the objective.

Despite the difficulty, being specific is necessary. Systems objectives must ultimately be stated in terms of the objectives of the department, group, function, or manager to be served, or in terms of the functions the information system is to perform. In other words, systems objectives should be expressed in terms of what managers can do after their information requirements have been met. Such expression may use descriptive statements, flow charts, or any other means that will convey to management the objectives that the systems designer must meet in order to develop the system. If possible, the objectives should be stated in quantitative rather than qualitative terms, so that alternative system designs as well as system performance can be measured for effectiveness. In other words, a statement of objectives should include exactly what it is that the systems is supposed to accomplish and how it will be subsequently evaluated.

Table 4-3 contains a statement of objectives for the material control system of one of the nation's major manufacturers. Notice how specific objectives are defined.

TABLE 4-3. Objectives of Material Control System—Major Manufacturer

Subsystem	Objective
Routings	Establishment of a system to capture routing information and time values that can be used by manufacturing for cost of completes, labor status by contract, effect of changes by rerouting, etc.
Status	Establish a system that can be used by manufacturing to determine workload in shop, effect of accepting additional work, overload in various cost centers, status of self-manufactured work in process, etc.
Tools	Establish a system to capture all tool information that can be used by manufacturing to determine tool status *prior* to release of work to shop and maintain a tool inventory by contract for auditing purposes.
Cost Control	Establishment of an overall system that can be used by manufacturing to very quickly determine labor costs, material costs, tool costs, overruns, etc. by contract.
Exception Reports	*Of primary importance*, any establishment of mechanized systems will be predicated on the basis that when information is

TABLE 4–3. (*cont.*)

Subsystem	Objective
	required by manufacturing, the system will have the ability to provide selective feedback immediately.
Scheduling	Establishment of a general-use scheduling system that can be used by manufacturing to determine effect of engineering changes, lack of material, tool shortages, etc.
Make or Buy	Establish a system that can be used by manufacturing to make intelligent decisions on those items to subcontract based on cost, load, schedule, etc.
Request for Proposal	*Establishment* of a system that will be used by manufacturing to determine break-in points, effect of breaking in changes, and configuration of units when shipped.
Elapsed Time Reporting	Analyze, improve, and prepare an orderly procedure that can be used by manufacturing to report elapsed time, if required by contractual obligation.
Inventory	Optimize inventory costs through the design of decision rules containing optimum reorder points, safety stock levels, and reorder quantities, each capable of continuous and automatic reassessment.
Accounts Payable	Pay 100% of invoices before due date.
Purchasing	Provide performance information on buyer's price negotiations with suppliers so purchase variance can be controlled within set limits.
Production Control	Identify cost and quantity variances within one day in order to institute closer control over these variables.
Project Control	Identify performance against plan so that events, costs, and specifications of the project can be met.

In summary, the first step in systems design attempts to answer the questions: What is the purpose of the system? Why is it needed? What is it expected to do? Who are the system's users, and what are their objectives? These questions relate to the *what* of systems design; the remainder of the steps relate to *how* the systems design will do the *what*.

Determine Information Needs

A clear statement of information needs is fundamental and necessary to good systems design. Too many companies spend lavish sums on hardware and software to perpetuate existing systems or build sophisticated data banks without first determining the real needs of management for information that can increase the perception of managers in critical areas such as problems, alternatives, opportunities, and plans.

Unless managers can provide the specifications for what they want from an information system, the design effort will produce something less than optimum results. If, on the other hand, the manager-user can define his objectives and spell out those items of information that are needed to reach the objective, he is then at least halfway home in systems design. Failure to be specific on these two steps probably accounts for the downfall of more design efforts than any other factor.

Too often systems design begins without a clear-cut statement of objectives and information needs. If this happens and the manager fails to provide them, the systems analyst or technician will provide *his* objectives and *his* information needs.

Information requirements should be stated as clearly and precisely as possible. Yet it is not easy for a manager to spell out the specific information requirements of his job, and therein lies a basic frustration in the improvement of systems. In an attempt to get a clear statement of information needs, the analyst frequently meets with an interviewing situation somewhat like the one represented in this typical exchange:

ANALYST: *Could you tell me what the objectives of this cost accounting system are as you see them?*

FINANCIAL MANAGER: *Sure ... to get the reports out faster ... to do something about keeping the costs in line ... to keep management informed ...*

ANALYST: *Yes, I understand ... let me put it another way. What are your responsibilities as you see them?*

FINANCIAL MANAGER: *Whatta you mean?... I'm in charge of the treasury department.*

ANALYST: *Yes, I know, but we need to get a better statement of your department's objectives, how the cost accounting system can further these objectives, and what information is needed to do this.*

FINANCIAL MANAGER: *Well, we need the information we've been getting but we need it faster and with a lot more accurate input from those fellows in operations.*

This hypothetical conversation reflects the difficulty of getting managers to be specific about information needs. One approach, sometimes used by consultants, is to get top management to require in writing from subordinate managers a statement containing: (a) a list of four to five major responsibilities for which the manager believes himself to be responsible, and (b) the four to five specific items of information that are required to perform the responsibilities. These requirements could be framed in terms of duties performed or decisions made; the idea is to get the manager to think of information needs. If this can be done, the information system is well on the way to being designed.

Determine Information Sources

The step of determining information needs is hardly completed before it is necessary to consider the information sources. Indeed, these two steps are overlapping and, as we stated before, iterative.

Although some systems require considerable external information, for the most part the natural place to turn for information is inside the firm: books, records, files, statistical and accounting documents, etc. Thus, most analysis refers to the step of determining information requirements as analyzing the present system.

The extent to which the *existing* system should be studied in a redesign effort for a *new system* has long been the subject of debate. One school of thought maintains that detailed analysis of the existing system should be a preliminary step to determining information requirements and that as much information as possible should be gathered and analyzed concerning the in-place system. This approach is justified on four grounds:

☐ A minor modification in the existing system may satisfy the information requirements without a major redesign effort.

☐ A look at the existing system is required in order to determine the specific areas that need improvement.

□ Since most systems utilize some common sources of input, a study of existing systems is necessary to determine these common inputs.

□ A study of existing systems is necessary to determine the data volume and costs associated with new designs.

The second theory of systems design, sometimes called the "fresh approach" or the "logical approach," holds that detailed analysis of the existing system is not necessary because the new system will be substantially changed and should not be predicated on the restraints of the existing one. Moreover, too close an identification with existing systems may compromise objectivity in the construction of logical methods to satisfy the information needs required to meet the systems objectives.

Whether the manager or the designer chooses one or a combination of these approaches is probably a matter of the state-of-the-art of information systems in the company under study, the objectives and existing information sources of the subsystem being designed, and the preferences of the manager himself. Sooner or later during design, some examination of existing company files as well as of external sources will become necessary if only to determine the source in order to satisfy a portion of the new information needs. It will also be necessary in order to integrate the subsystem under study with the total for the organization.

Detail the System Concept

At this point, sufficient information has been accumulated to begin a more detailed description of the system concept. This description includes essentially a flowchart or other documentation of the flow of information through the system, the inputs and outputs, and a narrative description of the operations.

Here we are describing the manager's participation in systems design and not the detailed specifications and documentation included in subsequent expansion by the designer. The manager's involvement in the design process is analogous to the homeowner's participation in the architect's planning. As with such plans, the basic design and many of the details are shaped by the wishes and needs of the person buying the house. So it is with a computer-based information system. The manager should be involved to the extent that the system provides information for his needs; the designer is concerned with the nature of the materials and equipment as well as with the technical processing considerations. Later details will be worked out by the designer. These details will include explicit instructions that will dictate what *data* are to be captured and *when*, the *files* that are to be used, the details of how *processing* is to be done, what *outputs* will be generated by the system, and how the outputs and files are to be *distributed*.

SYSTEM INPUTS

From the user's point of view, the inputs have been structured mainly when information sources were determined. However, there remains the task of design of input format. Since inputs frequently have to be accepted in the form in which they are received from outside the firm (e.g., sales orders, shipping documents, receiving papers, personnel information), input design becomes a matter of converting these to machine-usable form. When inputs are from other subsystems within the firm, the problem becomes one of integrating these systems through common data elements and other means.

More detailed input data specification includes the sources of data—i.e., where they come from, what form they are in, and who is responsible for their production. Because *forms* are so often used in collecting inputs and for other aids in operating a system, they are indispensable in modern business. Forms design is a major consideration for the systems designer.

Although the manager is not concerned in detail with these input specifications, he should be aware that the designer must specify the source of each input, its frequency, volume, and timing, plus its disposition after processing is completed. Since input must be checked for validity and volume, the editing procedures for accomplishing this are also required. Another important consideration is the specification of how inputs are to be converted into machine-readable form. These and other details of input design are usually contained on forms designed for that purpose.

SYSTEM OUTPUTS

From the technical standpoint, output-data definition includes the specification of destination—i.e., where they go, in what form they are, and who is responsible for receiving them. Included in these specifications are the distribution of output (who gets what, how many copies, and by what means), the frequency with which output will be called for and its timing, and the form the output will take (tape, hard copy, data terminal, etc.). Questions that the designer will ask in the process of developing output specifications include:

☐ What form are the output reports to take? Can it be offline?

☐ Should the information be detailed or summarized?

☐ What can I do with the output data that will be reused?

☐ What kind of output form will be required? How many copies?

☐ Are reports generated on demand? By exception? On schedule?

Despite the need to answer these details of output specification, the manager is concerned primarily with getting his information needs as previously determined in some type of output format. In other words, the consideration is how to *present the information to the eye or the ear of the manager.* The answer to this question lies in the content and form design of the output document. This form design is a direct function of information needs and should be designed to provide those needs in a timely fashion. Care should be taken not to ask for *too much* information *too frequently.* "Management by exception" and "information by summary" should be the guiding principles.

Remember—the system output is the most important element in an information system. It is the reason why we design an MIS, and the system exists for the sole purpose of providing the output. Information for decision making and for planning and controlling operations is provided by the output, and it is therefore of primary concern to the manager.

PEOPLE &
PRODUCTIVITY
Motivation &
the Quality of Work Life

Organizations don't have objectives—people do. Organizations don't achieve productivity—people do. An organization is nothing more than the combined efforts of the people who are its members. Despite this obvious truth, many managers hesitate to delegate or allow people to participate in decisions affecting them and the company.

CHAPTER 5

MOTIVATION AND THE WORKFORCE

The Workforce of
the 80s
The Employee of
the 80s
"The New Breed"

THE WORKFORCE OF THE 80s

It is widely agreed among successful and profitable firms that the greatest potential for increasing productivity lies in the motivation and untapped abilities of the workforce. Even the economic experts concerned with productivity indicate that in the years ahead industry will benefit even more from investment in human capital than in plant and equipment. This idea, somewhat slow to catch on, is now being promoted by management and labor alike. At General Motors, the "organization person's organization," many managers believe that recapturing the interest of their workers—or at least getting them to tolerate life on the assembly line—is one of the crucial problems to be solved in the remainder of the century. Most chief executives will freely admit that their most important decisions are about people. Even unions, historically concerned with little more than pay and benefits, are now adopting policies regarding the quality of work life as it relates to motivation and participation. Quoted here is a portion of a recent policy statement by the United Automobile Workers (UAW):

Achieving job satisfaction includes not only decent working conditions, it must move to a higher plateau where the worker is not merely the adjunct of the tool, but in which he participates in the decision-making process which concerns his welfare on the job. This calls for a departure from the miniaturization and oversimplification of the job, symbolic of "scientific management" to a system which embraces broader distribution of authority, increasing rather than diminishing responsibility, combined with the engineering of more interesting jobs, with the opportunity to exercise a meaningful measure of autonomy and to utilize more varied skills. It requires tapping the creative and innovative ingenuity of the worker and his direct participation in the decisions involved in his job.

The modern manager must consider not only what is right for the company but what is right for the individual as well. In the past we have ordinarily considered these two requirements as conflicting. The problem now is to combine them into a single approach that meets the needs of the company as well as its personnel. It can be done.

In 1980 Yankelovich, Skelly & White, the firm that prepares trend reports based on comprehensive social monitoring, identified *bottom-up management* as one of the ten most important emerging trends for the 80s.[1] The employee is no longer content with the traditional rewards offered up by the company or by labor unions such as more pay, four-day workweeks, more fringe benefits, and so on. What he or she really wants is deep human satisfaction from work. Managers should not view this as a problem, but as an opportunity.

In this chapter we will examine those factors which affect productivity and relate them to modern motivational philosophy and practice. Throughout, a *management by results* approach is the central theme and the operational vehicle by which we can achieve productivity. Results management motivates the manager and the subordinate to action because each decides the job necessary to get the results demanded by the work. It is a philosophy of management that rests on the concepts of human action, behavior, and motivation.

THE EMPLOYEE OF THE 80s

In 1902 Samuel Gompers, the first president of the American Federation of Labor, described what the union wanted for its members: "We want more, we demand more, and when we get that more, we shall insist upon again more and more." Today's "new breed" of workers want more too, but not simply more money and benefits. They want more psychological satisfaction, more skills, more possibilities to accomplish something on the job that is satisfying and worthwhile.

In a 1939 book, *The Future of Industrial Man,* Peter Drucker wrote, "Any workable social order such as the corporation must confer status and function upon all its members." Apparently it has taken forty years for this advice to catch on because today's manager has come to realize that *status* and *function* must be accommodated if the worker is to be productive and achieving.

In previous times the value system of the "old breed" of worker traditionally included the following ideas:

☐ A job was a living and a person would put up with its drawbacks for the sake of economic security

☐ People owed their loyalty to the organization for which they worked

[1]Other trends that were among the top ten that are of interest in terms of productivity are: an information society, decentralization, human technology, and participatory democracy.

□ People were motivated to work by money

□ People defined their personal identities through their work role (e.g., "I work for GM," or "I am a salesman")

THE "NEW BREED" OF WORKER

This value system no longer holds for today's "new breed." A recent survey of 23,000 respondent readers was conducted by the popular magazine *Psychology Today* to determine the nature of modern work values. Some of the findings are typical of the many current studies and articles that center on this topic. Two interesting conclusions from the above study were these:

□ Two-thirds of the people were unwilling to accept a higher-paying job if it meant less interesting work

□ Most people would continue to work even if they could live comfortably for the rest of their lives without doing so

When given eighteen aspects of their job, and asked how important each of these was, the first five responses listed in order of importance were:

□ A chance to do something that makes me feel good about myself

□ A chance to accomplish something worthwhile

□ Chances to learn new things

□ Opportunity to develop skills and abilities

□ The amount of freedom I have on the job

Pay and fringe benefits were ranked No. 12 and No. 16.

Assuming that these responses fairly represent the values and work attitudes of the workforce at large, or at least of the "new breed" sector, we have some valuable clues on how to motivate for productivity.

It is clear that a growing number of people are unwilling to accept the old work values and the alienations that accompanied them. The carrot-and-stick approach (the carrot representing money and status, the stick the threat of economic insecurity) is no longer available as a motivational alternative. It has been replaced by the notion that an individual can and should achieve self-actualization *from his work.*

This is the managerial opportunity for productivity:

MOTIVATION AND PRODUCTIVITY
A Thumbnail Sketch of Motivation
Productivity and Self-Actualization
Factors Affecting Productivity

A THUMBNAIL SKETCH OF MOTIVATION

Most of the readers of this book have probably been exposed to the basic conceptual aspects of human motivation as it applies to the job situation. The fundamental notion is that when employees are provided an opportunity to utilize their talents and potential, they will perform at a higher level of productivity, make fewer mistakes, and achieve greater personal satisfaction. I will summarize the mainstream of existing theory by presenting a thumbnail sketch of the principles developed by three contemporary experts: Abraham Maslow, Douglas McGregor, and Frederick Herzberg.

Maslow, the father of humanist psychology, concluded that human wants form a hierarchy which runs from lower- to higher-order needs; from basic physical drives (hunger, thirst, sex) to psychological needs (self-esteem, accomplishment). He called the highest-order need *self-actualization*. As one level of the hierarchy is reasonably satisfied, the next level becomes the more potent motivator. Maslow's statement that "man lives by bread alone—only when there is no bread" illustrates the point that as the economic wants become increasingly satisfied, it becomes less and less satisfying to obtain more economic rewards. Hence the promise of money or other economic rewards is no longer a motivator once basic needs are met.

Maslow's theory has two important lessons for the manager. First, within most organizations, sizable numbers of employees move swiftly to satisfy lower-order needs but become frustrated because their opportunities for self-actualization (growth and development) are thwarted and full utilization of their talents is blocked. They must either be content with something less than optimum job satisfaction or find outside involvement to fulfill their needs for meaningful accomplishment. The second lesson to be learned from Maslow's ideas is that money is not the motivator people once thought it was. This may be hard to accept, but a moment's reflection may convince you that although a person may work harder because of the promise of money, he or she is not motivated. There is a substantial difference. The problem with money is that the worker must constantly be recycled by some form of behavior reinforcement with either the carrot or the stick. Neither case illustrates motivation. The worker "moves" but isn't motivated. Only self-actualization related to the job will achieve that.

A second highly popular theory of motivation and human behavior has been advanced by Douglas McGregor: the concept of the Theory X and the Theory Y managerial styles. The classical approach to management is represented by Theory X, which maintains that there is no satisfaction in the work itself, that human beings avoid work as much as possible, that positive direction and tight control over workers is necessary, and that workers possess little ambition or enthusiasm for their work. The human-relations approach of Theory Y, the antithesis of Theory X, states that workers exercise self-direction and seek responsibility if they are properly motivated. Theory Y is a *participative* approach. We will talk more about this theory when we examine leadership styles.

It remained for Frederick Herzberg to show how managers can move toward adopting Theory Y assumptions while seeing that their workers can work toward achieving self-actualization. He pointed out that when economic rewards and other lower-level needs are met, they diminish in importance as positive incentives; however, their capacity to create dissatisfaction rapidly increases if they are not satisfied. Economic rewards cease to be "incentives" and become "hygiene factors." If not properly taken care of—that is, if there is dissatisfaction with the economic rewards—they become deterrents. On the positive side, Herzberg postulated that another group of factors, the *motivators*, tended to produce job satisfaction and productivity. These motivators center around the job itself or the job content and include *achievement, growth, participation,* and *responsibility*.

Figure 5-1 summarizes a simplified version of Maslow's general theory of motivation (hierarchy of needs) combined with Herzberg's notion of hygiene and motivational factors in the workplace. The combination of these two approaches explains much about how barriers to motivation can be removed and how we can facilitate work so that people are *working willingly to achieve common goals*.

Herzberg's role in motivational theory cannot be denied. He has refocused management's attention from the classical Theory X assumptions and hygiene factors (e.g., pay, benefits, environmental conditions) to the far more important motivator factors of

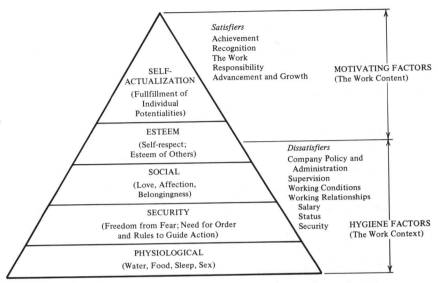

Figure 5-1. The hierarchy of needs combined with motivating and hygiene work factors

achievement—recognition, and the work itself. These factors are the ones that hold promise for increased productivity and job satisfaction. Too often in the past, management's motivational attempts have been limited to the "hygiene" areas.

It is important to understand the difference between hygiene and motivational factors surrounding the subordinate's job. To illustrate these differences, Table 5-1 contains a list of potential assignments for a staff secretary. These have been identified as motivator (M) or hygiene (H).

What does all this mean in terms of our *system for managing productivity*? It means that first, we must identify those job factors that motivate and hence affect the productivity of subordinates. It means that second, we must operationalize these factors. In other words, we combine theory and practice in order to achieve results through managing subordinates.

PRODUCTIVITY AND SELF-ACTUALIZATION

Let me propose a simple but operational definition of motivation:

A person is motivated when he or she is working willingly *to achieve* common *goals*.

108   *People & Productivity: Motivation & the Quality of Work Life*

TABLE 5–1. Hygiene and Motivational Factors Surrounding Job of
Staff Secretary

Job Assignment	Motivator	Hygiene
Go to lunch with boss		X
Set objectives for office routine	X	
Select incoming letter for self-reply	X	
Provide advice to department on policy	X	
Set own working hours		X
Have own office		X
Present recommendations at meetings	X	
Attend departmental meetings		X
Eliminate coffee-making duties	X	X
Get new typewriter		X
Farm out copy-machine work	X	X
Get salary increase		X
Prepare expense accounts		X
Approve expense accounts	X	
Change title to Staff Coordinator		X
Attend convention	X	X

   Although this definition may be simple, I have found that it gets to the heart of *practical* productivity improvement. At the risk of offending hundreds of behavioral scientists I would like to state two objections to many of the current motivational concepts. First, they are so *complex* as to be impractical—the typical supervisor finds them difficult both to understand and to use. He or she is usually so busy keeping up to date on maintaining technical skills (e.g., accounting, sales, engineering) that it isn't possible to apply complicated motivational notions. Second, most of the motivational theories assume *manipulative* behavior on the part of a superior toward a subordinate: "Boss is smart, subordinate is dumb." I hope that the concepts advanced in this chapter overcome both of these objections. We are seeking a practical, easy-to-use method for achieving both motivation and productivity.
   Notice that the two essential concepts in my proposed definition of motivation: *willingness* and *common goals*. The common goals, of course, involve productivity improvement. These must be common

to the individual, the team members, and the company. We are not interested in goals that differ between individuals and the organization. A person can be motivated to participate in a variety of actions such as striking, absenteeism, grievances, sabotage, and so on—but these do not represent *common goals*. Our second concept is *willingness*. If people are forced to move toward a goal that is not their own, they are not motivated according to the definition above. The actions are not taken willingly.

All this brings us to the question of *money* as a motivator. Almost everyone will tend to agree, at first, that money does motivate people. But does it, really? Assume for a minute that you are held up by an armed robber at 4:00 A.M. in a dark alley. He puts a gun to your head with the command: "Give me your wallet!" You will probably deliver the wallet to the robber with no questions. But are you *motivated*? If your answer is yes, consider these questions: Are you doing it *willingly*? Does your action involve *common* goals? The answer must be No! Your goal is to save your life, but the robber's goal is to relieve you of your money. These are quite different goals and are therefore not common. You are hardly surrendering your money willingly. You must be "moving," but you are not "motivated"—not, at least, in accordance with my definition. You are moving because you have a *gun to your head*. So in this instance, the goals are not common and the action is not taken willingly.

Is the carrot-and-stick approach a "gun to the head"? Is the promise of a raise for a good job, the threat of being fired, even the paternalistic management style, a "gun to the head"? Perhaps the analogy is extreme, but it demonstrates that the negative approach to motivation will not work. People will not perform if they are driven. The positive approach involves *working willingly toward common goals*. The individual is then headed for self-actualization on the job.

Essential to the understanding of motivational theory is the admission that it is not the boss, the supervisor, the manager who motivates. The employee involved can only be motivated if the driving, motivating goals are *internalized* within him- or herself. Goals and objectives cannot be imposed from outside. If people are not driven from inside themselves to achieve a goal, the exhortations of the boss, though they may *move* the employees, will not *motivate* them. The best that a manager can do is remove the barriers to motivation and set a climate in which self-motivation can flourish. The supervisor must apply the motivating concepts illustrated in Figure 5-1 and provide a working environment in which the individual can motivate him- or herself through achievement, recognition, responsibility, and advancement and growth resulting from the *job*.

FACTORS AFFECTING PRODUCTIVITY

Today's company and manager face a paradox. The many benefits enjoyed by today's worker, undreamed of a generation ago, are now accepted as basic rights. It is the age of entitlement. James Lindheim, senior vice president of Yankelovich, Skelly & White, says that the vast majority of workers feel *entitled* to good wages, health benefits, insurance, profit sharing, tuition benefits, legal assistance, and many other benefits. These are taken for granted. Now they want job satisfaction. They don't want to be treated like numbers. So if traditional rights and benefits aren't enough, what motivational factors are available to today's supervisor?

The most important question in the field of management remains: *How do I motivate employees?*

Research and observation tell us that there are nine important factors (motivators) that need to be taken into account if an organization is to effect the changes that are necessary to increase productivity and profitability. These are summarized below:

- □ *Work* that is challenging, creative, and interesting and provides an opportunity for "stretch" performance
- □ *Participation* in decisions that have a direct effect on the individual's job
- □ *Compensation* that is tied to performance and to sharing in productivity gains; this requires realistic *appraisal*
- □ *Communication and authority* channels that are simplified
- □ *Supervision* that is competent
- □ *Recognition* of achievement
- □ *Self-development* opportunity
- □ Opportunity for *stewardship*, care of and attention to customer and co-worker needs
- □ *Organizational styles* and patterns that are more flexible

Providing for these job satisfaction and motivational needs is not a simple task. Indeed, it is very complex. No single simplistic change or group of changes, such as revised pay schedules or job enrichment, will suffice, nor will any vague and misdirected notions of "human relations" or paternalism.

We do know that certain basic techniques, methods, and programs are available to the organization and to the individual manager which, taken together, can go a long way toward creating the proper climate for productivity. We will call these *Results Management Methods*, and they form the basis of our system of managing subordinates. They are:

☐ *Job Development.* Matching the content and level of an employee's job responsibility to his or her skills and abilities.

☐ *Performance Appraisal.* The process of appraising a subordinate's performance against previously established goals. This provides feedback on performance, a tool for self-development, and a device for recognition for performance.

☐ *Subordinate Development.* Providing the environment for continuous learning, self-development, and growth on the job.

☐ *Communication.* Improving the communication process, using upward communication so that subordinates are informed about matters that affect their jobs.

☐ *Leadership Style.* The adoption of leadership and supervisory styles that promote "results thinking" and hence productivity and job satisfaction.

☐ *Delegation and Control.* Learning and practicing the art of delegation utilizing subordinates' self-control.

☐ *Organizational Style.* Adopting an organizational form that provides for flexibility in authority and communication and overcomes the inflexibility of the classical bureaucracy.

The matrix shown in Table 5–2 indicates how our factors affecting productivity can be achieved by use of the seven results-management methods listed above.

The remainder of this book will discuss in more detail the principles behind these methods and the ways of achieving greater productivity. These seven methods provide the central core of our system for managing subordinates.

The Japanese Lesson

I have already pointed out in Chapter 1 that Japan's productivity is outpacing our own by a wide margin. Indeed, we might say that they

TABLE 5–2. Management Methods and Factors Affecting Productivity

Management Methods

Factors Affecting Productivity	Job development	Appraisal	Subordinate development	Communications	Delegation and control	Leadership style	Organization style
Work that is challenging, creative, and interesting	X	X	X		X		X
Participation in decisions affecting the job	X	X	X	X	X	X	X
Compensation tied to performance	X	X	X	X			
Simplification of channels of communication		X	X	X	X	X	X
Competent supervisor	X	X	X	X	X	X	
Recognition for achievement	X	X	X	X	X	X	X
Opportunity for self development	X	X	X	X	X	X	X
Opportunity for stewardship	X	X	X	X	X		X
Organization style that is flexible			X	X	X	X	X

Note: X indicates the management method that can be effective in implementing the factor affecting productivity.

are running circles (quality circles) around us in the rate of growth of productivity.

The typical Japanese firm realizes that *planning* and *doing* need to be united in the same person. Unlike American workers, the Japanese are given freedom to plan and execute their own work and are encouraged to solve problems and develop innovations without reference to managers except when needed as a resource. They practice *bottom-up* management. They understand what motivates a worker; that given a chance, workers can be self-motivated.

When the Matsushita Company took over a bankrupt Motorola plant and began to produce the Quasar television set, they reduced the supervisory level from 600 to 300 but kept the 1,000 workers. After two years, production doubled, the reject rate dropped from 60 percent to 4 percent, and warranty costs went down from $14 million to $2 million.

THE QUALITY OF WORK LIFE (QWL)
What Is the Quality of Work Life (QWL)?
Components of a QWL Program:
PARTICIPATION
TEAM ORGANIZATION
JOB DEVELOPMENT
INCENTIVES AND FEEDBACK
Incentive Plans
QWL and the Unions

So far in this chapter we have developed a thumbnail sketch of the worker of the 1980s and beyond, and I have suggested that the factors affecting motivation are the same as those that increase productivity. In the remainder of this chapter we will examine what I call the Quality of Work Life (QWL) concept and programs that make possible its integration with motivation and productivity. There are substantial untapped human resources in every organization, and improvement is there virtually for the asking.

Quality of Working Life is a term made popular by Richard Nixon. It is an accelerating movement in the United States and in Europe as well. It is being promoted by employees, by some unions, by government, and by many management groups and companies. Those individuals who take the time to understand the principles of QWL recognize that the concept goes hand in glove with productivity improvement. Each reinforces the other. In the words of Theodore Mills, director of the American Quality of Work Center, "I don't know of a single instance in which improved quality of working life didn't lead to improved productivity."

"Spacetronics" [a pseudonym] is the primary supplier of airborne computers required for the guidance system of Minuteman ICBMs. Quality is essential and quality assurance a major concern. In an effort to improve quality and productivity, the firm established a QWL program that included the elements of participative management and problem solving and group or team goal setting accompanied by feedback and training. Three thousand people were eventually involved, and the results included a 20 to 30 percent increase in productivity with a 30 to 50 percent improvement in quality. [2]

WHAT IS QWL?

To help you understand QWL, we will summarize what it *is* and what it *is not*. What QWL *is not* is the concern with the environment and corporate social responsibility reflected in the Messianic movement of Ralph Nader. What it *is not* is the philosophical movement in which greater understanding of self, of relations to others, and a closer relationship with nature are stressed. What QWL *is* is the approach to a working environment that increases output by better human-resource management while at the same time achieving a *more satisfying and rewarding life at work.*

One of General Motors' most successful QWL efforts has been at the Tarrytown (N. Y.) assembly plant where the company's worst facility turned around and won GM's highest quality award as the firm's top unit. The United Auto Workers local president said, "The grievance load has been cut from 2,000 to 20 and everybody is more of an integral part of the structure than ever before. What the [QWL] program has done is create an atmosphere at the workplace that is no different than it is at home. You're not turned off when you walk in the factory gate."

The actions that need to be taken to provide a satisfying and rewarding life at work are fortunately the same actions that are

[2]Adapted from John R. Hinrichs, *Practical Management for Productivity* (New York: Van Nostrand Reinhold Company, 1978).

required for human-resource motivation and hence productivity. I repeat that this is fortunate because it simplifies both the QWL and the productivity problems. We have already commented on the connection between them.

COMPONENTS OF A QWL PROGRAM

The major components can be summarized as follows:

☐ *Participation and Participative Management.* This involves the sloughing off of the old-fashioned idea that management is omnipotent and that labor can be manipulated. It involves a recognition that employees can be responsible, mature, and knowledgable about work affecting them, that they want to be involved. It is possible to implement managerial approaches and programs that build employee involvement and *common goals.* Employees have both the potential and the desire to contribute to problem solving and innovation for improvement.

☐ *Team Organization.* QWL problem-solving groups, which are referred to as "quality circles" or "productivity improvement teams" (PITS), are a recent organizational innovation designed to break through the structure of the functional departments or to improve the operation of an ongoing but specific task or problem. Aside from contributing to the adaptability of the team and its receptivity to new ideas, membership in such groups can heighten motivation and commitment to effective performance.

☐ *Job Development.* This component of QWL ensures that individuals use their talent, ability, and knowledge. This means that employees are allowed to have the maximum amount of autonomy concerning how a job is to be done. A person's commitment to a job is a function of the amount of control he or she has over it. Job-design concepts also take account of the skills and knowledge of the team or group in order to take advantage of diverse abilities and the synergy of the group.

☐ *Incentives and Feedback.* Continuing motivation and productivity depend upon the formulation of realistic objectives or targets and the existence of feedback concerning progress. The "loop" is therefore a process of goal setting, feedback, and reinforcement. These three elements, along with possible QWL techniques, are shown in the table below:

Element	QWL Technique	Chapter
Goal Setting	Management by Objectives	7
	Individual Productivity Improvement Objectives	2
	Company Productivity Measures	3
	Team Goals	6
Feedback	Individual Self-Control	7
	Supervisory/Company Feedback	8
	Team Performance Measures	3
Reinforcement	Recognition	8
	Performance Appraisal	8
	Incentives	7

A WORD ABOUT FINANCIAL INCENTIVES

For decades, incentive plans have been commonplace in the United States and abroad. Experience has shown that many of these plans (but by no means all of them) can improve productivity. Because all incentive plans encourage performance above standard, individual earnings depend on increased efforts.

Group plans, as opposed to individual plans, are based on total plant or company performance. The most popular of these is the Scanlon Plan, devised in 1937 by an Ohio open-hearth worker named Joe Scanlon. This approach encourages cooperative relations between union and management, and productivity gains are shared with the workers. Other plans include profit sharing and employee stock ownership (ESOP).

Desoto Chemicals & Coatings achieved a 49 percent increase in productivity after installing a Scanlon production-incentive plan in four plants. Employees received cash bonuses and higher morale was reported to be a fallout benefit.

At Texas Instruments, profit sharing is dependent on two variables: PEI (People Effectiveness Index) and ROA (Return on Assets). PEI is calculated by dividing net sales billed by total payroll plus payroll-related benefits. ROA is the conventional figure derived by dividing net after-tax income by the average assets employed during the year. PEI and ROA are combined to arrive at the profit-sharing percentage.

Individual incentive plans, in which each individual's incentive is based on his or her performance, is more difficult to administer. Moreover, the plan may obscure the relationship between work and pay.

One manufacturer found so many problems with his system that he dropped it. When an employee was absent, for example, other employees became reluctant to move to the unfamiliar job for fear their own output might drop. Further resistance developed when production bottlenecks developed and employees had to be transferred to other areas. Likewise, considerable resistance and friction resulted from rate adjustments, design modifications, and production changes. Quality control began to slip as items of marginal quality were passed to help meet incentive quotas. Everyone, including workers, managment, and the union were glad to see the plan fold.

QWL AND THE UNIONS

Labor unions today face a paradox. On the one hand, they tend to frown on many elements of QWL programs because of the traditional fears that productivity means speed-up, job security will be threatened, standards of performance will be tightened, and QWL is a union-busting activity. On the other hand, union management is beginning to realize that members are no longer content with the traditional union benefits.

The attitude of many unions has begun to soften toward QWL programs. Today the United Auto Workers offers general support for the programs. Experience at several auto plants indicates that QWL programs have dramatically improved relations between worker and manager and reduced chances of local strikes. Other unions that have endorsed such programs include the Bakery & Confectionery Workers, the Newspaper Guild, the American Federation of State, County, and Municipal Employees, and the United Food & Commercial Workers. The Communication Workers of America are in the developmental stage of endorsing QWL methods.

In 1980, the bargaining pact in the steel industry became a landmark event in labor negotiations. The settlement moved labor relations away from the traditional adversary confrontation between workers and bosses toward a more cooperative approach to common problems in the workplace. The United Steel Workers (USW) and the companies agreed to set up "labor-management participation teams" in an effort to make jobs more meaningful for workers and more productive for the companies. The problem-solving teams discuss such items as production efficiency, product quality, safety and health, employee morale, absenteeism, and how supervisors deal with workers. This was the first union-management agreement adopted on an industrywide basis to deal with work-improvement ideas to relieve worker alienation and to speed up lagging productivity.

It is very unlikely that a QWL program can be successful in a unionized organization without union involvement. Both management and the union should avoid the traditional adversary relationship and cooperate in a program that will benefit everyone. A beginning can be found in establishing a *labor–management QWL and Productivity Committee.*

At a New York plant of one automaker, the situation was desperate. Operating costs were skyrocketing and the plant was at the bottom of the company's system in quality, production, and efficiency. Labor-management relations were polarized into a climate of entrenched conflict.

Then everything changed. During a meeting to review a production reorganization, the usual management groups were present: industrial engineers, plant engineers, staff planners, and so on. Someone raised a simple point that had never been asked before: "Maybe we should ask the people who are actually going to be directly involved. They probably know a lot more about it that will help us too." This led ultimately to the involvement of workers on the line and eventually to "rap sessions," expanded involvement, and a joint union-management committee to oversee quality of work life in the plant. There have also been joint labor-management problem-solving committees. Out of this union-management cooperation has come spectacular results. Grievances have been reduced by 98 percent, absenteeism by 36 percent, and selected production problems have been reduced by from 50 to 95 percent![3]

SUMMARY

In this chapter I have attempted to integrate the concepts of productivity improvement, motivation, and the quality of work life. None of these is in opposition to the others. All are interactive, and

[3]Adapted from Hinrichs, *Practical Management for Productivity.*

together comprise the *people* dimension of productivity. If a firm organizes a QWL effort it will inevitably improve productivity. If it organizes a productivity effort, it must be sensitive to QWL. An understanding of the concepts and principles of motivation are essential.

Taken together, productivity, motivation, and Quality of Work Life represent change in an organization. Change cannot be achieved by dictum; it cannot be nurtured by lip service. Productivity should be accepted as what it is—*a way of managerial life.*

PEOPLE & PRODUCTIVITY
Work Teams & Work Design

"Take this job and shove it. I ain't working here no more." —Johnny Paycheck, *Country singer*

These lyrics from a popular country song reflect the dissatisfaction many workers feel with their jobs. A growing number of employees perceive their work as impersonal and unrewarding in terms of job satisfaction and personal identification. This is unfortunate because the workforce, at all levels, represents a huge untapped resource.

Increased productivity in the 1980s will depend on improving the commitment to goals and the effectiveness of the individual employee. To reiterate, many organizations have attempted to improve human-resource utilization by cutting back on *inputs*—reduction in force levels or substitution of less expensive equipment for people. This approach has yielded limited results. For example, clerical costs may have been saved by computers, but the perception of people as a direct expense has not increased productivity significantly.

There is now evidence that many enlightened organizations realize that the productivity of the human resource can be improved without reducing inputs. The approach simply means establishing an environment that leads to *greater employee outputs.*

PEOPLE AND PRODUCTIVITY, I

Participative vs. Bureaucratic Management
Productivity Improvement Teams (PITs)
ORGANIZATION AND DUTIES
TRAINING
BENEFITS

PARTICIPATIVE VS. BUREAUCRATIC MANAGEMENT

In Chapter 4, I argued that productivity was inhibited by the traditional style and structure associated with the classical pyramidal form of organizational structure. The focus on structure and chain of command, and labor specialization and attention to activity rather than results, were two characteristics that tended to discourage innovation and the natural inclination of people to suggest change and improvement. This inflexibility in managerial style is representative of another era. This type of classical manager, when confronted with the idea of participation, becomes uncomfortable with the thought of giving up control to the workers. C. Jackson Grayson, founder of the American Productivity Center, describes it this way:

What has happened is that autocratic, bureaucratic organizations in business and public service have suppressed the desires and ability of the individual to feel that he or she is contributing. People do not mind contributing to the success of an enterprise so long as they feel that they have had a hand in helping to shape it and are rewarded.

A recent study by the American Management Associations concluded that "the 1980s will become the decade of the employee." Americans are demanding some voice in the decision process, and if they don't get it, they will not be productive.

What does "participative management" mean? It means the adoption of an organizational philosophy, and a managerial style which recognizes that most employees are responsible and react positively to the opportunity of sharing in decisions regarding productivity improvement. It means that the vitality and growth of the organization is not solely a concern of top management.

Employees have the potential for caring and contributing. This potential can be substantially realized by two approaches suggested in this chapter: (1) the idea of work teams, and (2) work design or job development.

PRODUCTIVITY IMPROVEMENT TEAMS

The idea of work teams is not new. The British, Japanese, and West Germans developed productivity teams shortly after World War II, but the Americans, inventors of the management process, have been slow to catch on.

Lately, the movement to work teams in the United States has gained momentum. They have a variety of names and take on a number of acronyms such as VIPs (Volunteers Interested in Perfection), IMPS (Improved Methods and Products Seekers), TOPS (Turned Onto Productivity and Savings), PICs (Performance Improvement Circles) and PLUS (Productivity Leads Us to Success). In Japan, where the idea gained worldwide prominence, the work teams are called *quality circles*.

Whatever the name, the objective is to apply the teamwork principle to improve productivity. For the sake of simplicity, I shall call the concept the Productivity Improvement Team (PIT). The acronym PITs is clearly appropriate because it is in the workplace— the "pits" or "trenches" where productivity improvement must ultimately occur.

Organization and Duties

The productivity team is based on the premise that the workers often know best how to improve productivity and quality, as well as solve on-the-scene problems. This holds true in manufacturing, clerical or service areas, knowledge work, or in the dozens of functional departments.

Groups of from five to twelve employees voluntarily gather for an hour or more each week on company time, and engage in problem-solving sessions on how to increase output per hour worked, improve quality, or solve work problems. The team leader, frequently a supervisor, leads the discussions and helps put the recommendations into practice. Unlike a committee, the team as a whole is responsible for the mission and tasks. The mission is productivity, and the task is problem solving. Each member contributes his or her particular knowledge and skill.

At IBM's San Jose, California facility, "productivity circles" have been assigned these responsibilities:

☐ Develop problem list

☐ Assign data-gathering teams

☐ Present resolutions to management

☐ Assign priorities to problems

☐ Develop problem resolutions

☐ Document activity and savings

Many people mistakenly assume that the work-team concept applies only to production or factory work. In fact, organizations in banking, insurance, government, and hundreds of other service departments in industrial firms have found the team approach valuable.

Under Texas Instruments' Team Improvement Program (TIP), more than 80 percent of the employees meet regularly at their workplaces to discuss and implement more productive ways of doing their jobs. Teams work on indirect *expense as well as products. For example, every time net sales double, a 14 percent decrease is achieved in general and administrative expense as a percent of sales.*

At IBM, where productivity teams are a way of corporate life, computer programmers in a complex development laboratory formed a team to reduce costly errors in program logic and code. The result: Errors in program code were reduced by two-thirds, accompanied by a 70 percent increase in programming instructions per man-month.

Scientific management and labor specialization gave us the *functional* organization, in which work was organized into discrete units of homogeneous tasks (e.g., cut, weld, assemble, design, sell, ship). The functional arrangement of activities has been around for a long time, and is still the overwhelming form of organizational structure. Indeed, it has been around for so long that we find it difficult to see how the team concept can operate within the functional setup. Functional organization and team organization are commonly assumed to be opposites, with the "modern" team being opposed to the "traditional" functions. However, it must be emphasized that the choice is not between one form or the other; the two are *complementary.* The best organizational form is one that allows people to perform and contribute. The *productivity team* achieves the best of both worlds for the purpose of problem solving and innovation surrounding the "how" of productivity improvement.

Each team has a "quarterback," a leader who is usually, but not always, a supervisor. It is the leader's job to clarify objectives and the roles of team members. Additionally, he or she ensures that there is coordination and communication. This includes providing feedback on progress, and a means for all members to identify problems and provide input.

One of the earliest work-team projects, organized in 1970 at Alcan Aluminum Corporation's rolling mill in Oswego, New York, is still going strong. Teams of four and five workers run six rolling mills. Each team has a leader who is cross-trained to know all the other jobs so that no backup people are needed. All production workers are cross-trained, rotate jobs, and do their own maintenance. This experience shows that manufacturers needn't be locked out of work-design programs by equipment constraints.

Training

Although the team members bring technical skills to the productivity team, these are usually not enough to contribute to the new work dimension. Employees need to be trained in new skills, whether they are unskilled, skilled, or knowledge workers. Training allows the employees to contribute what they have learned to a more rational way of working and hence the improvement of their own jobs as well as others'. Moreover, training has the additional advantage of overcoming resistance to change—in this case, the change required to innovate for productivity.

There are many areas for training and development in both supervisory and technical skills (see Figure 4-1), but we are concerned here with those that are appropriate for team members in order to function effectively in the group.

Productivity improvement implies that productivity levels are currently less than what they should be; suboptimal is the word among industrial engineers. This, in turn, suggests a problem. It follows that some basic training in problem definition and analysis would help identify the *cause* of suboptimization. Following the identification of the *cause* of the problem, a next step would be to determine a course of action to remove the cause and increase productivity—an approach to be learned by rational *decision making*.

In gathering information and data for *problem solving and decision making*, it is helpful to be aware of analytical tools and some courses of action to improve workflow.[1] A familiarity with such

---

[1]These methods are discussed in Chapter 11.

basics as data collection, frequency histograms, statistics, check sheets, process charts, graphs, quality control, and work simplification aids the problem-solving process.

At Bostich Textron (stapling machines), the productivity improvement effort was launched with one Performance Improvement Circle (PIC) of ten people. Members were given six hours of basic training in tools and techniques of problem solving. Also covered were motivation, creativity, and communications. A list of problems was developed and assigned priorities. Circle members were assigned data-collection tasks, and then suggested solutions to productivity problems. Several productivity improvements resulted, and employees in other departments asked that PICs be formed in their departments.

Benefits of Having Productivity Improvement Teams

Aside from the obvious objective of improving productivity, the team approach can yield these additional benefits:

☐ The "pass-the-buck" or "not-invented-here" syndromes are avoided when teams see a project through to completion or when people have a personal stake in action plans.

☐ There is better utilization of a wider range of knowledge and skills: "two heads are better than one." Participation among team members can also widen their own range of individual skills.

☐ Synergism is promoted. Team members understand their individual roles in relation to other operations in the organization.

☐ A sense of competition, if properly handled, can improve performance efforts as well as the fun dimension of the job.

☐ Potential supervisors are better identified and developed. Participants become "minimanagers." Many take their jobs home with them. Some come early and stay late.

☐ Morale and camaraderie are promoted. Team members identify with the project, department, or improvement, not just their "piece of the action." Part of this commitment results from continuous peer feedback.

☐ Job satisfaction is improved.

Huron Machine Products of Fort Lauderdale, Florida, manufacturer of chuck-top jaws, was operating at 70 percent of capacity, and there was extremely low morale, high turnover, and absenteeism.

In 1979, productivity teams were introduced and organized by job function with representatives from other departments as part of the team. Teams met every week for an hour for problem solving, negotiating, and goal setting. Results have been phenomenal. By 1980 productivity was up 57 percent, sales up 20 percent, and profit on sales up 25 percent with the same workforce. Productivity increases also allowed the absorption of substantial increases in raw-material prices without an increase in selling price. Says President Dave Lindemann, "It's mind-boggling what a company can achieve when it harnesses its human resources to tackle the problems of productivity. You certainly don't get it from machines alone."

QUALITY CIRCLES (QCs)

The Japanese Experience
The Operation of QCs
PROBLEM IDENTIFICATION
PROBLEM SELECTION
PROBLEM ANALYSIS
MANAGEMENT PRESENTATION

THE JAPANESE EXPERIENCE

Many American companies are losing a competitive race with the Japanese as they watch their marketplace being taken over and the dollar declining 40 percent against the yen. Now we are importing management techniques made in Japan and copying what many believe is the key to Japan's productivity growth: *quality circles* (QCs), small groups of employees that meet regularly and are trained to spot and solve production problems in their areas.

Quality circles in Japan now exceed 600,000, with a membership of over 6 million workers. Groups of managers and employees go through extensive training, and the teams of from five to ten employees meet regularly on a voluntary basis. At a circle meeting, 50 percent of the time is spent on topics related to quality control and improvement, 40 percent on productivity and cost improvement, and 10 percent on other topics.

There are tens of thousands of cases in which quality circles have made substantial improvements in productivity and quality. Comparisons with American operations can prove embarrassing. In one recent year, the 82,000 employees of Matsushita Electric turned in

663,475 written suggestions for improvement—an average of eight per employee. In the production of large-scale integrated circuits, Japan reduced defects to 0.2 to 0.3 percent compared to 2 to 3 percent in the United States. In almost every case in which Japanese management has taken over an American firm, productivity and quality have improved.

What is the Japanese secret? Many people think that Japanese workers are culture-bound and perform like robots. This is not true. Indeed, they are given unusual freedom to plan and execute their work. The planners and the doers are the same. This is not "permissive" management, but "participative" management. This approach, plus continuous learning, produces a creative, self-motivated workforce. The concept of continuous learning and training encourages the workers to take responsibility for their jobs. The technician (e.g., the industrial engineer) uses the workforce as a resource, and functions as an assistant to the work group whose individual members achieve a knowledge of their own performance as well as that of the group.

Akio Marita, chairman, cofounder, and controlling stockholder of the giant SONY Corporation, says that productivity in SONY's U.S. plants is almost as high as it is in Japan. The difference, he says, should be attributed to the economies of scale that can be achieved in the larger plants, not to the fact that Japanese workers are more industrious. Such results prove, he says, that American workers can be motivated by Japanese management techniques. He concludes: "Japanese management tries to deal with the worker with a more personal touch. We try to be close to our workers."

U.S. Ambassador to Japan Arthur Mansfield, in commenting on the serious trade balance between the U.S. and Japan, concluded: "We are as good basically as the Japanese. We ought to be out there in the lead, and that calls for increased productivity and pride in workmanship."

THE OPERATION OF QUALITY CIRCLES

Because QCs have been so effective in Japan, interest in forming such teams is accelerating among U.S. companies. The Circle is a group of workers who voluntarily meet together on a regular basis to identify, analyze, and solve quality and other problems in their area. In most cases the seven to eight members of the Circle do similar work so that the problems they select for analysis will be familiar to all of them.

Individual QCs are usually part of an organizationwide system that also includes a facilitator (program coordinator) and a Steering Committee. The facilitator is that person responsible for coordinating and directing activities throughout the organization. A primary responsibility of the facilitator is the training of individual Circle leaders. The leader is normally the supervisor of the Circle members although this is not essential. The leader is responsible for the operation of the Circle and one of the primary challenges is to make sure that each member of the Circle is involved in group deliberations.

The four major steps involved in the operation of a Circle are:

☐ Problem identification

☐ Problem selection

☐ Problem analysis

☐ Management presentation

Problem Identification

During this initial phase of discussion, members are asked to generate individual ideas on problems that exist in their work area. In order to stimulate ideas and develop a problem list, *brainstorming* techniques are encouraged. Members are briefed on the brainstorming approach and guidelines are developed on how to conduct brainstorming sessions. The group leader makes sure that everyone participates. Other members are elected or volunteer as recorders and data collectors.

Problem Selection

Following the initial problem identification part of the Circle meeting, when all ideas have been exhausted and listed, the process of narrowing down the list is begun. The objective is to identify those two or three *most important* problems on which the members can begin the process of analysis.

Problem selection is achieved by a simple voting procedure. Individual Circle members vote on problem ideas that have the most merit in their opinion. Voting proceeds until those problems having the most votes are selected and prioritized for further analysis.

Problem Analysis

The objective of problem analysis is to identify a cause and effect relationship and arrive at a recommended problem resolution or action plan. This process involves *data collection, data presentation and analysis*, and *problem analysis* based upon the data.

Data collection is accomplished by one or more Circle members who have been trained in data collection techniques. These techniques include the use of *sampling* as well as such collection formats as check lists and drawings.

Data presentation and analysis is accomplished through the use of standard charting and graph forms. Among the more common of these are:

□ The *Pareto chart* (see discussion of 80/20 rule in Chapter 14) visually highlights the number one problem in a process.

□ *Control charts* (including $X \cdot R$ and Np) depict control limits and on-going control of a process.

□ The *histogram* is a representation of a frequency distribution and is used to measure the uniformity of a work process.

□ The *scatter diagram* shows the relationship between two problem variables or two kinds of data (e.g., height and weight).

Problem analysis based on the data is perhaps the most important phase of QC discussion and deliberation. It is here that the cause of the problem is identified and a decision made regarding a solution. The process is somewhat like the problem identification step described above.

Using the now familiar brainstorming technique, QC members attempt to identify the *cause of the problem*. Based upon their own experience and the data that has been collected, each individual offers his or her ideas on the cause or causes of the problem. For ease of analysis the causes may be organized into major groupings. These groupings may be general (e.g. manpower, materials, methods, machines) or more tailored (e.g. cutting, painting, assembly) in the case of a specific process.

Following the listing of possible problem causes the members are asked to vote on that which they think is a logical cause. This is the same process of elimination used for the problem selection step described above.

If the verification process indicates that the course selected is the most probable cause of the problem, the analysis process is completed by further brainstorming to select a recommended solution. The recommended solution or course of action then becomes part of the management presentation.

Management Presentation

This presentation serves a dual purpose. In addition to providing the occasion to make recommended solutions actionable, it is an important opportunity to reinforce communication between members of management and members of the QC. It enhances the participative management climate and provides many of the benefits outlined at the beginning of this chapter.

Presentations are structured and involve as many circle members as practical. The charts and graphs used during the data collection and analysis phases should be used during the presentation.

PEOPLE AND PRODUCTIVITY, II

Work Design

Job Development

Principles of Job Development and Work Design

VERTICAL LOADING

CLOSURE

FEEDBACK

Work Teams and Job Development

The new emphasis on productivity has given the concepts of work design and job development a new lease on life, and the application of the concepts of effective design of jobs is being increasingly used. Many companies are becoming interested in a methodology that improves the utilization of the skills of each worker. The same methods are used to design clusters of related jobs. Organizational methods are being refined to accommodate these changes. Related to the concept of work design is the accompanying use of goal-setting incentives and feedback in recognition of the principle that employees need to experience the achievement of self-established objectives (results expected) in order to maintain motivation and productivity.

WORK DESIGN

The story goes that the work-design concept was developed at IBM when the company's founder, Thomas J. Watson, Sr., saw a woman operator sitting idly at her machine. When asked why she was not working, the woman replied: "I have to sit and wait for the setup man to change the tool setting for a new run." Watson asked: "Couldn't you change the tool setting yourself?" The woman replied: "Of course I could, but I am not allowed to." Upon further examination Watson learned that in addition to waiting for setup men, additional idle time was spent waiting for inspectors to examine the finished products of the same workers. Watson reasoned, correctly, that little time would be required to train the workers to perform both additional tasks of setting up the machine and inspecting the finished product. He instituted these changes and the resulting job development and elimination of excess task specialization resulted in better quality, fewer losses due to scrap, and a steady increase in productivity. Moreover, workers reported greater job satisfaction and more interest in their work. This philosophy has pervaded IBM since that time.

There is little doubt that millions of employees at all levels of organizations are underutilized and misutilized in the United States today. This waste of human resources can result in serious consequences for company productivity. In the personnel management area it can account for turnover, tardiness, accidents, high rates of grievances, strikes, and even outright sabotage. In the product and service areas these consequences can range from low product quality to disinterest in or even antagonism toward customer requirements.

Another champion of work-design principles is General Motors. The company's commitment may have been given impetus as an outgrowth of the now-famous strike at GM's Vega plant in Lordstown, Ohio in 1972. The workers staged a 23-day walkout, not for more money or shorter hours, but to protest the pressure and monotony of their work on the assembly line. The stoppage helped make "worker alienation" a fashionable term in industrial, sociological and literary circles.[2]

Two actions can go a long way toward improving productivity through better personnel utilization: (1) match the job with the person, and (2) remove the boredom from the job.

[2]For an interesting and informative description of General Motors' experience with work design and quality of worklife programs at its Tarrytown, N.Y. assembly plant, see Robert H. Guest, "Quality of Work Life—Learning from Tarrytown," *Harvard Business Review*, July–August, 1979. Many academicians and managers equate Tarrytown with Hawthorne as a landmark in a new era in human relations.

Matching the job with the person involves developing or engineering the job so that the job responsibilities, content, and level match the employee's skills and abilities. It is worth noting the difference between *content* and *level* of the match. If a job calls for a level of responsibility that is lower than the person's ability, it is not a good match even though the job content and employee overlap. A good job–employee match includes a reasonable overlap between skill and job demands and a level of responsibility that provides room for growth and development of the individual.

Removing the boredom from the job is becoming an increasing challenge. Popular expressions like "blue-collar blues" and "white-collar monotony" are becoming commonplace, but these trite phrases mislead people into thinking that job monotony, boredom, and dissatisfaction are confined to the assembly line or the clerical level. This is not the case. In many organizations dissatisfaction occurs at all levels, from the floor sweeper to the executive.

The manager who wants to improve the job–employee match or remove some of the boredom from work is faced with two contradictory approaches. On the one hand, traditional "scientific management" and the industrial engineer call for the programming and standardization of specialized tasks using the techniques of work simplification, methods design, process and activity charts and so on. On the other hand, the behavioral scientists tell us that task specialization is bad and we should engineer the job so that employees want to channel their interests toward their work.

The two approaches have tended to exaggerate their differences rather than similarities, and a natural schism has developed. The route to overcoming the apparent contradiction between "scientific management" and "behavioral science" lies in a marriage of the two. The industrial engineer must recognize that the traditional view of the worker as a "hand"[3] must be changed because the whole person comes with it. The *integrated* approach is one that is based on job development. These three approaches to job design (industrial engineering, behavioral science, and integrated) are shown in Table 6-1.

[3]In high-technology industries, a technical worker, such as a design engineer, is frequently referred to as a "head."

TABLE 6–1. Comparison of Three Different Approaches to Job Design

Scientific Management	Behavioral Science	Integrated[a]
Specialization of tasks	Provide task variety to avoid boredom	Be allowed to monitor their own work pace
Minimize number of operations one employee performs	Enlarge the job to meet the skills and ability of the worker	Determine which methods are best for accomplishing a particular task
Eliminate unnecessary motions and operations	Provide feedback on performance	Be assigned primary responsibility for quality
No idle or waiting time	Provide job closure or job identification	Be encouraged to be the true job experts
Let the worker work and the supervisor plan and control	Self-control of significant aspects of the work	Be encouraged to become involved in decision making regarding unit problems and solutions
	Participation in problem solving, planning, and controlling	Be provided opportunity for more responsible, challenging, and self-fullfilling work assignments
	Opportunity to learn new skills	

[a]To the extent that long-term time or cost variables are not substantially increased, employees should exercise these opportunities.

WORK DESIGN AND JOB DEVELOPMENT[4]

At the outset, it is useful to distinguish between *job development* and *job satisfaction*. Many people are frequently under the assumption that job development is confined to improved working conditions, fringe benefits, and other "hygiene" factors associated with "job satisfaction." This, of course, is not the case. Job development means more—it means self-actualizing work.

Perhaps the best-known example of "job satisfaction" and quality of worklife involves Volvo, the giant Swedish automobile manufacturer. An entire plant was built to make the job of the workers more satisfying. Assembly lines were avoided wherever possible, and each employee could do a variety of tasks. Working conditions were designed to be the most pleasing of any auto plant in the world. But all this did nothing for productivity, despite the fact that employees were significantly more satisfied. The management of Volvo found out at great cost that increasing *job satisfaction* does not result in rising productivity.

Walter A. Fallon, board chairman of Eastman Kodak Company, gives one of the company's rules for productivity: "Realize that people enjoy working productively because they experience satisfaction through self-improvement. People like the sense of accomplishment that comes from doing a good job even better." This is job satisfaction *through* job development.

It has been estimated that substantially more than half of the jobs in both the private and public sectors, in both manufacturing and service industries, require little more skill than driving an automobile. There is no way to validate this estimate, but it does give us an indication of the potential for productivity increases if this reservoir of talent were put to work. A major possibility for achieving this potential is the use of *job development*.

Prudential Insurance Company has what is perhaps the largest job development and redesign program in the world, affecting hundreds of jobs and involving several thousand people. The reason given for

---

[4]The term "job development" is similar to, but more comprehensive than, the popular terms "job enlargement" or "job enrichment." It is unfortunate that the latter two terms have become associated with gimmickry such as horizontal loading of jobs, focus on salary aspects, and failure to deliver on motivational promises. Job development, on the other hand, focuses on all three areas of worker utilization: the job, the employee, and the team or work group of which the employee is a part. See William N. Penzer, *Productivity and Motivation Through Job Engineering* (New York: AMACOM, 1973).

undertaking such a project was the prediction that the company would find it more and more difficult to find people to perform "dumb" jobs. It therefore became desirable to change the nature of jobs—to enrich, expand, and develop them.

PRINCIPLES OF JOB DEVELOPMENT AND WORK DESIGN

There are three fundamental principles of job development:

☐ Vertical loading

☐ Closure

☐ Feedback

Notice that the application of each principle depends upon the establishment of targets or standards or *measures of productivity improvement objectives (results).*

Vertical Loading

Vertical loading refers to the job–employee match previously described wherein the employee's job responsibility and decision-making participation is enlarged to meet the individual's skills, abilities, and potential. This is in contrast to the "ratchet principle" or traditional *horizontal* loading, which merely increases the volume of work that an employee does at a particular level of difficulty. For example, the restaurant busboy who is assigned the additional duties of sweeping up the floor is experiencing horizontal loading without additional responsibility or discretion. However, if he is given responsibility for inventory control of dishes and tableware, he is experiencing vertical job loading. It becomes immediately apparent that *the delegation of the manager's own duties is the best way to enlarge the job of subordinates.*

The job development and vertical job loading approach is demonstrated in Table 5-1, page 108. Those job assignments identified as motivators involve the vertical job loading of the staff secretary.

At Citibank in New York, the entire production force of over 3,000 employees is being converted from functional (e.g., filing, editing, statements) work to a work-design format. Now each employee, instead of working at a somewhat boring task of limited scope, has his or her cathode ray tube (CRT) to handle all the account work, which includes research, processing, checking, and scheduling.

In one plant at Nabisco, Inc., a cookie line that was organized in assembly-line fashion was vertically integrated. Now one supervisor is in charge of the entire line, from flour mixing through baking and packaging.

Closure

Closure is the characteristic of a job that provides the employees with a sense of contribution to the organization and an identification with the end product of their work. The typical assembly-line job fails to provide closure because the workers perform miniscule, repetitive parts of the whole job, and begin to get the feeling that they are "nameless, faceless cogs in the big machine."

In the case of the busboy mentioned above, closure could be provided if his job were assigned the responsibility for purchase of supplies within a given budget. The budget is the measure or the productivity objective (result).

Many traditional managers think that when people punch a time clock they know they are working because being physically present means the same as working. This isn't necessarily so. Many workers perform their jobs while they are mentally a thousand miles away. What is happening is that the autocratic supervisor and the bureaucratic organization have suppressed the natural desire of the individual to feel that he or she is making a contribution. People contribute when they feel that they have a hand in shaping the final result.

At International Harvester's plant in Gulfport, Mississippi, instead of using the traditional assembly-line methods, work teams are assigned to equip tractors with front-end loaders, backhoes, and other components. Workers and managers believe that this method promotes identification with the finished product and the customer.

R. B. Barry Corporation, manufacturer of women's slippers, had a plant in Goldsboro, North Carolina that was organized according to modern assembly-line methods and industrial engineering techniques. The company scrapped the system and went to a more elementary mechanical team approach in which work teams handled the complete task. They also learned other operations and rotated jobs. They received same-day feedback on output and quality. Productivity went up 50 percent.

Feedback

The responsible worker, one who participates in setting his or her individual or team *productivity objectives* (results expected), requires information for *self-control*—performance against the target, standard, or measure. Such feedback must be timely, relevant to performance, and operational—not historical information from a variance report from the accounting department or the data-processing center. Obviously, information for self-control can only be relevant if it relates to a target or measure.

Feedback on performance is a necessary part of job development, and it makes good supervisory sense. Too frequently superiors depend upon variance reports or annual performance appraisals to provide feedback. These formal devices are not only too infrequent but in almost every case are too late to provide the type of "real-time" feedback required.

The notion of real-time feedback can be understood by using an analogy. A bowler ordinarily rolls the ball and gets immediate feedback on the number of pins he has knocked down. Now imagine that a curtain is thrown up immediately after the ball is rolled so that the bowler is unable to see how many pins he has knocked down. Somewhat in the manner of an employee, he shouts: "How did I do?" and somewhat in the manner of the manager, someone shouts from behind the curtain: "Don't worry, I will let you know [by variance report] next week." Obviously, no one would want to bowl under these circumstances because no feedback on performance is available.

The message here is that the supervisor should provide this feedback or, better still, build it into the job. Feedback is also a necessary ingredient of self-development, coaching, and counseling.

For many years, Emery Air Freight conducted unsuccessful industrial engineering studies to determine the optimum number of calls for a truck driver. Yet drivers, with little or no analysis could, in practically every case, control their own schedule and raise the number of calls significantly once they knew how many calls they actually made as compared to the numbers they had planned to make.

A number of firms are using electronic feedback for machine operations. For example, BRAM International, Ltd., of Scotland, has developed the BRAM Box, a computer-controlled machine that attaches to an operator's machine via a transducer. A visual display informs the operator of actual production against planned production. Electronics manufacturer Ferranti Ltd. is using the system for operators who stick silicon chips onto subframes. Workers on this delicate job used to produce 65 completed components an hour. Now they turn out an average of 135.

Summary

To make the principles of work design and job development (vertical loading, closure, feedback) operational, it is desirable to measure preformance against some target, standard, or measure. These may be in the form of productivity improvement objectives, but in any case, should track the *results* (not activity) *expected*. In other words, the job should *focus on results*. The concept of how job development is facilitated through a focus on results is illustrated in Table 6-2.

TABLE 6–2. Connection Between Job Development and Focus on Results

Job Development Principle	Focus on Results
Match the job to the employee	Results expected from the job provide yardstick of evaluation
Remove boredom from job	Integrated approach to job engineering requires definition of output in terms of results.
Vertical job loading	Enlarged responsibility defined in terms of results expected
Closure	Job results provide sense of employee identification with the job
Feedback on performance	Feedback is best provided in terms of performance against predetermined goal

WORK TEAMS AND JOB DEVELOPMENT

The principles of job development are equally applicable to individual workers and work teams. Indeed, the team approach provides the best of both worlds; job development *plus* the advantages of the Productivity Improvement Teams outlined earlier in this chapter.

It is not necessary that teams be comprised of employees with the same or similar functional work skills. Multiskilled teams can be equally effective.

At an automobile dealership with about 80 mechanics and body workers, there were major problems with space shortage, critical work scheduling, and customer complaints about delivery times. About 200 to 250 cars were worked on daily, and the variety of services (lubrication, shocks, electrical, tune-up, brakes, transmissions, etc.) required that each car be moved from five to eight times between order writing and final delivery. These movements were required to schedule the car to a particular location having the specialized skills required. It was not uncommon to consume an eight-hour day on a car that required only three actual hours in four different areas.

In an organizational change, shop teams were established; four mechanics with combined skills could provide most of the services on any given car. An apprentice was added as a parts runner and vehicle parker. This saved the more valuable time of the mechanic. Cars were now dispatched to a work team rather than to three or four different locations for specialized service. After nine months, the work team almost doubled its output per man-hour, the critical space problem was relieved, and completion times met with fewer complaints from customers. (Unfortunately, the teams were disbanded because of friction with other personnel, who resented the increased incentive pay of team members.)

SIXTY YEARS AGO

By dealing intelligently and squarely with labor, Fayette R. Plumb, Inc., Philadelphia tool manufacturers, have more than doubled production, reduced working hours and cut down the yearly turnover of the company's 500 workmen 75%. By a system of representative government and a series of welfare features, all unrest and discontent in the working force ... has been eliminated.
—From *Forbes* Magazine–May 29, 1920

PEOPLE & PRODUCTIVITY Management by Objectives

"A seat-of-the-pants approach to objectives will lead inexorably to failure."
—George Odiorne, *Professor of Management*

CHAPTER 7

It should be clear by this time that in order to tap the potential of the entire workforce some commitment to productivity improvement through results management is necessary on the part of all. One approach for achieving this commitment is called *Management by Objectives* (MBO). It is also called variously by such terms as management by results, participation, or commitment. Hereafter I will simply call it MBO. Although many organizations already have a system of MBO, few, as we shall see, have properly organized it for the specific purpose of *productivity improvement*.

Since Peter Drucker first coined the term "Management by Objectives" in 1954 it has become far and away the most prevalent approach to the emerging discipline of organizational development and promises to become the most pervasive managerial system of the 1980s. Literally thousands of companies around the world are practicing various styles of MBO. This chapter is not an exhaustive treatment of the subject but is sufficient to provide an understanding and for laying the groundwork for application in practice. Our objective is to integrate the concepts of MBO with the aims of productivity improvement. Since the behavioral science foundation has already been laid in previous chapters, I will focus here on the structural methodology.

MANAGEMENT BY OBJECTIVES, I

What is MBO?
MBO: A Philosophy of Management
MBO: Past and Future
Objectives
Hierarchy of Objectives

WHAT IS MBO?

MBO is commonly described as a process whereby superior and subordinate jointly identify the common goals of the organization and define each individual's major areas of responsibility in terms of the *results expected*, and then use these measures as guides for operating the unit and assessing the contribution of each of its members. Since the major organization goal with which we are concerned here is *productivity improvement*, the approach in this case would be the method whereby this goal is established for individuals and Productivity Improvement Teams (PITS). These goals would be expressed in terms of the improvement to be achieved or the results to be expected.

MBO: A PHILOSOPHY OF MANAGEMENT

Drucker calls the MBO approach a philosophy of management:

Management by objectives and self-control may properly be called a philosophy of management. It rests on a concept of the job of management. It rests on an analysis of the specific needs of the management group and the obstacles it faces. It rests on a concept of human action, behavior, and motivation. Finally, it applies to every manager, whatever his level and function, and to any organization whether large or small. It insures performance by converting objective needs into personal goals.

Drucker is correct. Results management and MBO are new and different ways of management. For many managers this calls for a reorientation of thinking, a different set of assumptions about how human resources should be utilized within an organization, and a new concept of delegation and control.

Utilization of the MBO concept does not depend entirely upon the installation of a formal companywide system. Individual managers can develop objectives for themselves or for the work groups for which they are responsible. Their individual "minisystems" would introduce priorities, furnish internal feedback, and trigger results-directed behavior. However, a much better foundation would be provided by a system throughout the organization. This would assure that everyone's objectives would be consistent with and support those of the total company.

On the other hand, MBO is not a panacea. Many companies have installed formal systems that have failed. In almost every case this has been the result of emphasis on the system rather than on results. The cause has been lack of management support and follow-up.

MBO: PAST AND FUTURE

MBO has been around for a long time. Despite its popularity, a large number of users have reported something less than success with the concept and practice. Others have predicted its ultimate demise. George Odiorne, the number-two proponent of MBO (after Drucker) has summarized two main reasons why the practice has not lived up to its promise. First, the practice of MBO requires that a manager's characteristic orientation be changed from a focus on *activity* (doing things right) to a focus on output or *results* (doing the right things). This change can be disturbing for those who are accustomed to ad hoc behavior or for those "creative" people who enjoy "winging it" on the job. MBO, like productivity improvement, requires an advance commitment to results.

A second reason for the failure of MBO to deliver as much as promised is the behavioral dimension, which has never been fully understood. The idea that communication is essential has never really caught on. It requires boss-to-subordinate, one-on-one, or group face-to-face discussion. The failure to achieve this degree of under-standing and communication has been due partly to the reluctance of managers to delegate or share authority and partly to the continuing practice of setting goals and objectives solely in terms of budgets or program plans. Another reason is that many managers simply don't know how to make the process work. It isn't enough to say, "We are going to have an MBO program!" The program must be organized.

The future of MBO is brighter. Much of this has to do with the increasing demand for productivity. The process, the technique, the theory and *practice* associated with MBO constitute a natural system for managing the productivity effort in the organization. Indeed, we might even call the approach Management by Productivity (MBP). Whether we call it MBO, MBP, or simply *results management*, the approach will surely accelerate in the 1980s. Here are a few reasons:

☐ The tighter competitive and profit requirements will demand a more rigorous style of management. Focus on efficiency versus effectiveness, intuition versus advance planning, and activity versus output will diminish.

☐ Workforce demands for participation and self-control will lessen the traditional autocratic managerial style of control and the dependence on variance reports against budgets. Managers will learn that self-control through MBO and individual results can be more effective.

☐ Incentive and pay plans will become more closely tied to productivity ratios and hence results.

☐ The growth of the tendency to make productivity an integral part of corporate strategy and the acceleration of strategic planning in general will result in action-committed derivative plans. These will require that results be spelled out and integrated into business plans.

All these reasons argue for a brighter future for the MBO philosophy and practice when the approach becomes integrated with productivity improvement objectives.

OBJECTIVES

Many managers pay lip service to objectives and when asked will declare: "Of course, we manage by objectives." But when pressed, they are unable to define their objectives, let alone devise a plan to achieve them. Such platitudes as "increase market share" or "improve the operations" or "reduce turnover" reflect a catch-as-catch-can approach.

These managers may have a financial plan, or a rudimentary form of development plan, but it is not enough. In almost every case you will find that managers and supervisors at lower levels are at best unclear about and at worst totally unaware of company goals. It is unlikely that this environment will give us the two benefits of the systems approach: focus on results and organizational integration.

A simple definition of the work objective would be phrased in terms of *results expected*. It can also be defined as a temporary estimate of a desirable future result that cannot be predicted with accuracy that you are willing and able to pay for and that you believe can be achieved through effort. This definition focuses on a commitment to resources in order to achieve results. It therefore implies a more formal approach than a mere statement that "Sure, we manage by objectives." I can't imagine a manager who would admit to not having an objective. What we need is a system to achieve those objectives.

The system in use in most large companies is directed to the more tangible and measurable targets of a financial or business plan. There is, of course, no objection to these targets. However, I have suggested that the financial or business plan does not always reflect the tangible, measurable targets required for productivity improvement. By including the productivity dimension in the business plan, operating managers are required to "buy into" productivity and track results in the same way as for financial measures.

Smaller firms are frequently guilty of depending on their accountants to define budgetary goals, which they then rely on as indicators of directional change. The same caution applies in this case as well. *Operating* managers should define *operating* plans, which may be financial in nature, and these too should contain the productivity dimension.

HIERARCHY OF OBJECTIVES

Despite the inhibiting structure implied by the word "hierarchy," the *integrative* requirement demanded by MBO is achieved through the concept of the hierarchy of objectives. This implies that objectives are arranged in descending order much like the lines of authority shown on the organization chart. Assuming that the board of directors or the chief executive has established broad, overall company goals, these can be broken down into lower-level supporting objectives. The result may be imagined as a "cascade effect."

The entire system of MBO depends upon the eventual integration of closely understood company objectives at the top. Once again, you are reminded that platitudes will not suffice. Statements like "be a better supplier" or "have the best product in the industry" are not meaningful and cannot be divided into smaller increments for meaningful goals at lower levels. Objectives must be operational; they must be capable of being converted into specific targets and assignments at lower levels.

Many companies have set overall company objectives in these eight key result areas:

□ *Marketing.* Following a clear determination of strategy (product-market scope and competitive edge), objectives should be set for existing and new products and services in both existing and new markets.

Example: Improve market position in product line B from fourth to third in the industry in two years.

□ *Innovations* in management, product, and operations.

Example: Design, produce, and commercialize new product B by November 1983.

□ *Human organization and resources* including the basic structure, policies, and management of the business. Also, worker attitude, union relations, managerial development, and performance.

Example: Install human-resource planning system.

□ *Financial resources* concerned with the supply and utilization of capital.

Example: Increase raw-materials inventory turn from 3 to 4 by the end of the year.

□ *Physical resources* concerned with the physical facilities, fixed assets, and raw material.

Example: Increase production rate per thousand square feet of plant space.

□ *Productivity* measurements for comparing management of different units within the company as well as the company with others in the industry regarding the productivity of labor, capital, materials, energy and overall productivity.

Example: Improve ratio of sales per employee.

□ *Social responsibility* related to the company's existence within the society and economy.

Example: Cooperate with local authorities to develop regulations for pollution control.

□ *Profitability* in terms of earnings per share, return on investment, or other measure.

Example: Achieve return on investment of 16 percent.

Figure 7–1. The "cascade effect" of a hierarchy of objectives

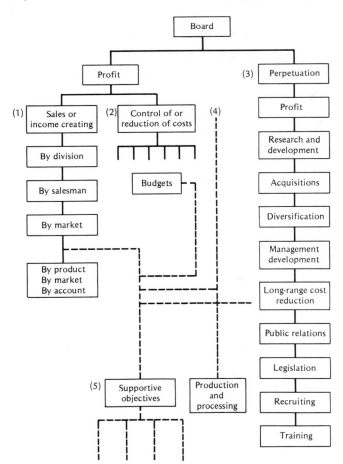

The goals of employees' jobs are defined in terms of the contribution they have to make to the success of the larger unit of which they are a part. It is therefore clear that, whatever objectives are established, at any level, it is important to be as specific and accurate as possible. The multiplier effect of an inaccurate goal at a higher level can be demonstrated by the principle of "cumulative compounding of error." For example, you may think that 90 percent accuracy in goals is reasonable, but at the end of a twelve-step sequential process of goal setting (twelve levels down the hierarchy) 90 percent gets to be 25 percent, 80 percent gets to be 6 percent, and so on.

The "cascade effect" of establishing objectives at the top and converting them into increments at lower levels in the organization can be seen in Figure 7–1. In this particular breakdown, objectives are organized around these areas:

□ Sales or income creating

□ Control of and reduction of costs

□ Perpetuation of the organization

□ Production and processing

□ Supportive objectives

Figure 7–2. The hierarchy of objectives

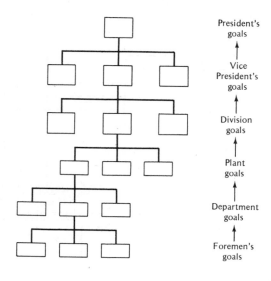

Figure 7–2 illustrates another breakdown by organizational hierarchy. Each goal supports a higher goal of which it is a part.

MANAGEMENT BY OBJECTIVES, II

Integrating Organization Objectives
Linear Organization Chart

INTEGRATING ORGANIZATION OBJECTIVES

Synergism (syn-er-gism) is defined in Webster's Dictionary as "the simultaneous action of separate agencies which, together, have greater total effect than the sum of their individual effects." The "hierarchy of objectives" described above and its "cascade effect" will serve the purpose of *vertical integration* but leaves unresolved the question of horizontal integration—synergism. We want to integrate each department and each individual, if possible, with all other elements in the organization.

Individuals and Productivity Improvement Teams (PITS) need specific targets and measures for improved results. Although this concept is essential for the practice of productivity improvement and MBO, the establishment of individual objectives alone is not enough. These must be coordinated and integrated with other individuals and departments.

This type of organizational synergism is rarely achieved. In the past, the effectiveness of business organizations has been somewhat less than optimum because managers failed to relate the parts or functions of the systems to each other and to the whole. The sales function was performed without a great deal of integration with design or production; production control was frequently not coordinated with financial or personnel planning; and the classic management information system was concerned largely with variance reporting on a historical basis and was constructed around the chart of accounts without too much regard for the integration of organizational components.

Individuals, teams, and departments have two kinds of objectives. The first is involved with maintaining an *ongoing* process or activity with a predetermined standard of performance. This may be called an *ongoing* objective and refers to the day-to-day performance necessary to maintain a given level of output in an activity or function. The second kind of objective is concerned with bringing about a change or improvement in an ongoing function or activity. This may be called the *productivity improvement objective* and is perhaps more important for our purposes here. The two kinds of objectives can be illustrated:

Ongoing Objective	Productivity Improvement Objective
Keep accounts receivable at a level of 45 days	Improve cash flow by reducing accounts-receivable level to 40 days
Meet the sales forecast of $8 million	Improve sales in target area by 10 percent; increase high-profit items from one-third to one-half of sales within the existing level of distribution costs
Stay within the maintenance budget	Reduce downtime on line #1 by 10 percent; improve the ratio of machine hours to maintenance hours from 16/1 to 24/1

The typical functional organization is not designed to achieve synergism. On the contrary, it frequently inhibits it. The structure is designed to operate the routine and specialized tasks of the business—designing, selling, shipping, assembling, operating machines, accounting, and so on. The focus of these tasks, these *activities*, is on neither objectives nor the relationship or integration of related activities in different organization components. The whole effort is directed to specialization and vertical authority relationships.

THE LINEAR ORGANIZATION CHART

The chart, or grid illustrated in Figure 7–3 can help overcome the lack of integration. The vertical columns of the chart can represent three types of objectives. For example:

□ Key Result Areas (I, II, III, etc.)

Example: Increase market share

□ Ongoing Functional Objectives (1, 2, 3, etc.)

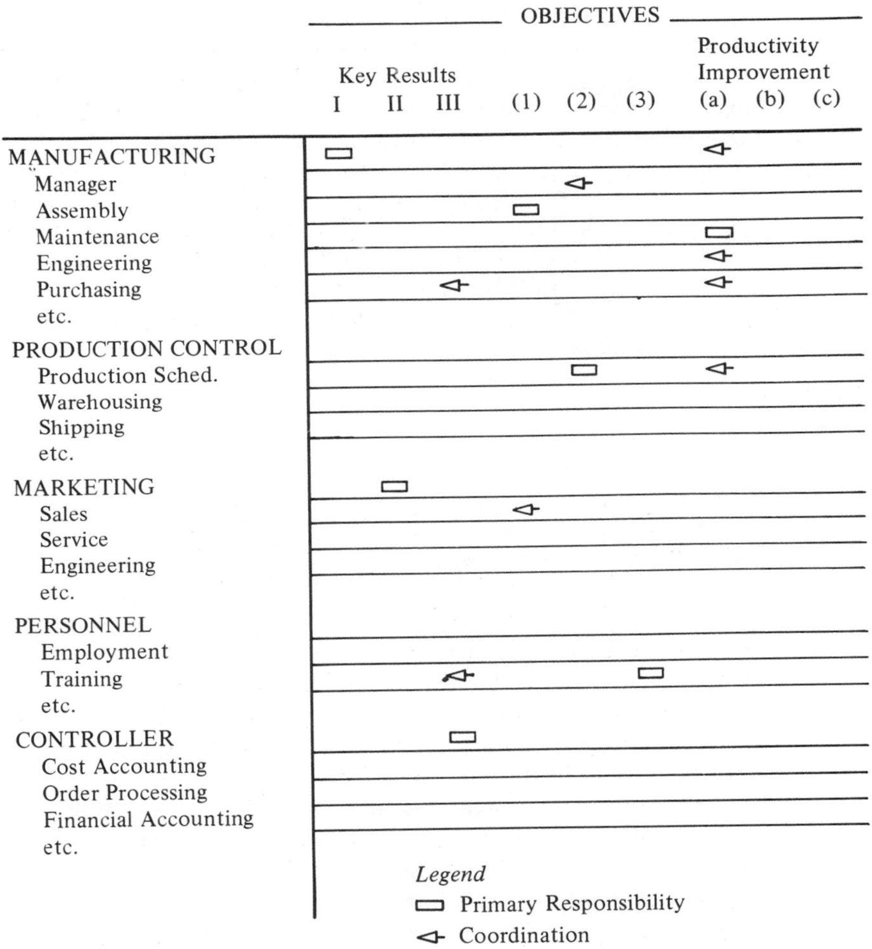

| | OBJECTIVES | | | | | | Productivity Improvement | | |
| | Key Results | | | | | | | | |
	I	II	III	(1)	(2)	(3)	(a)	(b)	(c)
MANUFACTURING	□						⊲		
Manager					⊲				
Assembly				□					
Maintenance							□		
Engineering							⊲		
Purchasing		⊲					⊲		
etc.									
PRODUCTION CONTROL									
Production Sched.						□	⊲		
Warehousing									
Shipping									
etc.									
MARKETING	□								
Sales					⊲				
Service									
Engineering									
etc.									
PERSONNEL									
Employment									
Training		⊲				□			
etc.									
CONTROLLER		□							
Cost Accounting									
Order Processing									
Financial Accounting									
etc.									

Legend
□ Primary Responsibility
⊲ Coordination

Figure 7–3. Linear organization chart

Example: Reduce accounts receivable to level of 45 days

□ Productivity Improvement Objective (a, b, c, etc.)

Example: Reduce downtime

Naturally, one or more charts would be used for each category of objectives. The functions or job titles are listed along the left-hand margin of the chart and represent the functional organization. The arrows where the columns (objectives) intersect the functional job titles indicate the function or person whose contributions are needed to achieve each objective. For example, the *productivity improvement objective* "Reduce downtime" listed above is assigned to the maintenance supervisor but must be coordinated with manufacturing, engineering, purchasing, and production scheduling.

MANAGEMENT BY OBJECTIVES, III
Service and Staff Jobs
Measuring the Unmeasurable
Setting Key Objectives

SERVICE AND STAFF JOBS

As American industry has shifted from a manufacturing to a service economy, fewer and fewer workers are engaged in physical production. More have been needed to produce ideas, patents, scientific formulae, invoices, market research, sales presentations, letters, computer programs, and a thousand other forms of data or symbolic output. America is a nation of information-handlers. We are now in the post-industrial age. We work in symbolic factories.

Well over half of the workforce in the United States is employed in service industries. This does not include those who work in "service" departments and jobs in manufacturing firms. The makeup of this workforce represents a real, but not insurmountable, problem in productivity measurement and objective setting. Work measurement, and the related traditional techniques of measuring productivity in manufacturing industries, is infrequently used in service industries, and where it is used it only measures about one-third of the activities.

From the point of view of productivity measurement and improvement, the shift to service work is a two-edged sword. On the one hand, the shift is characteristic of a highly developed economy. On the other hand, we have made a few inroads in improving productivity among service jobs. Office costs alone have swelled to 40 to 50 percent of all costs in some companies.

Managers of these activities have traditionally attempted to measure the efficiency of the operation with some cost control or budgetary allocation. Some have resisted efforts to set the necessary goals or to measure productivity. Personnel departments have generally operated in a "reactive" mode to the inroads of government regulations; computer departments have wandered over the map of technology without much effort at planning and controlling the function; research departments have thought in terms of cost, not value. It is time to bring *productivity improvement* to the service and staff job.

SETTING OBJECTIVES TO MEASURE
THE UNMEASURABLE

Some advocates of MBO say that if you can't count it, measure it, or describe it, you probably don't know what you want and can forget it as an objective. While this may be a slight exaggeration, it does point up the need to devise some method of defining expected results.

Where the absolute measures of quantity, quality, time, and dollar value described above cannot be used, it may become necessary to invent some measure of present level of results in order to be able to estimate changes from that level. Three measures, in descending order of desirability, are: the index, the scale, and the description.

The index compares performance against some baseline level and can be expressed as a ratio, a percent, a fraction, or a batting average. Illustrations are: ratio of power cost to maintenance costs or percent of service calls.

The scale can be constructed to measure performance over time. It may be "on a scale of 1 to 10" or something less descriptive such as "better than–worse than" or "excellent–fair–poor."

The description is the least useful measure but is better than none at all for setting baselines for estimating expected results. "Better than the industry average" is different from "worse than the industry average" but the description can be used as an imperfect measure to state conditions as they should be and as they exist.

Measuring the Results

If the expected results have been adequately defined, measuring the actual results is not difficult. The measurement can be informal or formal.

The informal measurement is a matter of superior–subordinate face-to-face communication. Each understands the results expected and has frequent occasion during the performance cycle to achieve feedback. This is the most widespread and perhaps the most useful form of results management. Feedback is usually on a real-time or a continuing basis.

Formal measurement involves the many structured reports and control systems that are used to measure performance against standards. If these systems are to be used for MBO performance measurement, it becomes necessary to evaluate them for that purpose. Is the report providing the data that will measure performance? Does it contain the necessary quantitative figures? One of the by-products of an MBO program is that the company will frequently discover that its information and reporting systems are not doing the job. They are either not being used at the grass-roots level or do not provide the essential data for managing by results.

It may be useful to construct an MBO organization chart along the lines of Figure 7–4 to obtain an overall view of requirements for setting and measuring key objectives. This chart is useful for comparing existing information systems to determine whether they are adequate for the purpose of measuring expected results.

MANAGEMENT BY OBJECTIVES, IV

The System for Getting Results
How the System Works

DEFINE THE JOB

DEFINE EXPECTED RESULTS

MEASURE THE RESULTS

APPRAISAL

DOCUMENTATION

Dos and Don'ts of MBO

THE SYSTEM FOR GETTING RESULTS

Three major arguments have been advanced thus far in this book. Chapters 5 and 6 should have convinced you that it is entirely possible to integrate or reconcile the organization's objectives that are concerned with results and productivity (growth, profitability, cost reduction, and so on) with the individual's own needs. MBO is the system that can achieve this. It can balance the company's goals with the individual's needs to contribute and develop personally. If this can be done, everyone has the best of both worlds.

A second argument that has been made is that the manager can set the proper climate for motivation, job satisfaction, and productivity through these results management methods:

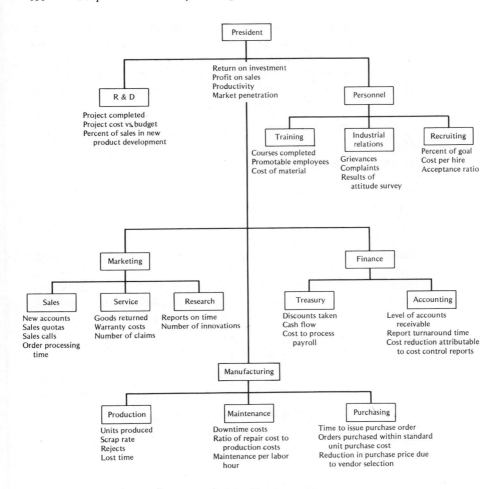

Figure 7–4. Organization chart of key result areas

- ☐ Job development
- ☐ Appraisal
- ☐ Subordinate development
- ☐ Communication
- ☐ Delegation and control
- ☐ Organization style
- ☐ Leadership style

A third point that has been made is the lack of organizational integration (synergism) provided by the classical or traditional bureaucratic organization form.

Stated simply, MBO is the system that provides the central element in all three of the foregoing requirements. It is a system of productivity management that integrates

☐ Organization and individual goals

☐ The managerial requirements for results management

☐ The subsystems of the organization

HOW THE MBO SYSTEM WORKS

Earlier, we constructed a system of productivity management that included the components of input, processor, and output. The MBO system can be depicted in the same manner. Figure 7–5 shows the components of the system, the output of which is results. Other components include input (define the job, define expected results), control (measure results), and feedback (appraisal):

☐ *Define the job.* Specification of the key responsibilities and duties for which the individual is held accountable.

☐ *Define expected results (objectives).* The performance conditions

Figure 7–5. The Management by Objectives system

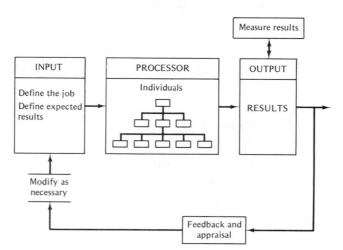

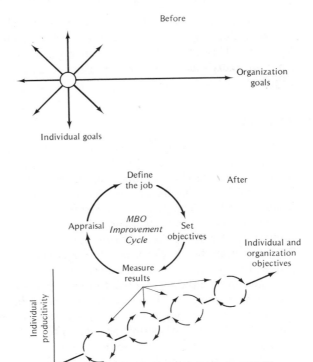

Figure 7–6. Before and after the MBO improvement cycle

(expressed in measurable, verifiable terms) that exist when the job is performed satisfactorily.

☐ *Measure the results.* Comparison of the actual results achieved against the established objective.

☐ *Appraisal.* The process of providing feedback on results and establishing the necessary modification to the job or the objectives in order to set expected results for the next performance period.

These basic four steps constitute the MBO *performance improvement cycle* for the individual. The cycle is repeated as often as necessary to maintain the desired level of productivity through the "stretch" performance process. Taken together, the performance improvement cycles of all the individuals in the organization comprise the route by which the total organization achieves its own goals. Without such a central integrating system, it is unlikely that the goals of the organization and those of its members will be in harmony. This concept of the route to growth and productivity for both individuals and the organization as a whole is shown in Figure 7–6.

Defining the Job

A number of years ago the American Management Associations conducted a survey among hundreds of superior–subordinate teams to determine whether common agreement existed regarding job responsibilities. The result of the survey indicated widespread disagreement. Indeed, the area of agreement was extremely narrow. The superiors' concepts of their subordinate's duties differed substantially from what the subordinates thought about the matter. Subsequent studies have supported the conclusion that millions of people are not clear about what they are expected to do.

Vague understanding of job definition is generally attributable to: (1) job descriptions that are stated in general rather than specific terms; (2) job descriptions that are "programmed" to such an extent that no flexibility in job definition is permitted; and (3) the total lack of any job description accompanied in turn by unclear authority delegation or confusion in assignment of responsibility.

Under the MBO system, the necessary first step in improving the productivity and development of an individual is to identify the key elements which describe the areas for which he or she is held accountable. This is an "individualized," not a "programmed" or mass-production process. Employees should therefore write down the duties, actions, and responsibilities of their jobs as they understand them. These can then be grouped for the purpose of summary into key job duties. This will provide the basis for superior–subordinate understanding.

THE 80/20 RULE

The "80/20" rule, known more formally as Pareto's Law, says that in any group of activities, a vital few account for the bulk of the benefits. In other words, a few of the activities (10 to 20 percent) are more important in achieving results than all others put together. This can be applied to almost any area of the organization. For example, 80 percent of sales are usually made by 20 percent of the sales force, 80 percent of the profit is usually made by 20 percent of the items, or 80 percent of overdue accounts are owed by 20 percent of the customers, and so on. The lesson here is that the important 20 percent should be identified and made the subject of particular management attention.

The 80/20 rule applies to a person's job as well. Eighty percent of an employee's time is usually spent on a few *key* duties that account for the major results of the job. It is therefore important that these key responsibilities and duties be identified so that particular attention can be devoted to them. The 80/20 rule will also provide a guide for homing in on the most significant areas for productivity improvement.

Defining and Measuring Expected Results

The general inclination to state responsibilities in such vague terms as "generate more business," or "reduce costs," or "do a better job of design" is not acceptable in the MBO system of results management. Objectives are not abstractions. They are the action commitments by which an individual's contribution to the next higher level of goals is measured. As such they must be capable of being converted into specific targets and specific assignments. They must be measurable. They should be quantifiable wherever possible.

HOW TO EXPRESS OBJECTIVES

Objectives can be expressed and results measured in terms of one or more of these basic yardsticks: quantity, quality, time, or dollar value. These are illustrated:

Yardstick	Illustration
Quantity	Sell a sales quota of 600.
	Produce two units per direct labor hour.
Quality	Improve the technical specifications.
	Reduce errors.
Time	Complete the project in six months.
	Reduce overhead by May 15.
Dollar value	Develop a training program at a cost of $25 per person.
	Achieve a return on investment of 10 percent.

The specific format for expressing individual productivity improvement objectives was covered in detail in Chapter 2 and the guide and examples are contained in Table 2-1.

CRITERIA OF ACCEPTANCE FOR OBJECTIVES

After objectives have been set in terms of expected results, they should be tested to see if they meet each of these acceptance criteria. Failure to meet one or more may disqualify it as an acceptable objective.

Criteria	*Yes*	*No*
1. Does the objective measure results and not activities?	( )	( )
2. Is it a stretch objective?	( )	( )
3. Is it realistic in terms of attainment?	( )	( )
Does employee have control over it?	( )	( )
4. Is it suitable? Does it support the objective of the next level in the organization?	( )	( )
5. Is it measurable and verifiable?	( )	( )
6. Is feedback built-in or can it be provided?	( )	( )
7. Is it acceptable to the individual (or yourself, if it is your objective)?	( )	( )

Appraisal

The process of performance appraisal is discussed in Chapter 8. It is important to note that appraisal is the action that closes the loop in the performance improvement cycle. It provides an opportunity for superior–subordinate communication, for individual growth and development, and for setting stretch objectives for the future.

Appraisal based on the measurement of actual against expected results is a realistic means of evaluating a subordinate in terms of what counts, his or her "track record." In order for this to be done, it is necessary that expected results (objectives) be recorded on the appraisal form and that the job description be written to reflect them.

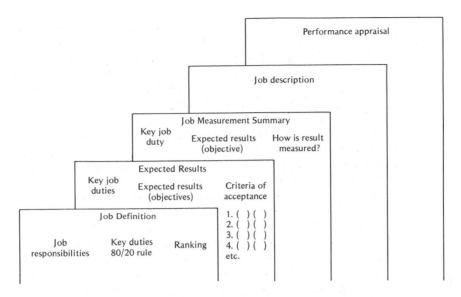

Figure 7-7. Documentation of individual employee's objectives

Documentation

Few people like to fill out forms and comply with detailed procedures and there is always the danger that the paperwork of any activity will become the ends rather than the means. Nevertheless, a minimum amount of documentation is necessary for the MBO program to succeed. Merely to announce that "we are going to manage by objectives" and not follow-up with some disciplined approach is not enough. A caution to remember is: "If you haven't written it out, you haven't thought it out."

The key documentation is contained in the forms shown in Figure 7-7. Each is briefly described below. The actual format and content can be designed to meet the needs of each individual organization. The purpose here is to provide the central idea.

WORKING PAPERS

☐ *Job definition:* On this form employees should list their various duties and job responsibilities as they interpret them. Be brief. These duties should be grouped and boiled down until a much smaller (no more than five) list of key duties remains. Follow the 80/20 rule and concentrate on the few duties that represent the most important part of the job. These key duties are then weighed and ranked according to their relative importance. Any reasonable scale (e.g., 1–10) will do. This form can then be jointly reviewed by the superior–subordinate team for agreement as the basis for setting expected results.

☐ *Expected results:* In this working paper the key job duties determined in the first step are entered in rank order of their relative importance. Then for each key job duty a measure of expected result (objective) is entered. This measure is designed according to the principles outlined in this chapter. Each objective is then checked to determine whether it meets the seven criteria of acceptance discussed on page 160.

☐ *Job measurement summary.* The purpose of this form is to summarize the source of data for measuring actual against expected results. After listing the key duties and expected results again on this form, the column labeled "How Is Result Measured" is used to describe the report (if any) used to measure the key duty, whether the data on the report can be used for measurement, whether new data may be required, or whether measurement is purely between superior and subordinate on an informal basis.

☐ *Personnel forms.* These include the job description, if used, and the performance appraisal form. Although it isn't essential to list key job duties on the job description, in almost every case the job duties and key results expected should become a part of the appraisal form.

SUMMARY

It is difficult to argue against MBO as a central method of achieving productivity. The approach is both theoretically sound and valid as a practical theme of management. It has been proven in hundreds of organizations. On the other hand, it has failed to live up to expectations in hundreds of others. These failures are not due to any weakness of the system. Rather, they can be traced to the way in which the system is managed.

From these successes and failures have come a gestalt of do's and don'ts that provide a handy guide for the success or failure of the program. For those who view MBO as just another technique, rather than as a philosophy of management, the guide below will serve as a checkoff list to hasten the failure of your program. For those who sincerely want to achieve productivity through results, the list will alert you to the roadblocks ahead.

THE DO'S AND DON'TS OF MBO

The Do's of MBO

☐ *Do design stretch objectives.* One of the most common mistakes is to design jobs so small that employees cannot grow. They become frustrated, bored, and "retire on the job." They take a passive attitude toward MBO or ignore it.

☐ *Do be flexible.* Plans and objectives are not set in concrete. Change occurs and individual results and plans must be adapted. Inflexibility encourages defensive behavior.

☐ *Do provide top management support.* Delegation of MBO to a staff assistant, a planner, or the personnel department will insure that it will be regarded as just another personnel or planning gimmick. MBO is a line responsibility. The action is at the middle management and frontline supervisor level.

☐ *Do provide feedback.* This is an absolute prerequisite to the success of the program. Feedback is not usually sufficient when provided by a formal chart of accounts or an incomprehensible reporting system. It should be achieved through feedback on individualized objectives established by each employee.

☐ *Do tie to compensation.* Although money alone is not a motivator, it does provide a yardstick of achievement and recognition. Tie compensation into the achievement of objectives, otherwise you may lapse into the practice of across-the-board compensation where everyone gets the same raise regardless of contribution.

☐ *Do follow up with plans.* It does little good to set objectives unless people develop some form of action plan to achieve them. The plan provides the necessary organization of effort and the feedback on progress toward expected results.

☐ *Do stress objectives and not the system.* Although the trappings of the system—the rationale, operation, forms, pitfalls—must be explained, be careful of the system becoming the end rather than the means.

☐ *Do tie to appraisal.* The same rationale applies here as it does under compensation. Job closure, ownership of results, and feedback are all essential to individual motivation. Performance appraisal is the primary vehicle through which these are provided.

☐ *Do train.* The concept and operation of the MBO system is not easy. It must be "sold" and people must be trained in its execution. Original orientation is not enough. Follow-up and refresher training is needed to keep the system "pumped up."

☐ *Do integrate and coordinate.* MBO is not an isolated method or system by itself. On the contrary, it is a very fine tool for coordinating other plans and programs as well as the subsystems of the organization. MBO should support the profit plan as well as the functional plans in marketing, personnel, production, and so on.

The Don'ts of MBO

☐ *Don't create a papermill.* If employees must spend a lot of time filling out hard-to-understand forms and complying with detailed procedures, you are unlikely to get support.

☐ *Don't emphasize techniques.* An emphasis on techniques, like the papermill above, sidetracks the real effort. People are hesitant to participate for fear of misunderstanding or noncompliance with a technique. Keep techniques at a minimum and emphasize that they are only a means to help achieve results.

☐ *Don't get caught up in techniques.* A manager who falls prey to this approach is the perfectionist who spends a disproportionate amount of time discussing, rehashing, and reworking the details of the program. This manager is more concerned with detail than content. He or she should realize that it is somewhat imperfect in terms of quantification and get on with the main idea—results.

☐ *Don't adopt the "busy" syndrome.* Many managers devote very little time to objective setting and appraisal because they put more importance on the activities of their job than they do on getting results. They are unable to delegate. Such a manager should schedule a time for getting activities accomplished and another time for MBO.

☐ *Don't adopt the attitude "Do what I say, not what I do."* This manager either discourages the participation with a "let's do it later" comment, or gives little time or assistance to make the system work. The result: a self-fulfiling prophecy in the department.

☐ *Don't be a copycat.* Although the experience of others may be very useful as a general guide, the system should not be a model of another organization. Avoid trying to make one plan or set of objectives fit all jobs.

☐ *Don't implement overnight.* A crash implementation throughout all levels of the company is likely to lead to confusion or disillusionment. Go slow at first. Try a "pilot" program in one division or department. Although "grass-roots" or "bottom-up" is the basic approach of MBO, you may want to adopt a "top-down" approach for the initial implementation or until your program is more mature.

☐ *Don't try to quantify every objective.* An insistence on quantification where it may not be appropriate leads to "creative numbering": assigning a number to an objective because it is a requirement. This is not likely to lead to commitment on the part of the employee unless the results expected have a realistic measure.

☐ *Don't "lay on" objectives.* MBO involves upward communication. The subordinate should establish personal expected results and to "assign" them is to kill the motivation and hence the real basis of the system. Don't be the autocratic manager who determines the objectives for subordinates unilaterally and attempts to "sell" them on the idea that the objectives are theirs. Take the time to discuss the objectives that are originated by the subordinate. Take the time to get commitment.

☐ *Don't consider MBO as a panacea.* The MBO system must be supported by good managers and a good management system that includes well laid plans, an organization style and structure to carry them out, and a sound basis for control. MBO is only as good as the management system it is built upon. This is the system for productivity management.

SUPERVISORY SKILLS
Communication &
Appraisal

CHAPTER 8

*"The three R's of productivity are: recognition,
responsibility, and rewards for workers."*
—Jackson Grayson,
Chairman, American Productivity Center

Communication and appraisal are two of the specific and essential skills that are necessary for effective supervision. If, as the opening quote suggests, productivity is a function of recognition, responsibility, and reward, then communication and appraisal are major tools for providing these essentials. I want to demonstrate in this chapter that the *results management* concept is the central approach to effectiveness in both disciplines.

SUPERVISORY SKILLS: COMMUNICATIONS

Why Improve Communications?
The Model and the Process
Formal vs. Informal Communications

WHY IMPROVE COMMUNICATIONS?

Few topics have been the subject of more research and debate. But the questions today still remains: "How do I communicate?" In dozens of seminars I have been told by supervisors that their primary problem is communications within the organization. "I communicate but nobody else does," is a common complaint. The more we seem to talk about it, the less we seem to experience it. Productivity suffers where poor communication exists, and there is every evidence that this is a major problem throughout industry.

There are two very important reasons for improving our communications with subordinates and superiors. First, there is the fact that the process of communicating takes up 75 percent of the time of the average manager; 75 percent of *that* time is spent in oral communications. It therefore makes a great deal of sense to improve the process, if for no other reason than to improve the effectiveness and utilization of our time. Second, since managers get results through constant communications, it follows that the impact on productivity makes this a vital area in which to seek improvement. Communications is the mortar that holds the "bricks" of the organization together.

There is no doubt that productivity is directly affected by the way we communicate in organizations. A communications breakdown is just as costly as a breakdown of machines, the loss of sales, a poor engineering design, or material stockouts. Indeed, the operation of all other subsystems of the business and the integration between subsystems depends on good communication. If we can draw an analogy between the company and the human body, organization structure is the anatomy and communication is the nervous system. Both are required to make the system work.

THE MODEL AND THE PROCESS

The word "communication" is a derivative of the Latin *communis*, meaning *commonness*, and it is this commoness of meaning in the message that the sender and receiver are trying to achieve through the process of communicating. The process is at once simple and complicated. It revolves around four basic factors: a sender, a message, a receiver, and feedback. The model is shown in Figure 8-1. The sender and the receiver can be either individuals or groups, since the process works irrespective of the numbers involved.

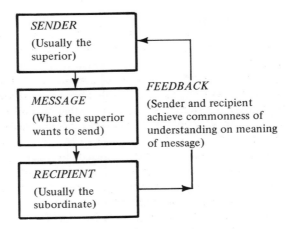

Figure 8–1. The communication process

Commonness in meaning is difficult to achieve, and it is not achieved until *sender* gets *feedback* that the message that was sent was received by *recipient* in the form that was intended. This feedback is critical and is infrequently achieved by many "senders." Most of us have played fall-guy to a small child's inquisitiveness when we try to answer a question such as: "Daddy, is there a sound in the forest if a tree crashes down but there's nobody around to hear it?" If we attempt to answer the question by using logic we do not communicate because the child's perception is quite different from our own. So we say: "No, there is no sound. There are sound waves but there is no sound unless someone hears it ... receives it." The moral of this story raises the question: How frequently do we *send* messages without getting *feedback* that the message has been received by the *recipient*? It is the recipient who communicates—not the communicator, the sender! Let me repeat:

It is the recipient who communicates—not the communicator!

FORMAL VS. INFORMAL COMMUNICATIONS

We face a curious paradox in communications today in organizations and in society in general. On the one hand there is an information explosion that is creating an accelerating volume of *data* but not *information*. Meanwhile, the communications gap widens—between sellers and consumers, between management and workers, between business and government, between professors and students.

Formal Communications

The paradox is nowhere more evident than in the specialized functional organization. The larger and more specialized it becomes, the more communications seems to *misdirect*. Consider, for example, the large university where specialization is carried to an extreme. This particular organization has been called "a collection of specialists held together by a common parking lot." The business organization is no different.

This complexity that is caused in part by the information explosion and size requirements has been accompanied by a number of complex, formal channels to handle the information and presumably to aid in the communication process.

One major oil company identified 130 formal channels of organizational communication which included staff meetings, employee forums, employee letters, manuals, bulletin boards, management notices, employee counseling, committee reports, recreation associations, informal talks, and a variety of information systems and reports. Anyone with experience in government or a corporate bureaucracy understands this dilemma. The larger an organization becomes, the more complex are its lines of communication, and there is always the danger that techniques and reports can become so institutionalized and inflexible that they take on an existence of their own. The system becomes the end, not the means. It becomes a classic case of thinking in terms of activities and not results.

Some managers believe that information means communication. Nothing is further from the truth. In order for information to communicate, there needs to be prior agreement on meaning and application, something that few reports and information systems achieve. Indeed, the more information, the greater the communication gap is likely to be. The chief executive of a major high-technology aerospace firm recently eliminated the company's centralized computer-based management information system (CBMIS). He said that the people doing the work at the grass-roots level weren't really using the system, and those who did were swamped with control reports that had become almost meaningless.

Organizations, by their very nature, tend to construct barriers to communication. Information systems, organization structures, authority arrangements, policies, controls, and the other trappings of formal organizational complexity make communication difficult, not easy. The challenge is to communicate despite this complexity.

Informal Communication

Communication, of course, is not all formal. The average supervisor concerned with a limited work group is equally concerned with the informal aspects because it is the superior–subordinate and face-to-face oral communications that usually get the job done. This is the way to overcome the formal organizational "trappings."

We communicate in both verbal and nonverbal ways. Our eye contact, physical touch, tone of voice, body posture, facial expressions and even silence can convey real messages to subordinates. These nonverbal messages can hinder as well as help. Most of us have experienced the "silent treatment" from a cold and uncommunicative boss. This sign of displeasure is frequently more effective than a verbal or written reprimand.

Eye contact is a particularly important conveyor of nonverbal communication. It can communicate concern or lack of it to the observer. In the experiment of the welding trainees described later in this chapter, the high-achieving welders were shown two photographs of their supervisor. They were exactly alike except that in one photograph the pupils of the eyes had been touched up and enlarged. All the trainees identified as high achievers felt that the photo with the enlarged eyes looked most like their supervisor. Five of the seven trainees identified as low achievers chose the untouched photographs. Could the pupil of the supervisor's eye communicate a message to the subordinates? Evidently it could.

The spoken word alone has no meaning and cannot communicate. It is merely a part of the total picture. The "silent language"—that is, gestures, tone of voice, plus the cultural and social refinements, cannot be distinguished from the spoken language. This phenomenon has been evident among the immigrants to the United States. Handicapped by difficulties of language and culture, most of them learned to communicate with gestures. One appropriate gesture can convey more than a hundred words.

SUPERVISORY SKILLS: FUNDAMENTALS OF COMMUNICATIONS

Communication Is Perception
Communication Is Expectation
Communication Makes Demands
Communication Is Information
Communicate Upward

Peter Drucker, today's most popular management writer, provides us with an excellent insight into managerial communications. He identifies four fundamentals:[1]

☐ Communication is perception.

☐ Communication is expectation.

☐ Communication makes demands.

☐ Communication and information are different; largely opposite, yet interdependent.

COMMUNICATION IS PERCEPTION

I have indicated earlier that it is the *recipient* (usually the subordinate) who communicates, not the sender (usually the superior). The sender sends a message, but there is no communication until the "percipient" perceives it. Percipient and recipient are one and the same; the message that is received is whatever the recipient *perceives* it to be.

Many teachers, public speakers, media "communicators" and managers overlook this fundamental principle; a recipient receives only that which is in terms of his or her own experience. Only those messages that are within a person's cultural and emotional "range of perception" can be understood. Yet we, the managers (communicators), continue to send messages in terms of our own limited experience. What we see so vividly, our subordinates do not see at all; what we argue so logically (we think) has little pertinence to the concerns of our subordinates. "Management" attempts to use logical arguments as to why the union should accept an agreement but "labor" perceives these arguments altogether differently. Consequently there is no communication and the result is impasse and confrontation.

Remember the old story of the three blind men and the elephant? Each man, encountering this strange beast, feels one of the elephant's parts—his leg, his trunk, his hide—and each reaches an unshakeable conclusion regarding what he has felt. What is the message here? The message is that you cannot communicate with the three blind men

---

[1]Peter F. Drucker, *Management: Tasks, Responsibilities, Practices* (New York: Harper & Row, 1974). See also *Managing in Turbulent Times* (New York: Harper & Row, 1980).

until you go over and feel the leg, the trunk, and the hide of the elephant. Then you can communicate, but only in terms of what the recipient, the true communicator, perceives and why.

The necessity to communicate on *results expected* becomes evident. If the recipient is truly the communicator, then the sender should send messages that are formed in terms of the recipient's perception. This can happen rather easily if both parties to the message agree on its meaning. This is unlikely to happen if either party communicates on activities in generalities or platitudes like "sell more" or "get costs down."

To illustrate how communications based on results might improve the process, consider this exchange between the manufacturing manager (sender/communicator) and the computer systems analyst (recipient):

MANAGER: *Design me a system that will keep the cost of raw materials down.*

ANALYST: *You mean a system that will report on hand balances against standard inventory levels? [The analyst's perception]*

MANAGER: *Yeah. That's right, I guess. Whatever you think is best.*

A year later the system is designed at great cost and installed. It doesn't do the job that the manager expected. Consider how much better the results might have been if a process of communicating based on results and common perception had been used:

MANAGER: *Our raw-materials inventory turnover seems to be much lower than in previous months. It's down to two turnovers per year. Could you design me a system that can reduce the costs of raw material and improve the turnover rate?*

ANALYST: *Yes, I think I can. The best system, in my opinion, is one that optimizes inventory costs through the design of decision rules that contain optimum reorder points, safety levels, and reorder quantities. Is that about what you want?*

MANAGER: *Yes. That's good. When do you think you could have it operational and at what cost?*

ANALYST: *I could do it in eight months at a design cost of sixteen man-months. It would return five times the cost in inventory savings. Specifically, it would improve inventory turnover from two to five times per year and reduce carrying costs by 50 percent.*

MANAGER: *That's great. Let me summarize. The results we expect are:*

Results Expected	Time	Cost
To design a raw-materials inventory system that will optimize levels and increase inventory turnover from two to five times per year and reduce carrying costs by 50 percent	8 months	16 man-months

ANALYST: *Agreed!*

COMMUNICATION IS EXPECTATION

The Pygmalion Effect (A Self-Fullfilling Prophecy)

It is frequently said that beauty is in the eye of the beholder. This cliché means that we perceive what we expect to perceive. We see largely what we expect to see, and we hear largely what we expect to hear. We don't like to be surprised with a message that doesn't fit into our expectations.

The principles of expectation and the self-fulfilling prophecies combine to provide us with two useful lessons. First, our expectations have an impact on subordinates and theirs have an impact on us. We should convert this into an opportunity to provide a positive influence and communication channel. Second, we should realize that before we can communicate we must know what the subordinates (recipients) expect to hear. We can then turn these expectations to our advantage in improving communication and at the same time avoid the shock that accompanies our attempt to make the recipients "change their mind" or perceive what they do not expect to perceive.

In Greek mythology, Pygmalion was a sculptor who carved an ivory statue of the ideal woman. Because his creation was so beautiful and lifelike, he fell in love with the statue and his steadfast belief led Venus to bring the statue to life. Later, this Greek myth was to inspire George Bernard Shaw's play, *Pygmalion*, which in turn formed the basis for the musical hit, *My Fair Lady*. In this play, Professor Higgins took Liza Doolittle, a London flower girl, and turned her into a charming and cultured lady. You may recall Liza's dialogue:

The difference between a lady and a flower girl is not how she behaves, but how she's treated. I shall always be a flower girl to

Professor Higgins, because he always treats me as a flower girl and always will, but I know I can be a lady to you, because you always treat me as a lady and always will.

Many managers, like Professor Higgins, unintentionally treat their subordinates in a way that leads to lower performance than they could normally achieve. This reflects the well-known principle that one person's expectations can influence the behavior of another. According to this concept—known as the Pygmalion Effect or the self-fulfilling prophecy—when one predicts an event, the expectation of the event changes the behavior of the "prophet" in such a way as to make the event more likely to happen.

The notion that one person's behavior is influenced by another person's expectations has been recognized for a long time by physicians and behavioral scientists but only recently by managers. Among physicians it is known as the Placebo Effect. (A placebo is a harmless preparation given merely to humor the patient, but if the patient believes it will help, it will.[2])

A Harvard University behavioral scientist, Dr. Robert Rosenthal, coined the term "Pygmalion Effect" and conducted a number of experiments to test his hypothesis. One of these involved the behavior of rats in solving the problems of a maze. He randomly chose two groups of rats and arbitrarily labeled them "maze bright" and "maze dull." Unaware of the random choice and arbitrary designation, student researchers adopted the conclusion that the rats were, indeed, "maze bright" and "maze dull" despite the fact that the rats were randomly chosen. The researchers even found the "maze bright" rats to be more pleasant to handle and more cooperative.

Another Rosenthal experiment tested the Pygmalion Effect in an elementary school. He randomly chose children from eighteen classrooms and labeled them "intellectual bloomers." Teachers were told that these children could be expected to show remarkable gains during the year. In actuality, the difference between the "intellectual bloomers" and the remainder of the children was solely in the minds of the teachers. Eight months later the "intellectual bloomers" showed an overall IQ gain of four points over the "normal" children. More remarkable were the attitudes of the teachers. They thought the brighter students were appealing, more affectionate, and better

[2]An opposite effect is also possible. Numerous people are afflicted with iatrogenic (physician-*caused*) illnesses. This occurs when the doctor is approached by someone complaining of a few symptoms. The doctor classifies these symptoms, gives them a name, and obligingly tells the patient he is sick. From that day on the patient becomes sick.

adjusted. The conclusion: the higher-performing and better-liked students had superior performance because it was what had been expected of them.

There is an important message here for managers. In the language of psychologist Rensis Likert, "If a high level of performance is to be achieved, it appears to be necessary for a supervisor to have high performance goals and a contagious enthusiasm as to the importance of these goals." Two examples will illustrate this: "Sweeney's Miracle" and the high-aptitude welders.

Professor James Sweeney of Tulane University believed that he could teach a poorly educated person to be a good computer operator. For a demonstration of his theory he chose George Johnson, an uneducated janitor. Johnson was doing very well under Sweeney's tutelage until the personnel department decided that computer operators must have a certain IQ score. Johnson's IQ indicated that he couldn't learn to type, much less operate and program a computer. But Sweeney insisted, even under the threat of resignation, that Johnson should be allowed to continue his training.

At last report Professor Sweeney is directing the computer center and George Johnson is in charge of the main computer room and is responsible for training new computer operators. Johnson succeeded because of Sweeney's expectations and what Sweeney believed about his own teaching ability.

In a Texas experiment, five welding trainees were selected at random and their supervisors were told that they had an exceptionally high aptitude for welding, despite the fact that they were no better or worse than the average. At the end of the six-month course, the supervisors rated these "high-aptitude" trainees significantly higher than the others. Remarkably, so did their peers. The groups also performed significantly higher on a standard welding test and on a written examination. By all measures they outperformed the control group. Why? Because of expectations of themselves and their supervisors. Their performance was a self-fulfilling prophecy.

Unfortunately, the reverse is also true. Negative expectations usually result in negative performance. Thus we have negative self-fulfilling prophecies. Indeed, these are more prevalent and far more damaging to productivity than positive expectations. The only way to break the cycle of negative self-fulfilling prophecies is to change the concept of work and superior-subordinate relationships. We must think positive!

If we assume, as we must, that the best managers are those who increase the motivation and productivity of their subordinates, then it follows that these managers should be "positive Pygmalions." They should expect more and communicate these expectations. They should try to develop these characteristics:

☐ Believe in themselves and have confidence in what they are doing. This confidence will be transmitted to subordinates.

☐ Have faith in their ability to develop their subordinates; to select, train, and motivate them. Subordinates will justify this faith because it is what is expected of them.

☐ An ability to develop "stretch" goals and communicate this expectation.

☐ Develop a preference for reward through achievement of the work group. If *group* rather than *self*-achievement is the higher form of reward, the group will have higher achievement expectations.

In summary, results management will shape the expectations and hence the productivity of subordinates. By communicating the expectations, the supervisor will be a positive influence on attitudes, self-confidence, and self-development.

COMMUNICATION MAKES DEMANDS

In recent years, the highest readership of any item in the daily American newspaper was enjoyed by the syndicated columns of two sisters: Abigail van Buren's *Dear Abby* column and that of Ann Landers. Why would anyone want to read these spicy self-confessionals? The answer is that these daily columns made no demands on the reader and we therefore have a case of excellent communication. We receive because there is a reward for doing so. Moreover, the message makes practically no demands upon our mental capacity.

Too many teachers fail to appreciate this principle. They demand retention, if not understanding, of historical dates, mathematical equations, financial ratios, and a blackboard full of what the student considers to be minutiae. Real understanding is unlikely unless the recipient is provided with some motivation, some reasons for learning. Communication has broken down. The learner shortly forgets because the mental demands of understanding and retention are too difficult.

If a message makes too many demands on the receiver, no communication occurs. On the other hand, the message will be received if it appeals to the receiver's motivation. If the communication fits in with the aspirations, values, or purposes of the recipient, it will likely be received in the form the sender intended. If it goes against these motivations, aspirations, or values, it will be resisted.

The conclusion to draw from this principle is that communication based on mutual *results expected* makes fewer demands and hence is more likely to be acted upon than generalities that are different to translate and mean little to the recipient. "Do something to get maintenance costs down" is a message that is either misunderstood or becomes frustrating to act upon. How much better and less demanding to get agreement on results expected:

Results Expected	Time	Cost
To reduce maintenance cost on line one by 10 percent to a rate of one man-hour for twenty machine-hours	By December 31	Stay within maintenance budget and no change in downtime

COMMUNICATION IS INFORMATION

When the U.S. Marine Corps drill sergeant barks: "Right face!" there is perfect communication because information exchange is perfect. Each command has only one possible meaning; it rests on pre-established understanding between sender and receiver regarding the specific response expected. Most formal information systems result in something less than the perfect communication exchange of the drill sergeant. Some company information systems serve to complicate rather than to enhance communication. We pay lip service to "management by exception" and demand concise reports that provide only information on the "critical variances." What we get is information overload or information blackout.

Information is always encoded. To be classified as communication the code must be understood by both the sender and receiver. This requires prior agreement on the code and to what the information pertains. This is not generally the case. The preparation of inputs for information reports is frequently misunderstood and is viewed as an unpleasant task at best. The output reports are rarely used because the information means different things to different people.

Once again, this principle demonstrates the need to communicate on *results expected*—objectives, goals, targets, standards, productivity improvement, and the like; predetermined measures that both sender and recipient have agreed upon.

UPWARD COMMUNICATIONS BASED ON RESULTS

The communication cycle is not complete until the sender receives some sort of feedback regarding the receipt of the message by the receiver. The sender must evaluate the impact of the message by some action or response that is appropriate to the message and the receiver. A lack of feedback appears to be the central problem throughout history; communication has almost invariably been *downward*. This cannot work.

Downward communication focuses on what we, the senders, want to say and makes the assumption that the sender—i.e., the manager— communicates. But in the overwhelming percentage of instances all the sender does is send. The sender cannot communicate downward anything connected with understanding, especially motivation to productivity. Communication is an act of a receiver and requires communication upward as well, from those who perceive to those who need feedback and understanding that a message has been sent and received. This does not take place when communication is one-way.

For too long the superior–subordinate relationship has been based on the quicksand of insufficient information and vague goals. Exhortations to "Sharpen up the operations" or "Do a better job" or "Get those costs down" are representative of communication at its worst. There is no message, no recipient, no perception, and no result.

Experience and common sense tell us that communication, motivation, and hence productivity can be improved by taking an approach that involves two fundamental ideas:

☐ Start the communication process with the receiver, not the sender. This requires a philosophy of upward, rather than downward communication.

☐ Focus upward communication on something that is common to sender and receiver, something that they both perceive alike. This is the expected result. This approach forces subordinates to think through logically and present to the superior their own ideas as to what contribution they are expected to make.

This communication by results approach provides a common perception between superior and subordinate, between sender and receiver, an essential requirement of good communication. Moreover, the subordinate is provided access to a new relationship that provides the essential ingredients for motivation: participation in an understanding of the realities of decision making, a choice between what the situation demands and what one ordinarily would like to do, a new understanding of one's role and responsibility, and a breakthough in organizational inflexibility.

Figure 8-2 illustrates the concept of downward versus upward communications. In the latter case, communications and results and hence productivity will be greater for the reasons outlined above.

SUPERVISORY SKILLS: APPRAISAL, I

Appraisal Problems

RESISTANCE TO APPRAISAL

SPECIFIC PROBLEMS

JOB DESCRIPTION

PERSONALITY APPRAISAL

Figure 8–2. Downward vs. upward communications

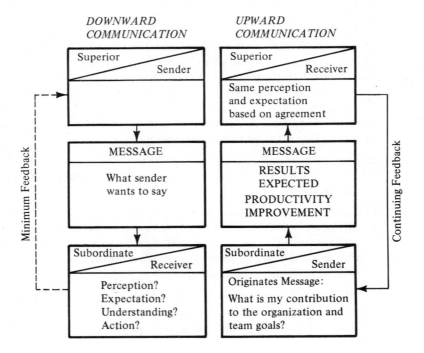

APPRAISAL PROBLEMS

The need to evaluate performance is present in all organizations. It may not be formalized or documented, but performance appraisal of some kind is the primary vehicle for *recognition and reward*. It can also be an instrument of developing *responsibility*.

Resistance to Appraisal

Any manager who has had "hands-on" experience with performance appraisal almost invariably finds the job distasteful. Research has shown that in those companies without a formal control system over the process, fewer than half of the appraisals are ever completed. In my own experience with hundreds of supervisors and middle managers I have found that the appraisal process and communication are the two most frequently mentioned problems. They don't like either role, whether it be the "appraisor" or the "appraisee." The process inhibits more often than it promotes communication.

In general, there are three reasons for supervisory resistance to the appraisal process: (1) Supervisors don't like to criticize a subordinate and have to handle the inevitable argument that follows; (2) they feel that they are not equipped to properly perform the appraisal of a subordinate or to handle the accompanying interview; and (3) they have a general mistrust of the techniques and procedures surrounding the appraisal process.

The subordinates usually dislike the process also. Unless they are one of the few selected for high praise, the employees almost always feel that their performance has been judged unfairly.

The general failure of the appraisal system to operate as expected is unfortunate. Properly used, the performance appraisal can become a fine tool for improved motivation, communication, self-development, and hence productivity.

Problems with Performance Appraisal

Most organizations with formal appraisal programs have two things in common. They follow the textbook definition, which considers the appraisal process as a formal evaluation of employee actions over a previous time period. Second, virtually all have some performance appraisal document, a form of some kind. The similarity among companies ends there. The systems in use represent a wide divergence. Some require supervisors to write broad essays describing an individual's strengths and weaknesses. A more common approach is the quantification of performance behavior or personal character- istics that requires a good/average/poor or a 1/2/3 technique for giving a value to a subjective judgment of performance or personal attributes.

Deficiencies in practice can be summarized under the five broad areas discussed below.

☐ Focusing on the *reward/punishment* aspect tends to detract from the real purpose of an appraisal session. When viewed this way, the interview frequently turns into either a whitewash job or a fault-finding session. If the former, the employee may go away with false hopes for promotion or pay increases or a false sense of job security. Fault-finding appraisals frequently regress into personality clashes resulting from statements about behavior and performance that have not been previously communicated. In any case, both the boss and the subordinate frequently depart with feelings of distress or ill-will.

☐ Appraisals based on *personality traits* (e.g., loyalty, initiative, cooperation, attitude, and so on) are bad news. They obscure the real purpose of appraisal which is focus on results. In practically no case is the subordinate motivated to better productivity. (More on this later.)

☐ *Emphasis on the system* is an all-too-frequent complaint. When it is viewed as a mandatory technique or procedure, or something the personnel department "dreamed up," the system becomes the end and not the means. Reflect upon our definition of the input managers in Chapter 2; they emphasized form and administration (doing things right) as opposed to process and management (doing the right things).

☐ There is a general *confusion about the objectives* of performance review. Rarely is improved productivity a stated objective of appraisal nor is it viewed as a vehicle to focus on results. Instead, its purpose is frequently seen as a catch-all of procedures related to general personnel administration: wage and salary review, place- ment, development, and advancement. When this occurs, both employee and manager become confused and adopt defensive behavior regarding the process.

☐ *Nonproductive behavior* is a frequent result of appraisal. Al- though the process implies precision, in reality it is quite imprecise (unless based on results) and filled with personal judgment and emotion. There is a tendency to do something *to* the employees, not *with* them. The appraisal becomes, at best, a hygienic aspect of motivation, at worst, an emotional letdown for both superior and subordinate.

These deficiencies are not universal, but one or more can be found in most companies. Usually they result from not adhering to the two main considerations in designing an appropriate system: determining valid factors for evaluating employee performance and making certain that the system is acceptable to both employees and management.

The Job Description Problem

More than fifteen years ago the American Management Associations conducted the classic study on communication, job descriptions, and boss–subordinate understanding. Hundreds of boss–subordinate teams were asked to *prioritize* a list of five job responsibilities and to match these with job results expected from each responsibility. Subordinates listed their perception of their own jobs and bosses listed their perception of their subordinates' jobs. The results were startling. There was little agreement between boss and subordinate concerning what the job was to achieve. You might rightfully ask: How can a superior–subordinate team ever accomplish a result if there is wide disagreement on what the result should be?

Some of the difficulty surrounding this lack of understanding can be traced to a great American industrial institution—the job description. Often these are written in terms of activities and general statements of responsibilities rather than in terms of what is expected from the job. An examination of Figure 8-3, a typical job description for a production foreman, will reveal that careful adherence to the language of the description tends to turn the employee's effort away from the real output of the subsystem.

A solution to this difficulty lies in including a statement of expected results in the job description. Aside from all the other advantages we have mentioned, such action would provide a basis for appraisal.

The Problem of Personality and Trait Appraisal

Regardless of how an organization views the purposes and needs of its appraisal program, many of them base all or a part of their employee evaluation on how the supervisor perceives the sub-

Job Description: Foreman, Line #1

General

The foreman of line number one is responsible for the manufacture of
assigned products in accordance with the applicable production
schedule. He or she is also responsible for cost budgets and quality
specifications as well as liaison with other departments considered
necessary to insure uninterrupted production. He or she will perform
these duties in accordance with company policies, procedures, and
instructions.

Specific Duties

1. Schedule tools for production line setup.
2. Schedule raw materials and manpower for production schedule.
    This applies to tools and maintenance also.
3. Take appropriate action to minimize absenteeism.
4. Maintain discipline for employees on the shift.
5. Maintain liaison with shipping to insure adequate finished
    goods shipments.
6. Communicate company policies, procedures, and other
    information as required.
7. Provide information to Personnel Department and Cost Accounting
    as required.
8. Comply with provisions of union contract.
9. Minimize downtime due to machine failure.
10. Take other action as required or as directed by company
    management.

Working Hours

First shift: 7:30 a.m. to 4:00 p.m. Monday to Friday
Second shift: 3:30 p.m. to 12:00 a.m. Monday to Friday

Immediate Supervisor

Plant Production Superintendent

Figure 8-3. Typical job description

ordinate's behavior, attitudes, personality, and job knowledge. This
traitist approach is designed to let the employee know where he or she
"stands" with the boss. This widespread approach is illustrated in
Figure 8-4, which is a typical company appraisal form. Many
managers express real misgivings about a system based on personality traits and are uncomfortable when put in the position of
"playing God" or "playing psychiatrist."

_____Corporation   Employee Appraisal Form

Name_____ Employee #_____ Date_____

Using the code below, rate the employee on each of the factors listed
with the code that most closely indicates his or her performance in
comparison with the requirements of the job.

1. Outstanding. The best possible for the job.   2. Very Good.
Beyond the requirements for good performance.   3. Good. Meets the
requirements for the job.   This is the basic standard.   4. Fair.
Performance is barely satisfactory and needs improvement in basic
aspects of job.   5. Unsatisfactory. Deficient.

Job Factor	Explanation	Rating
Judgment	Are his or her decisions based on sound reasoning?	( )
Human Relations	Does he or she cooperate with and effectively influence people?	( )
Attitude	Does he or she show interest and enthusiasm and a desire to improve performance?	( )
Quantity of Work	Does he or she produce an acceptable quantity?	( )
Quality of Work	Is his or her work accurate, thorough, and acceptable?	( )
Communications	Is he or she effective in written and oral expression?	( )
Initiative	Is he or she a self-starter, seeking out opportunities and responsibility?	( )
Leadership	Does he or she motivate fellow workers and subordinates?	( )
Cost Conscious	Is he or she interested in better performance at lower cost?	( )
Integrity	Is he or she reliable, trustworthy, and honest?	( )
Personal	Neatness, character, etc.	( )

What are the major positive aspects of the employee's work?

State the major area in which the employee should improve.

Figure 8-4. Typical appraisal form

Based on our discussion of productivity and motivation thus far, it is easy to summarize those reasons why the traitist approach to appraisal should be abandoned as the only device for employee evaluation:

□ It is resisted by superior and subordinate alike.

□ It doesn't measure performance in terms of results.

□ It focuses on activities rather than output.

□ Appraisal based on traits is not a motivator.

□ There is no proven correlation between traits and productivity.

□ Many managers are not qualified to "play psychiatrist."

□ It can be devastating to a person to go blithely on his or her way for 364 days without correction, praise, or admonition, only to find out on the 365th day that his/her performance is considered "substandard."

□ Appraisals tend to discourage and disgruntle employees when they can see no link between performance and pay. (One appraisal form I witnessed has this "trait" for appraisal: "How well-read is this individual?")

□ It is frequently the case among the growing number of knowledge workers that the employee is more technically and professionally knowledgeable than the supervisor or superior.

When discussing appraisal in class or in a seminar, I demonstrate the wide variation in the subjective judgments of individuals by asking the participants to appraise a situation. For example, I might ask them to write an answer to the question: "How big is a small town?" Opinions invariably range from 200 to 50,000, and this disparity points up the central shortcoming of subjective appraisals; they are nothing more than one individual's opinion of another. One opinion is as good as another.[3]

---

[3] Perhaps the best (or worst) example of the shortcomings of trait appraisals is the one used by President Carter's Chief of Staff, Hamilton Jordan following the housecleaning of high administration officials in July 1979. Members of the Executive Branch and White House were "appraised" with instructions such as these: "Rate this person on a scale of 1 to 10 on: (1) How confident is this person? (2) How mature? (3) How flexible? (4) Stable? (5) Open? (6) Bright?" Also: "How well does this person take direction? How well does he get along? How much supervision is needed?" Also: "List three things about this person that have disappointed you." Most experts agree that this system put appraisal theory back into the nineteenth century.

SUPERVISORY SKILLS: APPRAISAL, II

Appraisal Based on Results Expected
Results Appraisal and Motivation
Appraising Behavioral Qualifications

APPRAISAL BASED ON RESULTS EXPECTED

A *results management* approach to appraisal will help to overcome the several shortcomings of the traditional traitist system. It will also help to achieve the real objectives of appraisal: (1) improvement of productivity and results; (2) the development of people for both organizational and individual needs; and (3) improvement of the superior—subordinate relationship.

The results approach calls for the subordinate to determine personal performance goals in terms of expected results. At the end of the appraisal period, or as often as necessary, the subordinate makes a personal appraisal. This in turn provides the vehicle by which superior and subordinate jointly determine the nature of the job, the results expected, and the performance of the individual.

This approach will also significantly improve the process of communication. An appraisal based on what a person has done well and what can be done in the future, a discussion surrounding the individual's direction for self-development, provides basic foundations for communication. Taken in this light, appraisal is not a task to be resisted but an opportunity to jointly establish a future direction.

The shortcomings of traditional appraisal and a summary of how results management can help overcome them are shown in Table 8-1.

The organization that adopts an appraisal system based on results rather than personality traits is on the right road to productivity improvement. A companion system would include job descriptions that are written in terms of results expected rather than vague responsibilities relating to activities.

RESULTS APPRAISAL AND MOTIVATION

The most powerful argument in favor of an appraisal based on results and self-control is contained in the nature of motivation as outlined in Chapter 5. There I suggested that a person is motivated to perform

TABLE 8–1. Traditional vs. Results-Management Appraisal

Shortcomings of Traditional Appraisal	How Results Managment Can Help
Focus on reward/punishment for past performance	Focus on results for future
Emphasis on the system	Emphasis on productivity
Uncertain objectives	Objectives stated in terms of results
Nonproductive behavior	Motivation for achievement
Trait appraisal	Appraisal based on goals
Vague job descriptions	Superior–subordinate joint determination of job requirements

if such performance leads to a reward that meets his or her needs. It was suggested further that the money and the hygiene factors associated with a job are not truly motivators in the sense that although they are external movers or job satisfiers, they do not meet the higher-order need and reward of *self-actualization.* When the *results* of the job are designed by the individual and there is commitment to achieve those results, then the reward is valued and internalized. When this environment is set, appraisal can be a valuable tool for effectiveness.

It has been said that the best performance appraisal form is a *blank piece of paper.* On such a "form" the superior–subordinate team establishes on the top half of the page the productivity improvement objectives *together and jointly.* The bottom half of the page could contain the appraisal of actual performance against these expected results. This approach to mutual goal setting is growing. Figure 8-5 illustrates the appraisal form used by a major company that is generally known to be excellently managed. Although the form is not a blank piece of paper, the system does permit and encourage mutual goal setting by "appraisor" (superior) and "appraisee" (subordinate).

Some managers carry the blank-paper approach a step further and use an open-ended appraisal form that is originated by the subordinate. In what is a true *upward communication* style of management, the subordinate defines the objectives of the superior's and his (or her) own job as well. He also writes out what standards, in his

PERFORMANCE PLANNING

PERFORMANCE EVALUATION

RESPONSIBILITIES (Key words to describe the major elements of this employee's job.)	PERFORMANCE FACTORS AND/OR RESULTS TO BE ACHIEVED (A more specific statement of the employee's key responsibilities and/or goals employee can reasonably be expected to achieve in the coming period.)	RELATIVE IMPORTANCE	ACTUAL ACHIEVEMENTS	LEVEL OF ACHIEVEMENT				
				Far Exceeded	Consistently Exceeded	Exceeded	Consistently Met	Did Not Meet

CHANGES IN PERFORMANCE PLAN (May be recorded anytime during the appraisal period.)

ADDITIONAL SIGNIFICANT ACCOMPLISHMENTS

OPTIONAL ADDITIONAL PLANS (Where considered appropriate by manager and employee.)

Figure 8–5. An excellent performance appraisal form

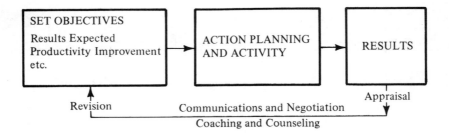

Figure 8–6. The performance improvement cycle

opinion, are being used to appraise his performance. He then lists the major steps or milestones that are necessary to achieve the self-imposed objectives. If the superior accepts this "action plan," it becomes the joint work charter for the coming period and the appraisal basis for the end of the period. The existence of the end-of-the-period appraisal does not mean that the document is forgotten during the course of the period. On the contrary, it becomes a tool of communication, negotiation, and revision during the period of the action plan. The iterative cycle of this process is shown in Figure 8-6. This cycle applies to all appraisals, whatever the format. As Figure 8-6 indicates, the appraisal can and should provide an ongoing opportunity for superior–subordinate communications, negotiation, coaching and counseling, and revision of action plans.

APPRAISING BEHAVIORAL QUALIFICATIONS

In a growing number of service organizations, the problem of appraisal is more difficult. What is good performance by the bank teller, airline stewardess, supermarket cashier, retail sales clerk, secretary and the many other jobs in which the customer judges the organization largely by the service employee? In many of these organizations the "up-front" service employee represents a major competitive edge.

Performance in these jobs has three dimensions. First there is the need to maintain standards of personal behavior (e.g., courtesy, grooming). Second, there is the need to set some quantitative standard of performance (e.g., transactions per hour). Finally, there is a need for *effective* behavior—the type of behavior that results in achievement of organization objectives.

It is this third dimension, *effective behavior*, that is more difficult to learn and practice. Many employees are unable to discern that type of behavior on their own because of their vague notions about how to do a good job. It is the purpose of the appraisal system to include descriptions of job behaviors that lead to good or bad performance and hence to achieving the organization's objectives. For example, if the objective of a bank is "to reduce customer waiting time at tellers' windows," the appraisal form may evaluate a teller's performance on a scale of 1 (extremely poor performance) to 10 (extremely good performance). The statement "Takes a coffee break with people standing in line" would indicate a 2 on the scale. Good performance, an 8 on the scale, might be indicated by the statement, "Identifies and stores all incoming transactions by five established categories."

The establishment of some rating scale based on effective behavior not only encourages that behavior, but, by identifying effective job-specific behavior, lets the individual know how goals can be achieved so he or she can develop an action plan accordingly.

SUPERVISORY SKILLS: APPRAISAL, III
Integrating Communication and Appraisal

INTEGRATING COMMUNICATION AND APPRAISAL

Properly performed, the processes of communication and appraisal provide the supervisor with powerful tools for achieving results. If superior–subordinate communications is essential to improving

Figure 8–7. The combined communication and appraisal process

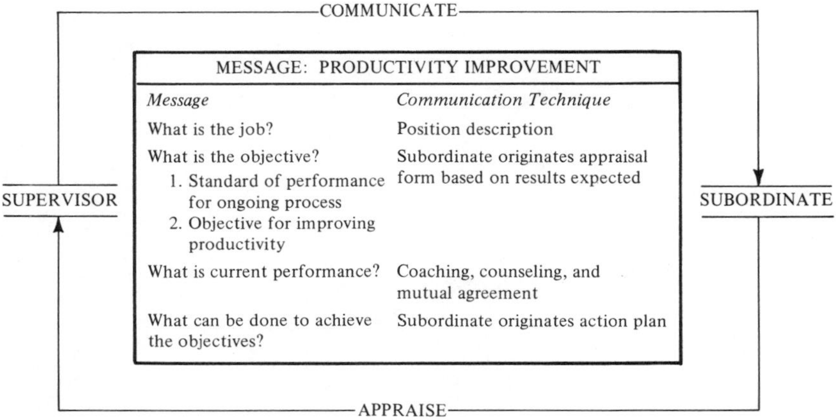

productivity, as it surely is, then the *combined* use of appraisal and communication can go a long way toward achieving this end. In other words, the message is productivity and the vehicle for communicating is appraisal.

The iterative process of superior–subordinate communications and the related communication techniques is summarized in Figure 8-7.

YOUR LEADERSHIP STYLE

"True leaders emerge from, and always return to, the wants and needs of their followers. The effective leader mobilizes new, 'higher' needs in his followers."
—James MacGregor Burns,
Distinguished Historian and author of Leadership[1]

CHAPTER 9

SUPERVISORY SKILLS:

LEADERSHIP STYLE, I

Approaches to Leadership
Requirements for Good Leadership
The Results Management Style
(Managerial Grid)
Integrating Requirements and Style
Evaluate Your Readiness

---

[1] *Leadership* (New York: Harper and Row, 1978).

There is almost universal agreement that individual productivity is significantly influenced by the superior–subordinate relationship in the work situation. This relationship can be productive or nonproductive depending on the leadership style of the superior. It is therefore important for all managers to examine their style and make changes if required. If changes cannot be made, managers can at least identify their style and understand what reaction it is likely to evoke on the part of the subordinates.

Although everyone agrees that leadership is important, there is far less agreement on what constitutes good leadership or the content of leadership theory. Over time, a number of approaches have developed.

APPROACHES TO LEADERSHIP

The *traitist* approach to leadership is the oldest and, to a large extent, the best known and most prevalent today, at least in terms of support by practicing managers. This theory can be traced back to the medieval period when Alfarabi identified the traits of a leader as intelligence, excellent memory, eloquence, firmness, and temperance. Later, in the sixteenth century, Niccolo Machiavelli wrote that leaders were born but could also be made, and he identified charismatic personality as a requirement for ruling as a prince. Subsequent writers and researchers have identified and tested literally hundreds of additional traits such as initiative, judgment, moral courage, perseverance, endurance, and so on. The list is endless.

There are two problems with the traitist approach to leadership. First, there is no evidence that any trait or group of traits correlate with productivity and results. Second, if an individual manager lacks these "born" traits, there isn't much chance that he or she can develop them. In conclusion, the traitist approach doesn't offer us much help in terms of an operational answer to productivity.

The Theory X and Theory Y approach of Douglas McGregor[1] continues to enjoy widespread attention. The theory identifies two extreme styles along a continuum, thus:

[1] Douglas McGregor, *The Human Side of Enterprise* (New York: McGraw-Hill, 1960). This book contains the original idea of Theory X and Theory Y. Since that time numerous other authors have popularized the theory.

Theory X   Theory Y

(Autocratic)   (Participative)

Traditional   Human Relations

Theory X assumes that people are lazy, dislike and shun work, have to be driven, and need the carrot and the stick. According to this assumption, most people are incapable of taking responsibility for themselves and should be looked after, presumably by the leader. By contrast, Theory Y makes the assumption that workers have a psychological need to work and want responsibility so that they can achieve. The manager should therefore locate his or her style closer to Theory Y along the continuum if required.

Perhaps one of the major contributions of McGregor's theory has been to highlight the inescapable fact that the traditional Theory X approach to leadership no longer works. Theory Y, on the other hand, does not give us an operational approach that fulfills our requirement for making work productive and the worker achieving. In other words, we know that Theory X doesn't work but we aren't sure how to put Theory Y to work on the job. It is not enough to merely adopt a participative philosophy. Something else is needed.

The *style* approach to leadership has also been very popular. Researchers have attempted to identify the characteristics present in styles of leadership behavior (e.g., autocratic, democratic, paternalistic, participative, custodial, supportive, collegial, and so on) and the impact of each style on organizational behavior. In management seminars, participants are asked to identify these types of behavior and the impact of the leadership style on subordinates by means of such questions as: "What would be your reaction to this style?" or "Under what conditions would this style be appropriate?"

There are two significant shortcomings in the style approach. First, it doesn't resolve the apparent conflict between task orientation and people orientation, despite the fact that task relationships and people relationships are not mutually exclusive. Second, the approach doesn't tell us how productivity can be achieved by results management and motivation. Somewhat like the traitist approach, the style approach leaves us with little more than a general impression of subordinate reaction to a given style.

The *situational* (or contingency) approach says that successful leadership is a function of: (1) the forces in the leaders; (2) the characteristics and types of needs of subordinates; and (3) the situation. Forces in the leader might include the person's value system, confidence in subordinates, inclination in terms of leadership style, and perception of how power and authority should be used. Subordinate characteristics and needs might include education and training, interest in the work, and group values. The situation for the practice of leadership is almost unlimited. It involves the nature of the work, level of management, organizational policies, problems to be solved, and environment. The variables are demonstrated in Figure 9–1.

While the situational or contingency approach cannot be denied (because it includes all possible variables), a casual examination will reveal that the interaction of these forces, variables, and situations presents the manager with an infinite and therefore impossible array of leadership situations. Understanding requires almost universal genius on the part of the manager. Most of us find it hard enough to know what we need to know about some technical area of expertise

Figure 9–1. Interacting forces that shape the manager's leadership style or the appraisal environment

FORCES IN
MANAGER

- Value System
- Background and Experiences
- Confidence in subordinates
- Leadership Inclination
- Tolerance for Ambiguity

FORCES IN
SUBORDINATE

- Need for Independence
- Desire for Responsibility
- Acceptance of Management Goals
- Skills and Commitment

FORCES IN
SITUATION

- Nature of Problem
- Availability of Time
- Economics of Decision
- Group Effectiveness

FORCES IN
ORGANIZATIONAL
SYSTEM

- Methods of Production
- Division of Work
- Certainty of Task
- Purpose and Mission of Job
- Structure of Organization

(e.g., accounting, engineering, sales, manufacturing) without the added problem of becoming a psychologist.

What is needed is a simple *operational* approach to leadership, one that achieves productivity by making the worker achieve. As background for the identification of such a style, it is desirable to set out some requirements for good leadership.

REQUIREMENTS FOR GOOD LEADERSHIP

From the foregoing discussion and what we know about the topic, we can discredit two old myths. One is that there is one best leadership style, or that there are leaders who excel under all circumstances. The other is that some persons are born leaders, and that training, experience, or conditions cannot materially affect leadership skills.

Saying what leadership is *not* doesn't tell us what it *is*. But if productivity is what we are seeking, then we can list a number of general requirements that have emerged over time. To be an effective leader, the manager should be able to

☐ *Resolve conflict* before it can become damaging to cooperation, organizational integration, and achievement of results. A major reason why conflict develops in organizations is that people do not understand the results expected of them or their co-workers.

☐ *Allow participation* in decisions for the common good, not for "permissiveness" or for reasons of "human relations."

☐ *Encourage creativity and innovation* in work methods that provide better results in terms of subordinate fulfillment and achievement.

☐ *Manage by results* based on upward communication and establishment of goals by subordinates.

☐ *Provide control and feedback* that fulfills the requirements of: (a) clear understanding of results expected; (b) information on progress; and (c) information for self-monitoring and control.

☐ *Maintain morale* that is grounded in good performance and not paternalism, human relations, or some "happiness index." Focus is on opportunities and not problems.

☐ *Negotiate and maintain commitment* to goals that are established in the superior–subordinate relationship. Results depend on commitment, not lip service.

☐ *Set stretch objectives* that require subordinates to "reach out" for productivity and satisfaction.

☐ *Develop subordinates* by providing opportunities for growth.

☐ *Utilize appraisal* as an opportunity for setting future objectives rather than focusing on reward or punishment based on past performance that is judged on traits.

☐ *Maintain a style and behavior* that have a positive impact on organizational longevity and growth.

THE RESULTS MANAGEMENT STYLE OF LEADERSHIP

If the foregoing requirements truly represent what we expect from a good leader, then we can examine an approach to leadership that may give us an operational answer to how we can achieve productivity while fulfilling these requirements.

Two psychologists, Robert Blake and Jane Mouton, have originated an approach to leadership styles that has gained widespread

Figure 9–2. The Managerial Grid. (Source: R. R. Blake and J. S. Mouton, *The Managerial Grid.* [Houston: Gulf Publishing Co., 1964], p. 10. Reproduced by permission.)

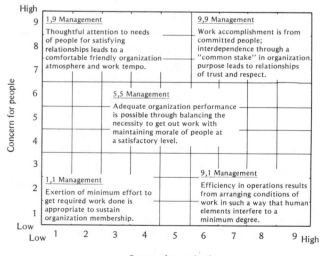

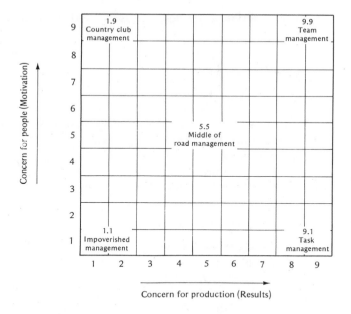

Figure 9–3. Styles of leadership

acceptance. It is known as The Managerial Grid.®[2] This innovative "school" of effective leadership behavior attempts to integrate the three basic "universals" of organizational life: (1) the need for production; (2) the need for satisfaction on the part of organizational members; and (3) the inevitable hierarchy of authority, the *boss* aspect of getting results. Blake and Mouton also attempt to balance the two ends of the managerial continuum that emphasize production on the one hand (Theory X) and people on the other (Theory Y). The basic contention is that organizational goals and satisfaction of workers' needs are not incompatible.

Figure 9–2 is the original Managerial Grid® figure. It identifies five leadership styles depending upon the manager's concern for production (results) and people (motivation). For a discussion of leadership styles, we can construct a model such as the one shown in Figure 9–3. As you can see there are eighty-one (9 × 9) "styles" on the

[2] R. R. Blake and J. S. Mouton, *The Managerial Grid* (Houston: Gulf Publishing Co., 1964).

grid but the five extremes are identified and discussed below for illustration.

9,1 THE TASK STYLE

These managers believe that there is a contradiction between production and the personal needs of people and since their concern is almost totally with production, they resolve this contradiction in favor of output. They are exacting taskmasters and achieve results by not permitting the human element to interfere. They know how to use their authority; they use it to coerce compliance. They represent the true *autocrat*, the "carrot-and-stick" type of manager.

1,9 THE COUNTRY CLUB STYLE

These managers, somewhat like the 9,1 managers, believe that the requirements for production and results are contrary to the needs of people. Unlike the 9,1 manager, they resolve the conflict in favor of people because to them, people come first. They arrange for the "happiness" of their subordinates by providing a comfortable and friendly atmosphere with a work tempo to match. They view themselves as the boss but don't use their authority to pressure subordinates. They lead by following. They are *paternalistic* leaders and have a high concern for the morale of "their" people.

1,1 THE IMPOVERISHED STYLE

These managers are usually found in some unimportant staff job or where operations have settled into a programmed routine. They assume that there is incompatibility between production and people needs but they have little concern for either. They are apathetic and self-defeating and summarize their supervisory role with the attitude, "I don't want to get involved." They think the best way to lead is to lead least and therefore they encourage subordinates to "do it your way." If forced to make a decision they will do it "by the book." They are waiting out retirement and social security. Oddly enough, these managers are frequently very highly motivated by activities unrelated to their jobs.

5,5 MIDDLE OF THE ROAD STYLE

These managers are excellent politicians and are fast on their feet. They believe that production and the needs of people are conflicting and view their job as resolving this conflict through negotiating, persuasion, and selling their own solutions. Since an imbalance exists between the need for results and the needs of people, they spend much of their time orchestrating an "in-between" position that is not the optimum for either requirement. They see themselves as motivator and communicator rather than as boss. If unable to resolve conflict they will take a vote. They are usually firm but fair. They are *democratic*.

9,9 TEAM MANAGEMENT

Unlike the other four leadership styles, the 9,9 managers see no inherent conflict between production and the needs of people. On the contrary, they believe that the needs of people can best be met by the provision of an opportunity for achievement. They know that production is in everyone's interest.

The 9,9 manager is *participative* but not in any paternalistic sense. Nor is participation a means for sharing responsibility or authority relationships. It is a means for organizing subordinate responsibility and achievement. The 9,9 managers view their role as establishing the conditions that integrate the potential for subordinate achievement and motivation through team action that is focused on *results*.

INTEGRATING LEADERSHIP REQUIREMENTS AND STYLE

In Chapter 5 I outlined nine factors that affect productivity in the work situation: challenging work, participation in decisions, compensation tied to performance, communication, supervision, recognition, self-development, stewardship, and organization style.

In this chapter I have established ten general requirements for good leadership: conflict resolution, decision making, creativity and innovation, management by results, delegation and control, maintenance of morale, negotiation and maintenance of commitment to goals, setting stretch objectives, appraisal, and subordinate development. Additionally, I said that another requirement for a good leader is to have a positive impact on organizational longevity and growth.

The conclusion should emerge at this point that the real job of the leader is to provide those factors that affect productivity by meeting the requirements of good leadership.

Table 9–1 compares these requirements with the five styles of leadership. An examination of Table 9–1 should convince the reader

TABLE 9–1. Comparison of Leadership Requirements and Styles

STYLE OF LEADERSHIP	Resolution of Conflict	Decision Making	Creativity & Innovation	Philosophy of Results Management	Maintenance of Morale	Negotiation of Commitment
9,1 TASK (Produce or Perish)	Suppresses or stamps it out. Establishes "win–lose" confrontation in which he/she always wins. Conflict simmers under surface.	Inner-directed. Subordinates not capable of participation. Makes decisions and enforces them.	"I am the boss and only I have the capability and responsibility to innovate."	Frequent demands to "get results," but these are not identified. Avoids joint goal setting and upward communication. No feedback.	Believes in tight supervision and "keep-busy" syndrome.	None. Subordinate reactions are 1,1 behavior or militancy or sabotage.
1,9 COUNTRY CLUB	Smoothes it over in order to relieve tension.	Solicits ideas of others in order to gain acceptance or avoid unpopular decision.	None expected and none encouraged except those that make work easier or "happier." Productivity is not the objective.	Approves because it is viewed as technique to lower supervision requirements. Sets "pseudo" but not organization goals.	Morale is primary focus and believes in taking care of "my people." Human-relations-oriented.	Committed to human relations and not goals. Desires subordinate commitment to "I like it here" attitude.
1,1 IMPROVERISHED	Avoids if at all possible. If forced to resolve, will resort	Avoids occasions for decisions. Defers to others.	Unrelated to company or productivity goals. May be quite innovative outside	Avoids!	People are happiest when left alone.	None to boss. Goal is "stay out of trouble."

(continued from previous page)	to "the book" on company policy or procedure.	As a last resort, consults "the book."	the work environment.			OK to pursue own private goals.
5,5 MIDDLE OF THE ROAD	Firm but fair attitude. Attempts to "cool off" conflict or reach compromise.	Compromises or sells his decision or takes a vote to get majority rule.	Encouraged unless it results in threatening conditions.	Generally approves but is faced with dichotomy when he can't reconcile personal goals with organization goals.	Attempts to "balance" morale and productivity. Measures morale by opinion survey or "happiness index."	Believes he or she is "go-between" to promote the company way. Attempts to sell commitment.
9,9 TEAM MANAGEMENT (People support what they participate in)	Gets the facts in the open and solves conflict based on how it is affecting results.	Gets best decision from team (group) on how to get results. Decisions based on facts and rational approach.	Encouraged for productivity and hence group goals. Innovation is motivation.	Views it as the central vehicle and basic philosophy for motivation and productivity.	Motivation is self-actualization through having a stake in results. Believes in team effort.	Has a sense of organizational purpose. Organization goals are same as personal goals. Negotiates commitment.

TABLE 9-1. *(Continued)*

STYLE OF LEADERSHIP	Feedback & Control	Setting Stretch Objectives[a]	Development of Subordinates	Appraisal	Long-Term Impact of Leadership Style on Organization
9,1 TASK (Produce or Perish)	Sets tight quotas and schedules with no participation. Frequent checking. Feedback after the fact and mostly for the "bad news."	Ratchet principle.	Believes human relations are soft. Development confined to training in company rules and procedures.	"Shape up or ship out."	1,1 behavior. Underutilization of people.
1,9 COUNTRY CLUB	Avoids specific standards and promotes "general" goals that everyone can support.	Sets mild stretch goals if they are "comfortable" and morale doesn't suffer.	Development devoted to "fitting in" or "getting acquainted." Uses company activities such as recreation indoctrination.	"How can I help my subordinates lead a rewarding life?"	OK for cost plus or monopoly situation. Ultimate result of "fat and happy" attitude is going broke.
1,1 IMPOVERISHED	Avoids both goals and controls. "I just want to make it to retirement."	Let the subordinates set their own. But don't bother me.	Nonexistent. Sends subordinates to development activities to "fill the quota."	Comply with company appraisal policy and system. Appraise not too high and not too low.	The classic bureaucracy.

5.5 MIDDLE OF THE ROAD	Balances personal and organization goals. Meets about 75 percent of targets.	Mild if acceptable to subordinate.	Attends personally only if nominated. Pays lip service but not convinced. Believes organization and product knowledge is more important.	Avoid confrontation. "I want my subordinates to go away from the appraisal interview with a good feeling."	OK if goal is to maintain the status quo but not if growth and innovation is desired.
9.9 TEAM MANAGEMENT (People support what they participate in)	Organization and individual goals are the same. Manage by self-control.	Mild stress through "reach-out" goals achieves self-development and self-actualization.	Believes in organization development. Learn by doing. Self-development through increasing responsibility.	Appraisal is opportunity to negotiate goal commitment, provide feedback, and develop subordinates.	Sustained growth for the organization and its members.

[a] See page 210.

Each of the following items describes some aspect of your relationship with your employees. Reach each item and then circle the response [1, 2, 3, 4, 5] which most nearly reflects the extent of your agreement or disagreement. Try to respond according to the way you would actually handle the situation on the job.

The best way to get good performance out of employees is to ....

	Response				
	Agree completely (1)	Mostly agree (2)	Partially agree (3)	Mostly disagree (4)	Disagree completely (5)
1. Allow them extensive freedom to plan and organize their own work.	1	2	3	4	5
2. Allow employees to set up special meetings and other ways to work out their differences and conflicts.	1	2	3	4	5
3. Not give them information unrelated to their immediate work.	1	2	3	4	5
4. Spell out exactly what their jobs are and what is expected of them.	1	2	3	4	5
5. Always insist that they solve their own work problems, but be available as a consulting resource to them.	1	2	3	4	5
6. Maintain tight controls on all work to be sure things don't get out of line.	1	2	3	4	5
7. Provide time, money and other resources so each person can develop his particular strengths and capabilities to the fullest.	1	2	3	4	5
8. Set up systems where information on performance results goes directly to the employee instead of through you.	1	2	3	4	5
9. Discourage employees from getting involved in the "why" of doing their job.	1	2	3	4	5
10. Bring employees together in joint meetings to make decisions and solve mutual problems.	1	2	3	4	5
11. Give them full information about their jobs, the department and the company.	1	2	3	4	5
12. Tell employees where they are going wrong and convince them of the merits of changing their attitudes and approaches.	1	2	3	4	5
13. Solve problems for employees as quickly as possible so they can get back to work.	1	2	3	4	5
14. Allow employees to take the responsibility for controlling and managing their own work.	1	2	3	4	5
15. Encourage employees to redesign their jobs around their own capabilities.	1	2	3	4	5
16. Leave employees alone and count on them to get their jobs done.	1	2	3	4	5
17. Clamp down on conflict and friction between employees.	1	2	3	4	5
18. Train employees to do their work according to standard procedures.	1	2	3	4	5
19. Insist that employees stick to their jobs and leave decisions and planning to you.	1	2	3	4	5
20. Discourage employees from introducing new ways of doing their work without first checking with you.	1	2	3	4	5

Instructions for Scoring: (1) Circle these questions: 1, 2, 5, 7, 8, 10, 11, 14, 15, and 16. Score 1 point for each response that was a 1 or 2. Add up your score and enter under the S/J heading in Figure 5-4. (2) For the remainder of the questions, score 1 point for each response that was a 4 or 5. Enter the score under the S/S heading, Figure 5-4.

Figure 9–4. Readiness questionnaire (Source: Glen H. Varney,
Management by Objectives [Chicago: The Dartnell Corporation, 1971]
Used by permission.)

that, in general, productivity can oest be achieved by a 9,9 managerial style. This is a general conclusion and, of course, does not apply in all situations.

EVALUATE YOUR READINESS FOR RESULTS MANAGEMENT

If you are interested in productivity and think that a results management approach can help achieve it, you may want to begin thinking of your managerial style. An indication of this style can be obtained by completing the questionnaire contained in Figure 9–4. After completing the questionnaire, you can score yourself according to the scoring key which is provided and enter your score on Readiness Profile shown in Figure 9–5.

If you score close to the Readiness Range or in the Readiness Range on the S/J scale, this indicates the way you perceive your employees working under such a system and means that you are on the right track in terms of your perception of how your subordinates are going to perform their jobs. If you score high on the S/S, this indicates the way you actually manage.

The S/S and S/J scales are not necessarily in line. For example, if S/S is lower than S/J, you might review the things you do in managing your subordinates which may be contradictory to what you have told them you would like them to do.

If S/S is higher than S/J, it may mean that although you are willing to manage by results, you may not be setting the environment in which this is taking place.

SUPERVISORY SKILLS:

LEADERSHIP STYLE, II

Delegation

Developing

Subordinates

DELEGATION

Studies of managerial failures almost invariably identify poor delegation as a major cause. Much of the reason for this lies in the

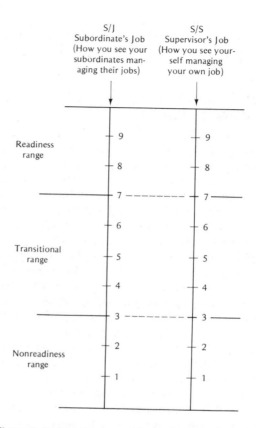

Figure 9–5. *Results management readiness profile*

manager's personal attitude and resulting inability to delegate. The manager confuses power with authority.

An extreme view of delegation is illustrated by the Army drill sergeant who announced: "Everything you are permitted to do will be ordered by me. Everything else is forbidden." Contrast this with the philosophy of a major division of the General Electric Company, which states: "All authority not expressly and in writing reserved for higher management is granted to lower management."

How to Delegate

Proper delegation can become a powerful motivator for productivity and job satisfaction. These six basic principles can go a long way toward overcoming the difficulty that most managers have in delegating.

☐ *Delegate by results expected.* To do otherwise is to confuse the subordinate as to what is expected. Assignments and jobs must be defined in terms of what results are to be achieved. This will also permit a finer degree of planning and communication.

☐ *Don't delegate upward* by passing the buck to the boss. The subordinate must be willing to accept authority and decision-making responsibility. Many top executives complain that their lower-level managers view their jobs as one of pushing their problems upward. If you accept the responsibility for results or a decision, don't pass the buck upward to the desk of the boss.

☐ *Match responsibility with authority.* Responsibility, once accepted, is the obligation to achieve a result. Therefore, you cannot assign more responsibility to subordinates than they have the authority to carry out. In other words, assign responsibility in terms of results and delegate the necessary authority to meet it.

☐ *Trust subordinates.* It is obvious that the manager who wants to delegate must be willing to release a certain amount of authority and decision-making rights to subordinates. It is said that the problem with most managers is that they "can't let go." When they are promoted they continue to perform the job they left. Others insist on approving the smallest detail of operations within their departments.

It is essential to trust subordinates (remember the Pygmalion Effect?). Moreover, subordinates must be allowed to make mistakes. It is the cheapest form of learning, provided the mistake doesn't endanger the company or the subordinate's position. This approach, accompanied by coaching and counseling, is far better than discouraging subordinates by criticism, intimidation, harping, or hovering over them with constant checks on their work.

☐ *Communicate.* Delegation doesn't mean abdication. Maintain open lines of communication so that subordinates have the information and feedback necessary to carry out the delegated authority.

☐ *Maintain some control.* These should be broad controls or self-control as discussed in the next section.

DEVELOPING SUBORDINATES

An essential requirement for achievement in an individual's work is a continuous learning process. This learning process is not only an effective motivator for improved performance (and, incidentally, self-satisfaction); it also fulfills the need that most of us have to keep abreast of new knowledge and avoid obsolescence. A side benefit is that workers who are engaged in learning will be much less resistant to change. Indeed, the chances are good that they will recommend innovation and change.

It is the job of every supervisor to provide the environment for and encourage self-development of subordinates. We have already seen how coaching and counseling during the appraisal process is one means to provide this encouragement. Another is formal training. But in terms of our system of productivity management, two additional principles of subordinate development should be remembered:

□ The motivation of a "stretch" objective.

□ The Pygmalion Effect or the self-fulfilling prophecy.

Setting a "Stretch" Objective

Procter & Gamble has long been recognized as a citadel of excellent management and financial success. The chief executive says: "We don't believe in mothering our managers. We like to give people responsibility very quickly, and that means putting them in jobs they aren't quite ready for." The results of such a philosophy of development was summarized by one middle-level manager: "You believe you can succeed because you know the company thinks you can. Each successive assignment, which at first seems like a crisis, reinforces that feeling."

This Procter & Gamble philosophy of a "reach-out" goal is to be admired, but it reflects a curious dilemma for the managers. On the one hand, they know that their subordinates will not be motivated to reach high levels of performance unless they consider the boss's high expectations realistic and achievable. On the other hand, goals that are easy to achieve and do not represent any challenge are not only nonproductive but fail also in the other motivational aspects of the job. The trick is to maintain in the subordinate a state of *mild stress* by mutually setting goals that make him or her "stretch" to achieve them.

My golf handicap is 18. This means that on the average my score is 96. Now if my goal were to reduce my average score to 95, I would not be motivated because the target is too easy; it doesn't make me "stretch." On the other hand, if I were required to shoot an average score of say, 80, I would simply stop playing the game of golf. Instead of "stretching," I would be in shock! The goal is clearly beyond reach.

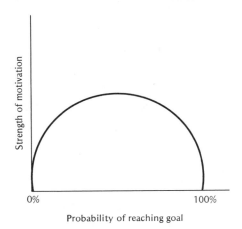

Figure 9–6. *Relationship between motivation to succeed and probability of goal success*

Research has shown that targets that are set too high generally result in negative attitudes and a drop in performance by employees. The old "carrot-and-stick" philosophy, the practice of dangling the carrot just beyond the donkey's reach, is not good motivational practice.

The relationship between motivation to succeed and expectation of success can be represented by the curve shown in Figure 9–6. The degree of motivation and effort will rise until the probability of reaching the goal reaches approximately 50 percent, then begins to fall even though the expectation of success continues on a lessened basis. Thus the employee can be expected to have little or no motivation to succeed when the goal is perceived as being practically certain or practically impossible to attain.

The message is clear. The results expected (not the activity) of subordinates should be mutually agreed upon at a level that keeps them under mild stress for their attainment; a "stretch" objective. It follows naturally that since the expectation of success is substantially less than 100 percent, reasonable failure to meet the target is not cause for recrimination or punishment. Progress should be measured periodically through feedback and the target adjusted as required to maintain mild stress but not shock.

CHAPTER 10

PROBLEM DEFINITION & ANALYSIS

"A problem well-defined is a problem half-solved."
—Anon.

Problem definition and analysis is an essential skill for supervisors and employees. The process is particularly useful for both individuals and Productivity Improvement Teams (PITS). If an objective or standard is set to improve over the existing level of productivity, by definition, there is a variance, a deviation, a shortfall from the results that are expected. Discovering the cause of this variance is the first major step that precedes decision making and action planning in order to achieve the objective.

SUPERVISORY SKILLS: PROBLEM SOLVING

What is a Problem?

The Process

THE LOGIC

There is an old Laurel and Hardy comedy routine that has been used successfully by generations of comedians and still gets a laugh today. The audience roars with delight as the comedian opens his closet door while the contents pour forth and crash around him in utter disarray and confusion.

Many managers view their job in this way. As the door to the "problems" closet is opened, out tumbles a disorganized array of crises brought on by subordinates who can't, or won't solve problems for themselves.

How many times have you gone to your boss with the statement: "Boss, I've got a problem." And how many times have your subordinates come to you with a similar complaint? Too many times, we must admit.

There is an abundance of evidence to indicate that problem solving and crisis management take up the vast majority of the typical manager's time despite the textbook admonition that planning, organizing, and controlling should take precedence. Indeed, many theorists and practitioners define a business organization as a set of problems to be solved. This suggests that the primary role of the manager is the definition and solution of problems through the process of information gathering and analysis.

Nobody knows how much effort is wasted and how much productivity is lost due to the failure to identify and find the cause of organizational problems. We do know that if problems are not defined and the causes identified, subsequent decisions and action plans are misdirected. This can lead to large cost increases and significant losses in productivity.

WHAT IS A PROBLEM?

Stated simply, a problem exists when there is a variance between expected and actual results; between that which is (or is anticipated) and that which is desired. It is an indeterminate situation in which doubt or uncertainty is felt, and a stimulus presses for a solution.

A second characteristic of a problem is that the variance concerns /ou, the manager. Either your attention is called to the variance by your superior or you sense that something is wrong and that something needs to be done about it. Although managers spend much of their time solving problems, one of their most important but frequently overlooked responsibilities is recognizing that a problem exists or is about to happen. Too often managers remain unaware of problems until a crisis is reached or affairs have gone beyond the point of no return.

From the point of view of problem definition and analysis, the subject of this chapter, we can also say that a problem exists when the cause of the variance is unknown. The essential objective of this chapter is to describe a method for problem definition and analysis that leads to the identification and verification of the *cause* of a problem. Subsequent chapters will treat the decisions and plans required for treating the cause.

THE PROCESS OF PROBLEM DEFINITION AND ANALYSIS

The central idea of problem analysis can best be explained in terms of the control process that we examined in Chapter 5. It was identified as a three-step process: (1) setting expected results (performance standard); (2) measuring performance against the standard; and (3) correcting the variance. The two basic ideas, a *standard* and a *variance*, provide us with a starting point; identifying the variance from standard or expectation and discovering the cause. The control process is important because it not only establishes the expectation but in many cases brings the variance to our attention in the form of a problem to be solved.

The role of problem analysis in managing work is shown in Figure 10-1. Following the establishment of expected results, subsequent control of activity may frequently uncover problems surrounding the

Figure 10–1. The role and process of problem definition and analysis

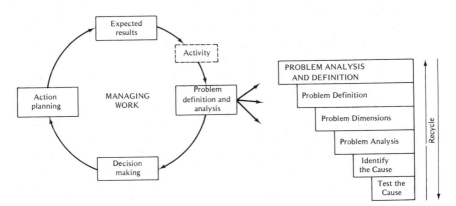

achievement of these results or the progress of an action plan. If so, problem definition and analysis will identify the cause(s) of the problem so that the decision-making process can identify a course of action to overcome the problem or form the basis for a revised action plan. The iterative nature of the process is also indicated in Figure 10-1, which lists the steps involved. These steps form the basis of discussion for the remainder of this chapter.

The Logic of Problem Analysis

The end result of the process is to identify the cause of the variance. Until this is done, nothing can be changed, no decision can be made, no plan devised, and no variance corrected. The process proceeds along the path of identifying the variance from expectation and then discovering the cause of the variance. For this reason we must avoid the tendency to state problems in platitudes and broad generalities (e.g., "The place is going to hell," or "We've got to reduce costs").

Problem analysis is nothing new. Its basic logic has been known for centuries and has been used in all of the sciences. One approach assumes that nothing will change or move and then asks the question: "What will happen in time?" The second approach, the one that is more appropriate to business problems, projects backward and asks: "What is it that could have been done or left undone at the time this problem first appeared that would have materially affected the present situation?" Either approach is an attempt to isolate and identify a cause-and-effect relationship. Both depend upon the basic logic that there is a relationship between cause and effect and this relationship can be determined by the evidence. Hence, if we can identify the event, the happening, or the effect, and trace it back to a cause, the analysis is complete.

In problem analysis, the effect to be explained or demonstrated is the variance. Since, by definition, a variance is a change from expectation, the cause of the variance is also a change of some kind. It follows logically that if the variance is to be corrected, we must know the cause-and-effect relationship between the variance and the change that caused it.

Figure 10-2 is a conceptual summary of the cause-and-effect relationship between change and variance and how these can be analyzed in order to get planned performance "back on the track." The process depicted in Figure 10-2 can be summarized:

☐ Performance moves along a standard preplanned path toward expected results.

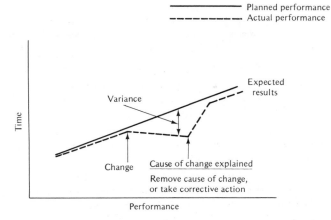

Figure 10–2. Cause-and-effect relationship in problem analysis

☐ Due to some change, actual performance varies from preplanned performance. The result is a variance.

☐ The variance is discovered and explained in terms of the change that caused it.

☐ Corrective action is taken to put the preplanned performance "back on the track" by removal of the cause or the change.

In summary, problem definition and analysis is simply the identification of the cause-and-effect relationship producing a problem. We begin with what is known—the effect, the variance. Then, using the logical approach described here, we work backward in order to identify the several changes that could have produced the effect. By a process of elimination we then arrive at the single change that did, in fact, produce the effect—the variance—and hence we arrive at the cause of the problem. The cause is what we are seeking.

The fundamental approach can be illustrated by the yellow fever experiment that followed the Spanish–American War of 1898. It is a classic case of problem analysis.

THE YELLOW FEVER EXPERIMENT

The Spanish–American War of 1898 ended swiftly and with remarkably few American casualties. However, by the year 1900, thousands of soldiers were dying of yellow fever. The job was to find the cause of the fever and eradicate it.

A two-pronged approach was taken to the problem. It was assumed that the disease was communicated either by person-to-person contact or through general unsanitary conditions. First, a program of microscopic research was undertaken. Autopsies were conducted on hundreds of victims. Blood, flesh, and the organs of the bodies were scrutinized microscopically in search of a clue. Clothing, linens, and personal belongings were analyzed with care in hopes of uncovering the cause of "yellow jack." All efforts were in vain.

A second approach involved a massive effort to clean up the dirt and filth of Cuba. This effort resulted in the cleanest and most sanitary Havana in history, but it did not affect the climbing death rate from yellow fever. The massive fatalities increased.

Later that year Major Walter Reed, in whose name the famous Walter Reed Hospital of the U.S. Army was later dedicated, was placed in charge of "the cause and prevention of yellow fever." He reasoned: "Perhaps we can't find out what causes 'yellow jack,' but maybe we can find out how it is spread." The problem was redefined. In other words, if they could keep people from catching yellow fever they would be successful even though they did not know what the basic cause was.

Reed set out to test the popular belief that the disease was spread through contact with other victims. As time passed he became increasingly frustrated because the evidence proved this hypothesis wrong. First, there were nurses who tended the yellow fever victims but were no more susceptible to the disease than any other group. Second, the pattern of disease was entirely random; it was extremely rare for all members of a family to be struck at the same time. Finally, his tentative cause-and-effect relationship was disproven when some of the totally isolated prisoners in the guardhouse contracted the disease, despite the fact that there had been not the slightest contact with outsiders.

One Dr. Carlos Finaly of Havana, considered by many to be a crank, persisted in his theory that yellow fever was carried by mosquitoes. Despite his skepticism, Reed decided to test this possible cause of the problem. A number of volunteers, including two medical doctors, allowed themselves to be bitten by mosquitoes that had previously bitten many yellow fever victims. The results, including the death of one of the doctor volunteers, indicated there might be something in the mosquito theory. Certainly a cause-and-effect relationship had been established, but the cause needed further testing and verification. So began the famous experiment.

Two houses were built. The first was very sanitary and was antiseptically clean. It had double-screened windows and doors that absolutely ruled out the entry of any mosquito. The volunteers in the house, each of whom had been bitten by mosquitoes that had fed on yellow fever victims, lived in spotless comfort, eating carefully prepared meals and having no contact with the outside world. In the second house lived another group of volunteers, none of whom had been bitten by mosquitoes. No mosquito was allowed entrance into this house but the volunteers lived in squalor and filth. They ate from dishes and slept in beds that were contaminated with the filth from the yellow fever wards.

The results of the experiment are now world-famous. The men living in the spotless antiseptic house and who had been bitten by the mosquitoes came down with yellow fever. Those who had lived for twenty days in the squalor and filth of diseased victims, although very uncomfortable, were still healthy.

By the process of problem analysis, Dr. Walter Reed arrived at the single change that produced the effect. Moreover, he tested and verified the cause of the change. He still didn't know the cause of yellow fever but he knew the cause of its transmission. The solution then became an engineering problem of eliminating the breeding places of the Aedes Aegypti mosquito.

PROBLEM DEFINITION AND ANALYSIS

Define the Problem

PROBLEM STATEMENT

SPECIFY THE VARIANCE

This logical relationship between cause and effect is the central notion of the problem definition and analysis process.[1] The steps in the process are shown in Figure 10-1 and are listed again below. These will form the basis of discussion for the remainder of this chapter.

---

[1] A complete bibliography on problem solving and decision making would run to more than a hundred pages. Three sources come to mind: Charles H. Kepner and Benjamin B. Tregoe, *The Rational Manager* (New York: McGraw-Hill Book Co., 1965); Robert G. Murdick and Joel E. Ross, *Information Systems for Modern Management* (Englewood Cliffs, N.J.: Prentice-Hall, Inc., 1975); and Kenneth E. Schnelle, *Case Analysis and Business Problem Solving* (New York: McGraw-Hill Book Co., 1967). The United States Armed Forces also teach an outstanding approach to problem solving, decision making, and planning in their various staff and war colleges. Here it is known as "the commander's estimate of the situation."

Assuming that we have *recognized* a problem (Is there a variance? Am I concerned?), we can then proceed to identify the cause as follows:

☐ *Problem definition.* Define the real problem and not the symptom. *State the problem* in specific terms, not generalities. *Specify the variance* in terms of who, what, where, when, and how much.

☐ *Problem analysis.* Analyze the boundaries and specifications in order to determine the cause of the variance. *Analyze the variance* in terms of problem boundaries; what is included and excluded from the problem. *Explain the cause* of the problem in terms of distinctive changes that have occurred that will explain the cause.

☐ *Test the cause.* Does the probable cause square with the facts? Does it explain the variance?

☐ *Verify the cause.* Verify the validity of the identified cause of the problem.

The discussion of the steps in the problem definition and analysis process are illustrated in the Office Systems, Inc. case at the end of the chapter.

PROBLEM DEFINITION

The most fundamental and important step in problem solving is to identify the right problem. Nothing is more futile than the right answer to the wrong question; nothing more frustrating than to spend time and effort on the wrong solution. This is why the problem definition phase of problem analysis is so important. For centuries, managers have been told that they cannot solve a problem until it is defined and that a problem well-defined is a problem half-solved. This is good advice.

Most of us are guilty of the common habit of attacking the symptom rather than the real underlying problem that the symptom represents. We blame inventory turnover; the real problem could be pricing, product obsolescence, or sales training. We may see a problem in cost control and begin a cost-reduction program; the real problem may be in design of the product. We conclude that communication is our problem, but this is a symptom of organization structure. And so it goes. We must resist the temptation to solve the symptom rather than the real problem it represents.

There is another reason for identifying the real or primary problem. It may lie at the root of a whole tree of secondary or related problems which represent symptoms of the real cause. The temptation is to get excited about the secondary problem, or symptom, and to waste time working on a temporary crisis rather than solving the root of the entire problem cluster.

Identifying the primary problem and its cause is somewhat like a medical doctor performing a diagnosis. If the patient complains of a sore throat, a symptom, the doctor goes beyond the symptom to seek out the real cause which might be infection, excessive smoking, or influenza. This in turn may be indicative of other "cluster" problems.

In summary, if problem analysis is to find the cause and develop a cure for a variance, we must first produce a clear problem statement.

The Problem Statement

A logical problem stating process will help to make sure that the problem and the variance that caused it are stated correctly. This involves the careful identification of the three problem elements: (1) the present situation; (2) the desired situation; (3) the constraints involved in solving the problem; and (4) the criteria by which the solution will be judged.

Consider the accounts-receivable problem in the Office Systems, Inc. case at the end of this chapter. Greg Peterson, the general manager, has identified a loan problem that is attributable to the level of accounts receivable and has asked the controller, Frank Jordan, to solve it. Perhaps you would like to play the role of Frank Jordon and develop a statement of the problem.

Despite the straightforward nature of the situation that exists with receivables, few managers in my experience are able to correctly state the problem on the first try. Typical problem statements include:

☐ "Improve the collection process."

☐ "Design a better receivables system."

☐ "Send out invoices faster."

☐ "Insist on faster payment or cut off credit."

☐ "The problem is morale and communication."

☐ "The problem is bank loans."

Problem definition can only be achieved by taking a logical step-by-step approach to arrive at a statement of the problem. This process is demonstrated below for the case of Frank Jordon in the Office Systems, Inc. case. By following such a process you avoid the waste of time that would normally occur from the identification and solution of the wrong problem, or worse yet, the symptom. Notice also that this process specifically identifies the variance.

Problem Statement

Describe the Present Situation (including identification and location of the variance)

The average level of receivables is $37.6 million.

The average collection days is 67.

Describe the Desired Situation

Reduce average level to industry average (10.8% of sales = $20.3 million).

Reduce average collection days to industry average (43 days).

Constraints (time, cost, manpower, equipment, organization, policy, customer, and so on)

Time: level must be reduced in six months.

Time: level must be reduced 5% below industry average in twelve months.

Resources: no additional personnel or equipment.

Criteria for Evaluation of Problem Solution (how will the boss judge whether problem is solved?)

Average collection time of 43 days and receivables level of $20.3 million to be achieved in six months. These levels to be improved by 5% in twelve months.

Statement of the Problem

The accounts-receivable level must be reduced to $20.3 million and the average collection days to 43 in six months, and these figures must be reduced by 5% in the following six months. There can be no increase in personnel or equipment to achieve these objectives.

Notice that the problem statement process identified the variance as well as the action necessary to solve the problem. We now proceed to get more specific regarding the dimensions of the variance. We want to know its specifications more precisely.

Specify the Variance

Earlier in this chapter we said that the central theme of problem definition and analysis was the identification of the cause-and-effect relationship and that this relationship could be determined by evidence; a careful examination of the facts surrounding the variance we wish to explain. This process means information gathering.

It has been said that the recipe for problem solution is "90 percent information and 10 percent inspiration." This statement may be overemphasizing the need to "get the facts," but it does point up the need for organizing the information surrounding the variance to be explained. It is necessary, therefore, to define the problem dimensions.

The admonition to "get the facts" does not mean that we should overlook opinion. Indeed, we need opinions regarding the problem in order to test them against reality. To avoid getting different opinions or asking questions is to fall into a common trap of seeking only those facts that support a conclusion that we have already reached. That is the worst possible approach to research or problem solving.

On the other hand, opinions should not be given too much weight unless they are thought out in relation to the problem at hand. "Top of the head" opinions are too frequently premature, self-serving, or representative of a parochial point of view.

Specification of the variance involves answering the traditional questions: Who? What? Where? When? How much? In other words, having identified the variance, we now proceed to describe it in such a way that subsequent analysis will allow us to trace the variance back in time to its underlying cause. Specification of the variance draws a factual picture.

In the case of Frank Jordan's accounts-receivable problem in the Office Systems, Inc. case, the facts and opinions contained in his problem file would fit into the standard specification format.

PROBLEM ANALYSIS, I

Analyze the Variance
Explain the Cause
State the Cause
Test the Cause
Verify the Cause

After reviewing these problem specifications, Frank Jordan should have a fairly good picture of what kind of trouble he has. He is now ready to focus his attention on analyzing the problem by limiting it to manageable details. He wants to eliminate the nonrelevant aspects in order to organize the pertinent facts that will help him identify the cause of the problem. He wants to get more specific by identifying the boundaries of the variance. In other words, he wants to know what is inside and outside the boundaries of the problem.

Question	Specification of The Variance
Who is the person, unit, or object involved in the variance?	The bank is disallowing credit. Customer accounts are overdue. Accounts Receivable department isn't collecting. Warehouse personnel grumbling about harassment. Sales department adding customers and processing orders.
What is the variance? What is wrong?	Average collection days increased from 42 to 67 days and outstanding receivables from $18 million to $37.6 million.
Where is the person, unit, or object located and where is the variance?	Overdue customers are located in all sales territories but confined largely to company items, not resale items.
When did the variance begin and what has been the pattern of the trouble?	The level of receivables started up in September and has grown steadily since that time. No irregular pattern of activity can be discerned.
How Much does the variance amount to and how many people, units, or objects are involved?	Receivables level exceeds industry standards and bank demands by 23 days and $17.3 million.

ANALYZE THE VARIANCE

	Variance Includes	Variance Excludes
WHO	Primarily customers for resale items	Few customers for company manufactured items.

WHAT	Exceeds standard by 23 days and $17.3 million	Above standard prior to September
WHERE	All customers and all territories	Not isolated to specific customers or territories (except as described under *who* above)
WHEN	Started in September and increasing steadily since that time	Not prior to September; not isolated instances
HOW MUCH	Majority of customers for resale items	Not isolated complaints

The variance now begins to take on a specific rather than a general form and the specific nature of the variance, as determined from the variance analysis above, provides us with clues as to the possible causes. These clues can be summarized as follows:

☐ The variance involves mostly resale items.

☐ The variance involves all customers and territories.

☐ The variance began in September and has grown steadily since that time.

The next step is to analyze these distinctions (clues) for possible changes that may lead to the cause of the problem.

EXPLAIN THE CAUSE

After the foregoing analysis of the variance, we are now ready to attempt the identification of a cause-and-effect relationship. This is done in two steps.

First we examine the distinctions between what is included and what is excluded from the problem boundaries. These distinctions are clues to problem cause. In the Office Systems, Inc. case, the Analyze the Variance step performed above points out two distinctions: (1) the overdue accounts receivable could be traced primarily to resale items rather than company manufactured items, and (2) the level of receivables began to increase in September and has steadily increased thereafter.

The second step in the explanation of the cause is to seek out some change that may have caused the distinctions. What is peculiar about the distinctions (resale items and September) and what changes occurred that might explain the rising level of accounts receivable?

A review of Frank Jordon's accounts-receivable problem file reveals four changes that might provide clues to the two distinctions we have identified. First, there is the growing dissatisfaction of warehouse personnel as evidenced by poor morale and the "hassle" from Sales and Order Processing. This could have resulted in a number of "foul-ups" that were planned or unplanned. Second, there is the addition of new customers during the past year. Possibly these new customers are not as credit-worthy as the old ones. Could the trouble be traced to a third possibility; the paperwork systems in Purchasing or Accounts Receivable? The answer must be no because there is no indication of any change in these systems. Last, we note that in July the inventory records for resale items were moved from the warehouse to Order Entry and a "pre-posting" procedure instituted. This was done to expedite the processing of orders and to provide adequate inventory and order information to answer customer inquiries.

Summarizing, we can compare variance distinctions against changes in order to explain the cause.

Distinctions		Changes
Overdue customers are complaining about resale items, not company items.	caused by	Morale of warehouse personnel went down in July & August.
Level of receivables started going up in September and has risen steadily since that time.		New customers added beginning January, a year ago. Moved inventory records from warehouse to Order Entry in July.

If the steps leading up to and including problem analysis have been performed correctly, the cause should almost jump out. At this stage you are ready to state, test, and verify the problem cause. Once again, we can illustrate the process by the example of Office Systems, Inc.

STATE THE CAUSE

Based on the comparison above of distinctive boundaries and changes, it can now be stated that there are three possible causes of a

rising level of accounts receivable: declining morale and performance of warehouse personnel, addition of new customers, or the movement of inventory records from the warehouse to Order Entry.

In a preliminary test, to discover the most probable cause, we can rule out the warehouse personnel because the potential cause doesn't square with the facts. The timing is wrong and customer complaints cannot be traced to any action or lack of action in warehousing. Likewise, the addition of new customers can be ruled out because the customers were added eight months before September when the level of accounts receivable began to rise. This leaves the third and most probable cause; the movement of inventory records. The cause can now be stated: "The cause of the increased level of accounts receivable is due to the change in inventory recording and posting procedures in July when records were moved from the warehouse to Order Entry. Subsequent clerical errors resulted in customer dissatisfaction and/or delay in payment."

This is the cause-and-effect relationship sequence we have been seeking.

TEST THE CAUSE

Now that the most probable cause is identified, it should be tested. Does it square with the facts? Does it explain the variance? To perform this test, we return to the statement of Analyze the Variance (page 224). If our most probable cause is the real cause, it will explain each item of what the variance includes and what the variance excludes. In other words, our cause must explain each effect that we have identified. The cause "moving the inventory records" does this.

VERIFY THE CAUSE

This is the last step in the problem definition and analysis process. The objectives are to verify the most probable cause you have previously identified and to lead up to the next step in problem solution; removing the cause or taking corrective action.

For this step additional information is needed. The questions must be asked: "What do I have to know to test the validity of this cause?" and "What would the facts have to be to verify this cause?" The answers to these questions involve getting outside the body of knowledge already collected and providing new and independent information. You need to ask questions, get facts, and perform tests.

In the Office Systems, Inc. case Frank Jordon might ask these questions:

□ *Warehouse supervisor.* What action do you take when sales orders do not agree with inventory balances? Are customers' invoices changed to reflect actual warehouse shipments?

□ *Sales Department.* Is the order-processing procedure for company manufactured items the same as for resale items?

□ *Accounts Receivable.* What reasons are given by customers for not paying on time?

□ *Order Entry.* How long does order processing take before and after the change in "pre-posting" procedure? What action do you take when there are discrepancies between sales orders and shipments?

Testing a probable cause can take a number of forms. In some cases laboratory experiments or sample runs can be made. If the variance is in manufacturing, the production process can be changed and tested. In the Office Systems, Inc. case, tests could be made by comparing invoices before and after the change that caused the variance or by "walking through" a sampling of sales orders to see for yourself what goes wrong.

PROBLEM ANALYSIS, II

People Problems

Problem Analysis as a Way of Managerial Life

Case Study

PEOPLE PROBLEMS

Most managers will freely admit that their "people" problems occur more frequently and have a greater productivity concern than the hard operational problems involving "things." Although less precise than other problems, those concerning people can also be solved through the process of problem definition and analysis. The difference is that in the operational variance we are dealing with facts, data that are verifiable and available, and observations that yield hard information. In problems involving people (motivation, morale, communication, organization, assignments, and so on), the information is 'soft" and we must rely largely upon opinions and sometimes emotions.

When using the problem definition and analysis to find the cause of people problems, certain cautions are advisable. These take the form of do's and don'ts:

Do	Don't
Address your analysis to problems over which you have some control	Play psychiatrist
	Jump to conclusions
Attempt to upgrade the bad, opinionated information you get regarding the problem	Make hasty generalizations that are colored by your own attitudes or experience
Attempt to get hard information about the specifics of the problem	

PROBLEM ANALYSIS AS A WAY OF MANAGERIAL LIFE

Did you ever sit down to discuss a problem with a subordinate and become frustrated because he didn't "do his homework"? Did his analysis overlook the basic facts? Was his conclusion based on opinion and speculation? Could you shoot holes in his written report? More important, did *your* boss ever have this feeling about your problem solution?

The answer to all these questions is probably yes.

Unfortunately, most of us jump to conclusions and reach out for evidence, however shaky, to support the conclusion. We don't go through the logical process of problem definition and analysis described in this chapter.

I recommend that this approach be adopted for all problem analysis, whether in oral or written form. The process will help insure that you, your subordinates, and your boss are agreed on a common ground. If your subordinates are required to use the approach, you can relax in the knowledge that he has done his homework and is using a rational method of analysis. The process provides both of you with a previously agreed upon set of rules for communication about problems. The same comment goes for you and your boss.

Never again should you have to hear, or say: "Boss, I've got a problem." Hereafter, you should hear, or say: "Boss, here is a problem and here is the cause."

CASE STUDY:
Office Systems, Inc., Part I

"Frank, I'm glad we've got somebody like you around to clear up this mess. The company is going to go down the drain unless we get organized.

"Your first job is to do something about accounts receivable. Unless we get receivables down to the industry level by June the first we're going to lose our line of credit with the bank. Do I have to tell you what that means?"

The speaker was Greg Peterson, general manager of Office Systems, Inc., manufacturer and distributor of a line of office furniture and related furnishings. The company manufactured approximately 250 items such as desks, chairs, credenzas, bookcases, and so on and was the distributor for an additional 1,450 items produced by other manufacturers. The company-manufactured items were commonly referred to as "company" items and those distributed for other manufacturers were called "warehouse" items.

The majority of company items, about 85 percent, were shipped from the factory directly to the customers without going through the warehouse. Distributed items were purchased by the company purchasing agent and were shipped from the warehouse. The company organization is shown in Figure 10–3.

Peterson was talking to Frank Jordon, the newly appointed controller, who had been recently hired from outside the company.

Figure 10–3. Organization of Office Systems, Inc.

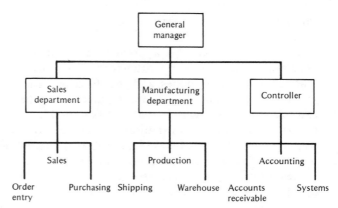

After only three weeks on the job, Jordon knew that something was wrong. In addition to the accounts-receivable problem, several large orders had been canceled recently because of inability to deliver on time and general confusion surrounding shipment.

Accounts receivable had been increasing at twice the rate of sales and the level of overdue accounts had reached the critical stage. The bank had recently indicated that the company's line of credit would not be renewed unless receivables were brought into line with the rest of the industry. Loss of the line of credit would seriously hamper plans for growth and damage the "good supplier" reputation that the company had carefully cultivated.

Greg Peterson continued, "Frank, today is February 1st. We've got until August 1st to get our receivables down to the industry average because that is the deadline for our credit renewal. I don't see why we couldn't beat the industry average by 5 percent in the six months following August 1st. Now Frank, I know you're new here and haven't got your feet on the ground yet, but I'd like to see you meet this target without spending any additional money on people or equipment or any of that stuff."

Greg Peterson concluded: "Frank, here's the file on the problem. Everything you need to know to get started is in the file. Good luck."

After returning to his office Frank Jordon sat down and opened the file labeled *Accounts-Receivable Problem*. He began to read the memorandums inside the file.

After reviewing the file, Frank Jordon began to wonder how he could define his problem and discover its cause.

INTEROFFICE MEMORANDUM

January 7

From: General Manager

To: Sales Manager
       Manufacturing Manager
       Supervisor, Accounts Receivable
       Purchasing Agent

Yesterday I received some very bad news from the First Bank and Trust Company, our bank for the past sixteen years. I quote:

Dear Mr. Peterson:

This will acknowledge your letter and supporting documents relating to your application for a continuation of your regular line of credit which has been in effect for the past sixteen years.
We regret very much to inform you that your supporting financial statements do not justify a continuation of the credit. Specifically, we note that your accounts receivable are growing at twice the rate of your sales and have reached what, in our opinion, is a dangerous level. This condition is substantiated by these statistics:

	Industry Average	Office Systems, Inc.
Sales in $ millions	174	188
Average collection days	43	67
Average accounts receivables outstanding	18.9	37.6

Gentlemen, I put it to you straight, this is one hell of a problem and we must solve it immediately. Please inform me by written memorandum immediately any information you have concerning this problem and why we are in this mess.

INTEROFFICE MEMORANDUM

January 11

From: Manufacturing Manager

To: General Manager

Subject: Level of Accounts Receivable

Regarding your memorandum, I can only say that we cannot trace any fault to production. As you know, about 85 percent of our production is shipped directly from the factory to the customer based on individual customer orders and does not go through the normal warehousing procedure. I understand that the order processing system of bookkeeping is also different. As you know, this business is built on service to the customer and we spend a lot of time expediting and putting out fires.

Since I also have the responsibility for the warehousing operation as well as shipping I asked each of these supervisors to give me their thoughts on this problem. Shipping has consistently met all scheduled dates so I don't see how the problem could be traced to that operation. You will notice in the memorandum of Pete Engels (copy attached), the warehouse supervisor, he speaks of poor morale and the "hassle" he continually gets from Order Entry and the Sales Department. Don't take this too seriously. Part of the so-called "morale" problem can be traced to the fact that for the past five weeks we have had to work all day Saturday to get the orders out. Pete and his crew are also somewhat miffed because we moved the inventory records up to Order Entry last July. This was so that the Sales Department could answer the customer inquiries and complaints without continuously calling the warehouse.

I notice that the Sales Department has added a lot of new customers over the last eight to ten months and this is causing us a number of headaches in design and delivery. Maybe that's the problem.

INTEROFFICE MEMORANDUM

January 9

From: Pete Engels, Warehouse Supervisor

To: Manufacturing Manager

Subject: Warehouse Operations

I'm not surprised that some of the customers don't pay on time. The Sales and Order Entry Departments must be really fouled up if the hassle they give us is any indication. My men are getting tired of the hassle and the overtime and if any mistakes are made you can't blame us.

We keep feeding the order entry clerks lists of items going out of stock and to be taken off backorder status. It doesn't seem to make any difference. Between purchasing and order entry we have to refigure about half of the invoices. No wonder the customers are mad. They get billed for items they don't receive and also get their bills marked "backordered" when they know we have it in stock. But what can we do? We can't control operations without the inventory records.

Incidentally, how is my request for two more warehousemen coming? We can't continue with this Saturday work.

```
INTEROFFICE MEMORANDUM
                                                    January 10
From:  Supervisor, Accounts Receivable

To:    General Manager

Subject:  Accounts Receivable
```

As you know, our system involves three basic steps: (1) customers
are invoiced weekly, (2) past due accounts are followed up by letter
after sixty days, and (3) after ninety days, personal telephone
contacts are made.

Regarding credit checks and approval of creditworthy customers, we
send a list of past due accounts to the Sales Department monthly and
that department determines who to sell to. There has been no
significant increase or decrease of accounts for which a cut-off in
credit is recommended based on our current credit policy.

We have a lot of small accounts that probably should be written off
because the trouble and cost of collecting the money is more than
the money we collect. Going through the customer account ledger
cards each month in order to flag delinquent accounts costs us a lot
of money. Also, many of our delinquent notices should never be sent
because the payment crosses in the mail with the notice.

An additional problem is the increased correspondence and telephone
calls connected with foul-ups in customer billing. This problem has
grown considerably in the past six months. Many incidents can be
traced to errors made in the warehouse. We spend a lot of time
chasing down errors because the customers won't pay until their bill
is straight.

According to your telephone request I am providing a recapitulation
of accounts receivable over the past twelve months:

Month	Average Collection Days	Average $ Outstanding	Month	Average Collection Days	Average $ Outstanding
Jan	39	19.1	July	39	19.1
Feb	38	18.9	August	45	22.6
Mar	40	19.4	Sept	51	24.9
April	39	19.0	Oct	57	26.8
May	41	19.6	Nov	61	31.7
June	39	18.9	Dec	67	37.6

INTEROFFICE MEMORANDUM

January 13

From: Sales Manager

To: General Manager

Subject: Accounts Receivable

As soon as I got your January 7th memo I put my sales analysis clerk
on the job of trying to identify the customers who were delinquent
and why. I think we have some good clues. After talking to most
of our salesmen and a few of our bigger customers, a summary of the
problem can be stated as follows:

> (1) Many of the late payments are due to the fact that customer
> invoices are erroneous. Prices are wrong, items marked
> "backordered" are shipped, and some items are shipped but not
> ordered by the customer.
> (2) There hasn't been too much trouble with shipments and
> billings of company items except when the order is combined
> with resale items from the warehouse.
> (3) We have added a significant number of new customers
> during the twelve month period ended December 31st. This is
> in accordance with the annual sales plan.

The new sales plan allowed us to drop a number of "bad" customers
while increasing sales. There seems to be no pattern of customer
complaints (ie., old versus new) and in general the problem is spread
over all territories.

Aside from the slow paperwork process in Accounts Receivable that
delays the customer collection procedure, I would suggest that we look
to warehousing for the problem of customer dissatisfaction. I don't
know whether it is a problem of morale or not but that crew in the
warehouse is confused and it is causing us a lot of trouble. This
trouble increased since we moved the inventory records from the
warehouse to Order Entry six months ago. However, the "pre-
posting" procedure we instituted should improve operations and having
the records up in Order Entry enables us to respond to customer
inquiries more rapidly.

TOOLS
FOR IMPROVING
WORK METHODS*

CHAPTER 11

"Getting people involved in improving their own work methods is a very common practice. Sometimes it's formalized as Methods Improvement Programs. Most often, however, it is simply a matter of an individual or a production team capitalizing on ideas that have developed out of experience on the job."
                                   Chairman, Hewlett-Packard

Hewlett-Packard's widespread use of productivity improvement teams grew partly out of their experience with their Japanese manufacturing operations, where quality-control circles meet to find ways to improve productivity and quality. The company is one of a growing number finding that the team approach to productivity combined with some exposure to the tools and techniques of work analysis can yield substantial results.

Thus far in this book we have examined a number of supervisory skills such as communication, appraisal, leadership, and problem solving. These skills of supervision should be accompanied by the tools necessary for problem analysis and subsequent action planning.

*This chapter was written by Jerry Jensen, Manager of industrial engineering in the Beatrice Foods Company. He has broad training experience and applications in the techniques discussed in this chapter.

Most people think that the tools of work-methods analysis are the province of the industrial engineer. That person is perceived as a "stop-watch jockey"—setting and updating work standards and incentives or focusing on *efficiency* improvement.

This perception of the industrial engineer is wrong in two ways. First, this professional discipline is really comprised of a broad range of skills and techniques all geared toward improving productivity. Short-interval scheduling, standards, methods engineering, motion economy, work simplification, materials flow, line balancing, plant layout, work sampling, and value analysis are all tools in the industrial engineer's aresenal. It is not just a matter of the stop-watch and the process chart.

The second misconception concerning the tools of work-methods analysis is that these below to the industrial engineer alone. This, of course, is wrong. A basic familiarity with just a few of these fundamental tools on the part of all individuals and team members will go a long way toward improving productivity. *Each employee must be his or her own industrial engineer.* The truly successful application of these programs comes when all employees become trained and involved in using the appropriate techniques to both identify and solve productivity problems and bottlenecks.

While a whole plant full of industrial engineers can be a frightening prospect to many people, it has proven to be successful in several companies.

At Sperry Univac, the company's PLUS (Productivity Leads Us to Success) program trains employees in work and procedures analysis, cost reduction, value engineering, work simplification, and group analysis techniques.

At IBM's Office Products plant in Lexington, Kentucky, every employee in the plant is given a fifteen-hour course in work simplification. Management's rationale was simple: "We decided that (1) a person who does a job knows that job better than any expert, and (2) work performed only by a person's hands—without the use of his mind as well—is a sheer waste of talent. What would happen if we helped people become their own industrial engineers? The basic principles of motion efficiency were not beyond the comprehension of anyone in our plant. After learning these principles, if each person were to decide for himself how to do his job better, he'd really do it better."

Coupling the work-simplification training with a productivity reward *system, the plant produced savings projects that totaled $1,130,000 in one year, of which $270,000 was reimbursed in employee awards.*[1]

Detroit Edison has instituted an extensive program of work measurement through the use of work sampling throughout the company. However, it is official company policy that "each department is responsible for carrying out its own work-measurement program in accordance with established methodology." The industrial engineering group is used to establish training programs and provide consultation services, but not to perform the actual measurement. It is interesting to note that in this largely administrative environment, only 6 out of 61 departments identified any jobs that could not *be measured through these industrial engineering techniques.*[2]

While some industrial engineers may view the statement as oversimplification, we hold that most industrial engineering work is really an organized application of common sense. To be sure, modern computer applications, linear programming, regression curves, etc. may be a little deep for the average production worker, but the basic industrial engineering principles are not. If we view the production worker as a *professional* in his or her field, and provide the formal training to support that profession, the results are powerful.

I remember an incident in my early idealistic career, in which we set up an in-plant training program for the workers in a new packaging department at a food plant. We were going to cover all the operating and technical instructions for the new capital equipment, as well as the indirect supports needed for the department. Our training committee decided that we would have the plant's production manager start off with a half-hour discussion entitled "What is Production?". Our intent was to emphasize that production is *not* just "cases-out-the-door," but includes quality, product value, scheduling, material control, customer satisfaction, cost control, and so forth. The discussion did not go well for the first 10 minutes, and the group was obviously uncomfortable. Finally, one of the veteran workers said, "I don't know why we're having this discussion. You must think we're a bunch of 'bubbleheads'! Of course we know what production is—that it includes all of these things. Production is our job, and this is what we do every day!"

---

[1]Clair F. Vough, *Productivity: A Practical Program for Improving Efficiency* (originally titled *Tapping the Human Resource*) (New York: AMACOM, 1975, 1979).
[2]Industrial Engineering Services Division, *Work Sampling Program Handbook* (Detroit, Detroit Edison Co., 1979).

The discussion ended right there, and we immediately started the training in technical methods. Let us do the same, and briefly cover an overview of basic industrial engineering techniques that can be put to use in an effective productivity improvement program. The techniques we will cover are these:

☐ Work simplification

☐ Asset productivity

☐ Controls   ᛁ

☐ Value analysis

WORK SIMPLIFICATION

Select the Job
Get the Facts
Question the Details
Develop a Better Method
Install Improvement

Work simplification has a lot of pseudonyms—methods improvement, work study, motion economy, job improvement—but they all boil down to about the same thing. Essentially, work simplification is "the *organized* use of *common sense* to find easier and *better ways* to perform a job." This definition almost seems to be too simple. If it is just common sense, why do we classify it as a discipline? The key word in the definition is "organized." There are certain steps of analysis and certain principles of improvement that can be applied in looking at a job.

The work-simplification process is traditionally defined in terms of five steps:

☐ *Select* a job to improve

☐ Get all *facts* about the job

☐ *Question* and challenge every detail of the job

☐ *Generate* alternatives and *develop* a better method

☐ *Install* the improvement

Let's go into each step in a little more detail.

SELECT A JOB TO IMPROVE

There are many symptoms of a job situation that indicate that it is ripe for investigation. Work is backing up at a workstation, or conversely, an operator is waiting for work to do. Obviously, there is a bottleneck that needs to be cleared up. Similarly, if an area seems either to be organized chaos or operating in slow motion, it is a likely candidate. Excessive material loss, lots of overtime, constant tool replacement, or even a high accident level could all be symptoms of a job that needs some improvement.

While every job can use evaluation or can undoubtedly be improved to some degree, it is best to use Pareto's 80/20 rule, and first go after the obvious. An early success in improving a problem gives validity to the work-simplification approach and stimulates other people to want to improve their jobs.

GET ALL THE FACTS ABOUT THE JOBS

This is the part that is the most tedious, and therefore, the most shortchanged. However, it is also the most important step in the work-simplification process. If opinions are substituted for facts, effects are confused with causes, or excuses are accepted instead of reasons, it becomes very difficult to do the "right thing." Gathering information up front gives us the perspective to look at the job. The work cycle, volumes, station layout, material requirements, and the tools needed for the job are all-important elements that should be documented.

There are several means to record the information. We will highlight three possible methods. There are literally dozens of variations to be found in the handbooks and textbooks, but these three are fairly representative.

Flow Process Charts

A flow process chart is used to define everything a person does as part of a job or everything that happens to a material in a job or process. In either case, the job is broken down into five basic elements. These are universally standardized by the American Society of Mechanical Engineers (ASME) as follows:

To change

Operation. An operation occurs where work is being done, or when an object is intentionally changed in any of its physical or chemical characteristics, is assembled or disassembled from another object, or is arranged for another operation, transportation, inspection, or storage. An operation also occurs when information is given or received or when planning or calculating takes place.

	NO. 1
	PAGE 1 OF 1

FLOW PROCESS CHART

JOB Receive air freight package and bring to outgoing freight area

☒ MAN OR ☐ MATERIAL Baggage handler

CHART BEGINS At receiving dock

CHART ENDS Outgoing freight area

CHARTED BY A.S.   **DATE** 9/26/—

SUMMARY	PRESENT		PROPOSED		DIFFERENCE	
	NO.	TIME	NO.	TIME	NO.	TIME
○ OPERATIONS	50	6.6				
⇨ TRANSPORTATIONS	43	21.3				
☐ INSPECTIONS	17	21.9				
D DELAYS	1	5.5				
▽ STORAGES	–	–				
DISTANCE TRAVELED	1471	FT.		FT.		FT.

DETAILS OF (PRESENT) METHOD	OPERATION	TRANSPORT	INSPECTION	DELAY	STORAGE	DISTANCE IN FEET	QUANTITY	TIME MIN.	WHAT?	WHERE?	WHEN?	WHO?	HOW?	NOTES	ELIMINATE	COMBINE	SEQUE.	PLACE	PERSON	IMPROVE
1 Other duties	○	⇨	☐	D	▽															
2 Goes to equipment area for hand truck	○	⇨	☐	D	▽	62		1.0	.	√				PLACE NEAR USE AREA				√		
3 Grasps hand truck and returns to receiving dock	○	⇨	☐	D	▽	62		1.0	√					"				√		
4 Loads packages on H.T.	○	⇨	☐	D	▽		4	.2	.	.	.	.	√	USE SEMI-LIVE SKID						√
5 Pushes H.T. to receiving dock scale	○	⇨	☐	D	▽	21		.5	.	.	.	.	√	"						√
6 Tips packages off H.T. onto scale	○	⇨	☐	D	▽		4	–	√					PAINT WEIGHT ON SKID	√					
7 Checks weight of each package	○	⇨	☐	D	▽		4	.8	√					"	√					
8 Checks packages for cond.	○	⇨	☐	D	▽		4	1.8	.	.	√			CHECK AS LOADED ON SKID		√				
Loads packages on H.T.	○	⇨	☐	D	▽		4	.2	√						√					
10 Pushes to check-in area	○	⇨	☐	D	▽	32		.3	.	.	.		.							
11 Tips packages off H.T.	○	⇨	☐	D	▽		4	–	√					LEAVE ON SKID	√					
12 Returns with H.T. to receiving dock	○	⇨	☐	D	▽	26		.3	.	.	.	.	√							√
Items 4-11 repeated 7 times	○	⇨	☐	D	▽															
Item 12 repeated 6 times																				
75 Rec. air bill from truck driver and checks no. of pkgs. with A.B.	○	⇨	☐	D	▽	32		1.1	.	.	.	.	.							
76 Goes with driver to billing office	○	⇨	☐	D	▽	48		.65	√					USE WIRE BASKET ON OVERHEAD CABLE	√					
77 Waits while bill is processed and lot labels prepared	○	⇨	☐	D	▽			5.5	√						√					
78 Returns to pkgs. with processed copy of bill and lot labels	○	⇨	☐	D	▽	48		.65	√						√					
79 Pastes lot labels to each pkg. and air bill to one	○	⇨	☐	D	▽	32		1.8	.	.	.	.	√	USE STAMPING MACHINE						√
80 Loads packages on H.T.	○	⇨	☐	D	▽		4	.2	√						√					
81 Pushes H.T. to outgoing freight area	○	⇨	☐	D	▽	41		.6	.	.	.	.	√							√
82 Tips packages off H.T.	○	⇨	☐	D	▽		4	–	√						√					
83 Returns with H.T. to check-in area	○	⇨	☐	D	▽	41		.6	.	.	.	.	√							√
Items 80-82 repeated 7 times	○	⇨	☐	D	▽															
Item 83 repeated 6 times																				
111 Returns H.T. to equip. area	○	⇨	☐	D	▽	30		.5	√						√					
	○	⇨	☐	D	▽															

Figure 11–1. Flow process chart (man type). (Source: H. B. Maynard, ed. Industrial Engineering Handbook, 3rd ed., [New York: McGraw-Hill Book Co., 1971].)

⇨

To move

Transportation. A transportation occurs when an object is moved from one place to another, except when such movements are a part of the operation or are caused by the operator at the workstation during an operation or an inspection.

☐

To verify

Inspection. An inspection occurs when an object is examined for identification or is verified for quantity or quality in any of its characteristics.

Delay. A delay occurs to an object when unanticipated conditions do not permit or require immediate performance of the next planned action.

To wait

Storage. A storage occurs when an object is kept idle while waiting for the next step or operation.

To protect

Combined Activity. When two activities are performed concurrently, or at the same workstation, the symbols may be combined. The example shown (circle within a square) represents a combined operation and inspection.

Each step of a job is listed and charted by type. Figure 11-1 shows a chart for a worker-oriented job in this case, a freight handler on a dock) and Figure 11-2 shows a chart for material-oriented flow (the example shows a comb moving through several operations). The flow process chart is then used to facilitate the third and fourth steps of the five-step process, which we will get to shortly.

Figure 11-2. Flow process chart (material type). (Source: H. E. Maynard, ed. Industrial Engineering Handbook, 3rd. ed. *[New York: McGraw-Hill Book Co., 1971].)*

American Hard Rubber Company

FLOW PROCESS CHART

PAGE 1 OF 3

JOB Saw, Inspect and Rub - Old Method

☐MAN OR ☒ MATERIAL Ace Combs (all types)
CHART BEGINS In Sawing Department
CHART ENDS In Polishing Department
RECHARTED BY W.R.M. DATE

SUMMARY		PRESENT		PROPOSED		DIFFERENCE	
		NO.	TIME	NO.	TIME	NO.	TIME
◯ OPERATIONS		26	57.8				
⇨ TRANSPORTATIONS		18					
☐ INSPECTIONS		2	7.0				
D DELAYS		9	960				
▽ STORAGES		2	7 da.				
DISTANCE TRAVELLED		429 FT.		FT.		FT.	

DETAILS OF (PRESENT) METHOD	OPERATION	TRANSPORT	INSPECTION	DELAY	STORAGE	DISTANCE IN FEET	QUANTITY	Min. TIME	WHAT?	WHERE?	WHEN?	WHO?	HOW?	NOTES	ELIMINATE	COMBINE	SEQUENCE	PLACE	PERSON	IMPROVE
1 Sawed and aside. Several kinds per battery of m/c	◯	⇨	☐	D	▽	100	24		•	•										
2 Packed in large box (several kinds) by sawyer	◯	⇨	☐	D	▽	500	2		•											
3 Delivered to Air Cleansing Unit by sawyer	◯	⇨	☐	D	▽	100			•											
4 Awaiting air cleaning	◯	⇨	☐	D	▽		480		•											
5 Removed from large box to bench by blower	◯	⇨	☐	D	▽	500	1/2		•	•										
6 Blown out to remove sawdust	◯	⇨	☐	D	▽	100	2		✓			✓		Dust blown on Inspectors	✓					✓
7 Loaded into large box on floor by blower	◯	⇨	☐	D	▽	500	1/2		•											
8 Carried to inspection by blower	◯	⇨	☐	D	▽	8				✓		✓		Move Inspector to Control room ?				✓		
9 Awaiting inspection	◯	⇨	☐	D	▽		120		•	•		✓		Congestion in aisles	✓					

Micromotion Analysis (or Simo Charts)

In situations in which a job is highly repetitive or short-cycled (less than a minute), a micromotion chart such as those shown in Figures 11-3 and 11-4 can be used. The examples demonstrate the original procedure and an improved procedure for a simple bolt and washer

Figure 11–3. Micromotion chart of bolt and washer assembly—old method. (Source: R. M. Barnes, Motion and Time Study, *5th ed. [New York: Wiley & Sons, 1963], p. 113, Fig. 69.)*

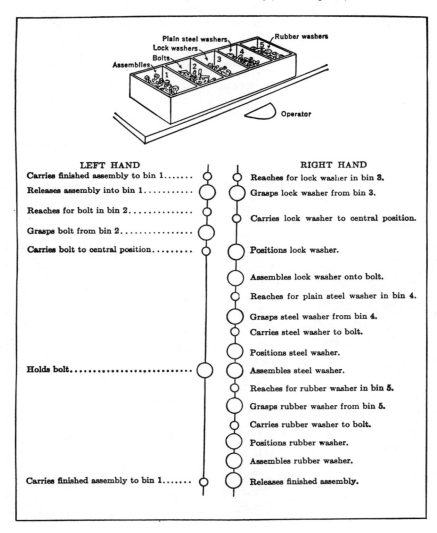

for identification or is verified for quantity or quality in any of its characteristics.

Delay. A delay occurs to an object when unanticipated conditions do not permit or require immediate performance of the next planned action.

To wait

Storage. A storage occurs when an object is kept idle while waiting for the next step or operation.

To protect

Combined Activity. When two activities are performed concurrently, or at the same workstation, the symbols may be combined. The example shown (circle within a square) represents a combined operation and inspection.

Each step of a job is listed and charted by type. Figure 11-1 shows a chart for a worker-oriented job in this case, a freight handler on a dock) and Figure 11-2 shows a chart for material-oriented flow (the example shows a comb moving through several operations). The flow process chart is then used to facilitate the third and fourth steps of the five-step process, which we will get to shortly.

Figure 11–2. Flow process chart (material type). (Source: H. E. Maynard, ed. Industrial Engineering Handbook, *3rd. ed. [New York: McGraw-Hill Book Co., 1971].)*

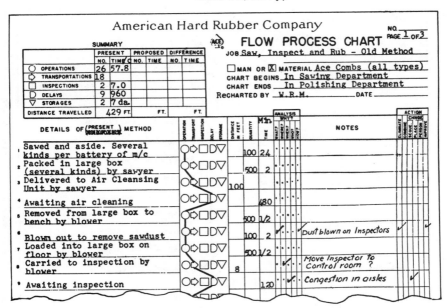

Micromotion Analysis (or Simo Charts)

In situations in which a job is highly repetitive or short-cycled (less than a minute), a micromotion chart such as those shown in Figures 11-3 and 11-4 can be used. The examples demonstrate the original procedure and an improved procedure for a simple bolt and washer

Figure 11–3. Micromotion chart of bolt and washer assembly—old method. (Source: R. M. Barnes, Motion and Time Study, *5th ed. [New York: Wiley & Sons, 1963], p. 113, Fig. 69.)*

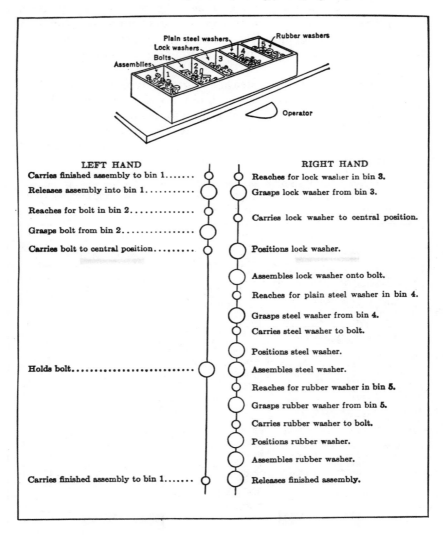

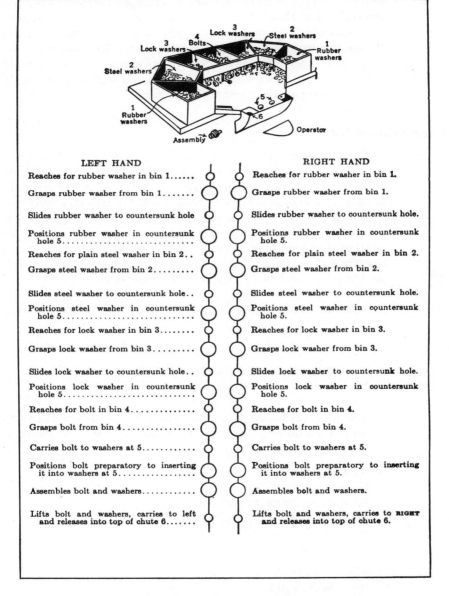

LEFT HAND

Reaches for rubber washer in bin 1......

Grasps rubber washer from bin 1.......

Slides rubber washer to countersunk hole

Positions rubber washer in countersunk hole 5..........................

Reaches for plain steel washer in bin 2..

Grasps steel washer from bin 2.........

Slides steel washer to countersunk hole..

Positions steel washer in countersunk hole 5............................

Reaches for lock washer in bin 3.......

Grasps lock washer from bin 3.........

Slides lock washer to countersunk hole..

Positions lock washer in countersunk hole 5............................

Reaches for bolt in bin 4..............

Grasps bolt from bin 4................

Carries bolt to washers at 5...........

Positions bolt preparatory to inserting it into washers at 5................

Assembles bolt and washers...........

Lifts bolt and washers, carries to left and releases into top of chute 6.......

RIGHT HAND

Reaches for rubber washer in bin 1.

Grasps rubber washer from bin 1.

Slides rubber washer to countersunk hole.

Positions rubber washer in countersunk hole 5.

Reaches for plain steel washer in bin 2.

Grasps steel washer from bin 2.

Slides steel washer to countersunk hole.

Positions steel washer in countersunk hole 5.

Reaches for lock washer in bin 3.

Grasps lock washer from bin 3.

Slides lock washer to countersunk hole.

Positions lock washer in countersunk hole 5.

Reaches for bolt in bin 4.

Grasps bolt from bin 4.

Carries bolt to washers at 5.

Positions bolt preparatory to inserting it into washers at 5.

Assembles bolt and washers.

Lifts bolt and washers, carries to RIGHT and releases into top of chute 6.

Figure 11–4. Micromotion chart of bolt and washer assembly—improved method. (Source: R. M. Barnes, Motion and Time Study, 5th ed. [New York: Wiley & Sons, 1963], *p. 114, Fig. 70.)*

assembly. A micromotion analysis breaks the job down into left-hand and right-hand elements, with associated times. The objective is to keep both hands working together with as little idle time or wasted motion as possible. While this type of analysis is a throwback to the "efficiency expert" era of industrial engineering, it is still a valid technique in repetitive situations, such as in a typewriter assembly line or packing an assortment of small parts.

Job Analysis Form

A more general type of chart, with which we have had good experience, is the job analysis form depicted in Figures 11-5 and 11-6. This is very useful in analyzing situations such as bench-top assembly or packing a large product, where the timing for each cycle may be a few minutes instead of a few seconds. The timing of each element is not quite as detailed, but there is a broader perspective in terms of materials-handling support and layout for the workplace. Sometimes an extra section is added, which lists the part numbers and quantities per assembly—sort of a miniature bill of materials.

Now that the documentation is done, what do we do with it? That's Step 3.

QUESTION AND CHALLENGE EVERY DETAIL OF THE JOB

This is a lot of fun for the "devil's advocates" in your group. Each step of the job should be put to the test of the following five questions (with an accompanying Why for each one):

□ *What* is being done?
   What is the purpose?
   Why are we doing it at all?

□ *Where* is the job being performed?
   Where is the best place?
   Why should we do it there?

□ *When* is the job done?
   When is the best time?
   Why should we do it then?

□ *Who* is doing the job?

JOB ANALYSIS FORM		
DEPARTMENT:		SECTION:
ACTIVITY:		
UNIT OF MEASURE:		TARGET:
JOB DESCRIPTION		
MATERIAL HANDLING REQUIREMENTS		
WORKPLACE LAYOUT		

Figure 11–5. Sample job-analysis form

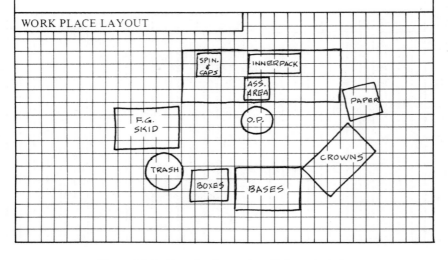

JOB ANALYSIS FORM		
DEPARTMENT: Packing		SECTION: Offline
ACTIVITY: Pack RH-8		
UNIT OF MEASURE: RH-8		TARGET: 30/hour

JOB DESCRIPTION

Assemble RH-8 box. Pack base, crown, spindler and cap and innerpack in box. Place layer of wrapping paper on top. Close box, staple stamp unit color on box and sit aside on skid.

MATERIAL-HANDLING REQUIRMENTS

Palletainer holds 30 Crowns. It must be replenished every hour. Skid will hold 42 completed units. It will need to be removed every 1-1/2 hours.

WORK PLACE LAYOUT

Figure 11–6. Sample of completed job-analysis form

Who should be doing it?
Why should he or she do it?
☐ *How* is the job done?
How should it be done?
Why should it be done that way?

These questions are sometimes actually formatted right into one of the flow process charts. However, they can be applied to any of the above methods. They get at the issues of the reasons for the work, the location, the sequence, the skills, and finally, the methods of the job. This questioning of every element then leads to Step 4.

GENERATE ALTERNATIVES AND DEVELOP A BETTER METHOD

This is the enjoyable step for the creative types in the group. It is best to brainstorm a lot of ideas for improving the job without criticism, and then analyze each alternative for practicality and appropriateness. Industrial engineers often cite another set of four questions to use in this process of analysis:

☐ Can the job be *eliminated*?

☐ Can the job be *combined* with another?

☐ Can we change the *sequence* or location of the job?

☐ Can we *simplify* the job in any way?

There are also twenty formal principles of motion economy that come into play in looking at improvements for the jobs:

☐ Move hands simultaneously.

☐ Use symmetrical motions.

☐ Use rotary wrist motions.

☐ Shift muscle tensions.

☐ Work within arm's-length.

☐ Move arms in circular paths.

☐ Slide, don't carry.

☐ Have a fixed place for everything.

☐ Perform make-ready work in batches.

☐ Use rhythm or smooth, flowing motions.

☐ Use foot pedal when possible.

☐ Use holding devices.

☐ Arrange for orderly disposal.

☐ Use ejectors.

☐ Shorten transport distance.

☐ Preposition the product.

☐ Preposition tools and supplies.

☐ Locate machine controls.

☐ Improve workplace height.

☐ Improve conditions of light, heat, dust, etc.

This analysis technique is not just confined to single-station, single-operator environments. It can also be applied to an entire multistation assembly line or even a progressive job-shop environment. The interaction of the jobs can be important. This is where the concept of *line balancing* comes into play. Figure 11-7 shows an

Figure 11–7. Line-balancing example

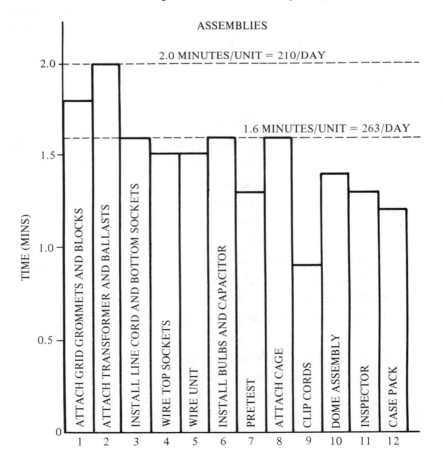

actual example of a twelve-station assembly line for a light electrical insect control device. The gross analysis indicated that the first two jobs on the line were slowing the entire assembly, but that there was ample slack time in the rest of the line to redistribute the work. By going through the elements of each of the jobs, questioning the "who," "where," and "when," the line was rebalanced by distributing some of the work content from Jobs 1 and 2 into other jobs further down the line. This resulted in a 25 percent increase in units/man-hour.

Once the analysis phase of Step 4 has been completed, the PIT can then decide on the best approach, determine the resources required, and then go for the payoff in Step 5.

INSTALL THE IMPROVEMENT

The first four steps are exercises in futility if we aren't successful in implementing the changes. For some reason, this is sometimes the most difficult step for American managers; however, this is where we get the results. Thoreau always admonished us to "Simplify, simplify, simplify!" I'd like to twist that to "Implement, implement, implement!"

Part of the implementation process should be a redocumentation of the new methods. In this way, it is both understood by and transferable to new personnel.

SUMMARY

This five-step approach to work simplification (select, document, question, improve, and implement) may seem to some to be too deliberate and time-consuming. However, the time invested is well spent. The process ensures that hidden details are not overlooked, that we give full consideration to alternatives, and that the ultimate solution has some consensus behind it. If we go back to our earlier definition, this is the *organization* of our common sense. There is nothing exotic in it, and thus the approach is very accessible to all production workers.

However, there is a very important step that must be done *up front* in order for a work-simplification program to succeed: It must be sold! A climate must be set that is nonthreatening and one that encourages creativity. The employee must be sold on the advantages that working better usually means a more interesting and rewarding job for the individual. However, if this climate has been established properly when the PITs are formed, work-simplification efforts are usually a natural follow-up.

One other point—work simplification is by no means limited to the factory floor. The office can also benefit greatly from it. Questioning the necessity of certain paperwork, looking at the flow of information through an order department, letting engineers use a template system instead of mechanical drawing, planning sales-call travel routes, or having your file clerks file documents in horizontal rather than vertical alphabetical order, are all examples of work-simplification activities that can yield substantial results.

ASSET PRODUCTIVITY

Machinery

UTILIZATION

EFFICIENCY

Materials Handling

Facility Layout

A frequent and deserved criticism directed at given industrial engineers is that they have studied factory labor to death. In many environments, direct labor is a very small portion of the total costs of a product or operation. In such capital-intensive situations, people must focus attention on improving the productivity of the plant and equipment. It is particularly vital in this era of high cost of capital. There are several approaches.

MACHINERY PRODUCTIVITY

Productivity of our equipment can be improved by increasing either its *utilization* or its *efficiency*. Some people confuse the two terms (as well as *productivity*) or think they are all the same thing, so let us clarify them:

□ *Utilization*—Percentage of time a machine is operating

□ *Efficiency*—Performance of the machine when it is running against its rated speed.

□ *Productivity*—Performance of the machine against the total time available.

These are all different forms of $\dfrac{\text{Output}}{\text{Input}}$ ratios.

EXAMPLE

If a machine has a speed of 1 piece/minute, runs 6 hours out of an 8-hour shift, and produces 288 pieces while it is running,

□ What is its utilization?

□ What is its efficiency?

□ What is the productivity as a percentage of total rated input?

a) 75%   b) 80%   c) 60%

There are many ways to improve both the efficiency and the utilization of the equipment.

Increase Utilization

□ *Reduce Time Required for Setups and Changeovers.* This can be done by effective scheduling of the work so that setup personnel, materials, and tooling are all available. Naturally, good training of setup personnel is essential.

□ *Increase Length of Production Runs.* Increasing the length of a run in relation to changeover time can certainly increase utilization. For example:

	Option A	Option B
Length of Run	4 hours	6 hours
Changeover	2 hours	2 hours
Total Cycle	6 hours	8 hours
In a 48-hour period:		
Runtime	32 hours	36 hours
Downtime	16 hours	12 hours
Utilization	67%	75%

It usually follows that unit costs can be reduced through longer runs—down to a point (see Figure 11–8). In this example, there is a pretty significant cost reduction running 4,000 pieces at a time instead of 1,000, but the savings on setup costs diminish over 5,000 pieces.

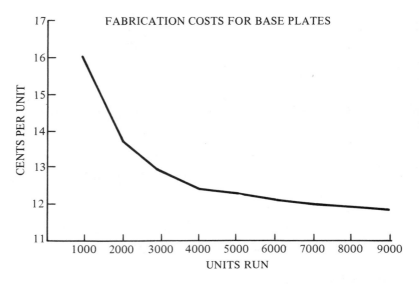

Figure 11–8. Example of tradeoff between setup costs and run lengths

The tradeoff is obviously to balance machine costs with inventory costs. Production foremen would be happy to run a five-year supply of an item for you, but your banker might not be overjoyed about that.

☐ *Monitor Utilization and Downtime.* A good record system for both "uptime" and downtime can highlight causes of problems and point out areas for attention.

☐ *Establish a Preventive Maintenance Program.* A regularly scheduled preventive maintenance program in accordance with the equipment manufacturer's specifications has yielded high utilization in hundreds of companies. If possible, maintenance should be scheduled for off-shifts to maximize the uptime.

☐ *Know Your Machine Costs.* Some equipment has very high costs per machine-hour in ranges of $20 to $50 or more. If that is the case, there may be very sound economic tradeoffs in actually adding a person to operate equipment during breaks and lunches or to perform required maintenance and changeovers. We must focus on *total* productivity decisions with equipment, not just one factor.

Increase Efficiency

☐ *Optimize Machine Speeds.* In some circumstances, relatively minor adjustments or modifications can often have a tremendous impact on increasing speed. A West Coast soft-drink bottler foreman recently took a hard look at his bottle spacing on a filling line, and found that with a relatively inexpensive turntable change, he could increase his bottle speed by 185 percent.

Conversely, a machine could be running too fast and generating too much scrap. Sometimes a slight reduction in speed can actually increase the *net* output of *good* units per hour.

☐ *Keep Amount of Time to Feed Materials to a Minimum.* Automatic feeds and ejectors often can shorten the cycle times for material through the equipment. If manual loading is required, materials should be as close to an operator as possible.

☐ *Utilize Your Labor Efficiently.* While we suggested earlier that an increase in labor hours could be leveraged toward greater improvement in machine utilization, the labor that is used might have some slack time. Some companies have been able to lay out machines to have an operator run more than one at a time, at no hardship to the operator. Similarly, with the great advance of automatic tooling and runnerless molds in plastic injection molding, many companies have found subassembly or packing work for operators to perform between machine cycles.

Your Productivity Improvement Team probably can identify dozens of productivity ideas, greater than the small list here. The important thing to remember is that it is a significant area of improvement opportunity.

MATERIALS HANDLING

Several studies have shown that materials-handling operations often operate at less than 50 percent of their potential. Obviously, with a ratio like that, this is also an important area. Some of the common problems are:

☐ Improper use of equipment
☐ Redundant and unnecessary handling
☐ Poor planning of handling

The approach toward improving materials handling follows some of the same pattern as the general approach to work simplification. If we select our materials handling as the work we want to attack, then we gather the facts. Figure 11–9 shows an analysis sheet that has proven successful for some companies. This summarizes the materials-handling requirements for a certain piece of equipment carrying a lot

PRODUCT	PRIMARY PACKAGE	PACKAGE SIZE L × W × H (INCHES)	WEIGHT (LBS)	PCKS PER LOAD	LOAD WEIGHT	SUGGESTED UNIT LOAD	

Figure 11–9. Sample materials-handling analysis form

	HAND CLASS	NORMAL DELIVERY QUANTITY	DELIVERY CYCLE	FIRST STORAGE LOCATION	PLACE OF USE	SPECIAL CONDITIONS OR REMARKS

of different loads. If the handling is relatively repetitive, then our old friends, the flow process sheets (Figures 11–1 and 11–2) might work better.

The five questions are expanded to seven questions for materials handling (see Figure 11–10) to really look at the specifics. Once the analysis is complete, some basic rules or objectives can be applied, similar to the twenty rules of motion economy. These principles are briefly summarized in Figure 11–10, following:

Figure 11–10. The seven questions of materials handling

1. WHY
    a. is handling required?
    b. are the operations performed as they are?
    c. are the operations performed in the current sequence?
    d. is material received as it is currently?
    e. is material shipped as it is currently?
    f. is material packaged as it is currently?

2. WHAT
    a. is to be moved?
    b. data are available and required?
    c. alternatives are available?
    d. are the benefits and costs for each alternative?
    e. is the planning horizon for the system?
    f. should be mechanized/automated?
    g. should be done manually?
    h. shouldn't be done at all?
    i. other firms have related problems?
    j. criteria will be used to evaluate alternative designs?

3. WHERE
    a. is materials handling required?
    b. do materials handling problems exist?
    c. should materials handling equipment be used?
    d. should materials handling responsibility exist in the organization?
    e. will future changes occur?
    f. can operations be eliminated, combined, or simplified?
    g. can assistance be obtained?

4. WHEN
    a. should material be moved?
    b. should I automate?
    c. should I consolidate?
    d. should I eliminate?
    e. should I expand (contract)?
    f. should I consult vendors?

Figure 11-10. (Continued)

5. HOW
   a. should material be moved?
   b. do I analyze the materials handling problem?
   c. do I sell everyone involved?
   d. do I learn more about materials handling?
   e. do I choose from the alternatives available?

6. WHO
   a. should be handling material?
   b. should be involved in designing the system?
   c. should be involved in evaluating the system?
   d. should be involved in installing the system?
   e. should be invited to submit equipment quotes?
   f. has faced a similar problem in the past?

7. WHICH
   a. operations are necessary?
   b. problems should be studied first?
   c. type equipment (if any) should be considered?
   d. alternative is preferred?

In General

□ Keep your materials-handling equipment in *motion* or *constant use* as much as possible.

□ Try for *continuous* material movement. Conveyors offer a great advantage in this respect.

□ Make use of *Gravity*—it's free!

□ Try for as *large* a load as possible. This reduces the number of trips.

□ *Standardize* methods. This provides ease of training and learning-curve experience.

□ Keep your equipment as *flexible* as possible to maximize the utilization of your assets.

□ Keep the ratio of *unloaded to loaded travel* to a minimum. Try for return loads as much as possible.

□ Use equipment *properly* and *safely*. In 1979, 23 percent of industrial accidents were on shipping docks and that cost industry $4½ billion. That's *not* productive!

In Manufacturing Operations

□ Reduce the materials-handling demands of your production personnel.

☐ Use your handling equipment to pace production, where possible.

☐ Establish your handling in the manufacturing area to allow the handling crew to work more or less at their convenience. If staging areas are provided, they can plan their work to bring loads in advance or take goods away on return trips.

In the Warehouse and Shipping Operations

☐ Operate your receiving, shipping and warehousing crew as a total manpower pool. Accounting managers sometimes like separate receiving and shipping crews, but if it is physically possible, the crews should be common.

☐ Set up information systems on receipts, shipments, and planned production for orderly assignment of people.

☐ Plan your storage methods and equipment to fit the items.

FACILITY LAYOUT

In some instances, during the process of either flowcharting or looking at materials handling, the issue of the facility's layout comes into question. Other times, especially during periods of peak activity, one gets the impression that the building is almost working against them. The proper layout and utilization of space can have a significant impact on both manufacturing and asset productivity.

The issues of a facility layout are quite complex. There are a number of objectives that must be assimilated into a good layout, some of which conflict. You probably want the facility to be flexible or easy to expand, yet have an orderly sequence of workflow for the business today. It must be convenient for the employees to use, and yet the machinery and equipment usually fixes most of the positions. It is necessary to have accessibility to all products and operations; on the other hand, the cost of building demands that we maximize the utilization of our space. An effective layout integrates all these factors into a successful compromise.

Planning a layout requires a systematic approach, and there are a number of fine courses and literature which delineate the process. Essentially, there are three fundamental steps to planning, graphically illustrated in Figure 11-11.

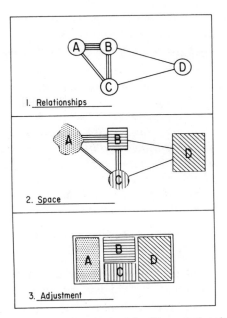

Figure 11-11. Fundamentals of layout planning.
Note: In the top chart, the heavy set of lines between departments A and
B indicates close interaction. (Source: Richard Muther, Practical Plant
Layout. [New York: McGraw-Hill Book Co., 1955].)

□ Establish the *relationships* among the various activities or functional areas. Departments with frequent involvement or interaction should be close together (such as departments A and B in the chart).

□ Analyze the *space* required to perform the activity—not just the amount of square footage, but the height, the shape, and type of space as well.

□ Finally, *adjust* the various elements to fit into a unified whole.

The important part of plant layout, though, is not the process, but how the layout activity can affect productivity. A couple of examples might be beneficial.

An injection molder perceived that the company was running out of space in a building it had occupied for only a few months. Analysis showed that there were too many aisles and these were too wide. In addition, material was only stored 8 feet high in an 18-foot-high building. Through a proper application of one narrow aisle lift truck, some pallet racking, and the resulting layout adjustments, the company has remained in the facility for another three years with a healthy increase in sales volume. In this case, the company improved the productivity of its current physical assets.

A custom window-covering manufacturer was planning a major new facility. During the planning, managers stood back and asked the question, "If we were starting our business from scratch, how would we produce the product?" This analysis yielded new methods of storing raw materials, a different procedure for cutting the piece goods, and a resulting simplification in the assembly process. These methods were tested and implemented in the old facility as the new one was built. The resulting savings totaled over $400,000 annually, and also resulted in a better-designed building. In this instance, a look at the layout precipitated many new methods.

In each of these cases, the operating people followed some basic steps:

☐ They looked at the whole operation and its impact, and then went down to the individual detailed departments.

☐ They asked the "what-if" questions up front, and therefore started "planning the ideal" and evolving into the practical applications.

☐ Finally, these layouts used the input from a number of sources to come up with a better plan than any individual had conceived. This is not to say there was not a project coordinator, but it was a participative process—an ideal project for a Productivity Improvement Team.

<u>CONTROLS</u>

Nonproductive Time
Setting Standards
Short Interval Scheduling

NONPRODUCTIVE TIME

Late in 1979, Theodore Barry & Associates published a five-year study of fifty companies that received a lot of media attention. The study showed that the average American worker spent his or her time in a typical 8-hour workday in the following ways:

	Time	Percent
Productive Work	4.4 hours	55%
Personal and Unavoidable Delay	1.2 hours	15%
Nonproductive Time	2.4 hours	30%
	8.0 hours	100%

This study included "blue-collar" and "white-collar" workers alike.

The reasons for the nonproductive time were many:

☐ Poor scheduling of workers
☐ Lack of clear communications
☐ Improper staffing
☐ Lack of material-flow coordination
☐ Slack starting and quitting times

None of the listed reasons are methods-related—they are all managerial shortcomings. However, this poor management is costing us at least 30 percent of our productive capacity.[3]

The needs for having clear objectives, good measurement for feedback, and good planning were discussed in Chapters 2, 3, and 4. The implementation of these concepts is the key toward gaining that 30 percent. But how do we translate these concepts into day-to-day action? A couple of specific industrial engineering techniques are useful.

SETTING STANDARDS

Much attention is spent in industrial engineering literature on the various methods of establishing standards. These range from historical standards to Detroit Edison's work sampling to predetermined standards, and finally, to the traditional stop-watch time study. All of these techniques are important and have validity in different circumstances. However, the methods are not of great importance to the readers of this book.

[3]Some experts feel that Barry's 30 percent nonproductive time is conservative, considering the fact that production time may be as little as 10 percent of the production process and waiting time about 90 percent.

The value of standards is *how* they are used in a productivity improvement effort:

☐ They provide the basic data for looking at the elements of a job, which, as we saw earlier, can be used as the basis for work-simplification or methods-improvement activities.

☐ They provide benchmarks of performance, from which improvements can be measured.

☐ They provide a basis for planning work in advance.

☐ They provide important feedback to the worker on how well he or she is doing the individual job.

This last point is probably the most important. Time and again, surveys of workers and attitudes toward work indicate that we all want to know how well we are doing in our jobs. We basically want to perform well. If we perceive the standard as being fair, then our performance against a standard is a very powerful feedback tool.

A colleague of mine is working with a company in an inspection and packing area. The first step they started with was merely to have the operators report their production. Standards were still in the process of being developed so the employees didn't know the target. However, productivity increased 25 percent, just from the element of reporting. Some layout and methods changes were introduced and the productivity jumped another 10 percent. Finally, standards were installed and the employees were told what was expected. Productivity increased another twenty percent in just six weeks and is now up almost fifty-eight percent over the base period. The department is averaging the new standard; the employees obviously know it is attainable. The lion's share of that improvement came from the feedback and articulation of what performance was expected. (See Figure 11–12)

SHORT INTERVAL SCHEDULING

The Barry study also emphasized lack of scheduling and improper staffing as a major cause of slack time. Many companies schedule only at a macro level—how much product is required for the week or month. However, if this is not translated to the details of what is required by an individual worker or work center, and how much time is needed, the macro schedule is doomed to failure.

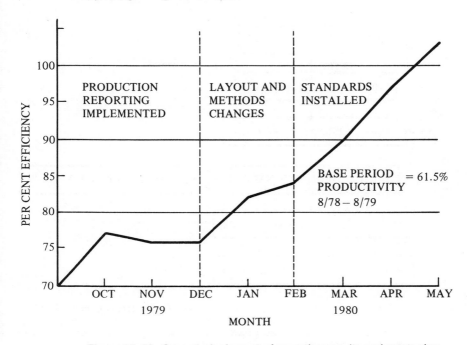

Figure 11–12. Case study: Impact of reporting results and measuring
results against standards

There is a formal structure called short-interval scheduling (SIS) which does this translation. The concept is very simple: The work to be done is translated to the number of hours required to perform the job. A time increment is chosen—the short interval—such as an hour, two hours, or half a shift. The output expected for that unit (e.g., pieces per hour) is scheduled, and production is checked at the end of each interval. An example might be a production requirement of 360 pieces of widget which can be produced at 60 widgets per hour (it should be noted that this 60 units per hour is the *achievable* or *expected* output for an average experienced operator). The job is scheduled for six hours and cumulative production is monitored on an hourly basis by the foreman. If there are significant misses—let's say only 45 units are produced in a second hour—the reasons for the 15 minutes' "lost time" are noted.

Figure 11–13 shows the schematic for the system. The daily schedule-control mechanism is integrated into the long-term production planning process as well as the summarized production

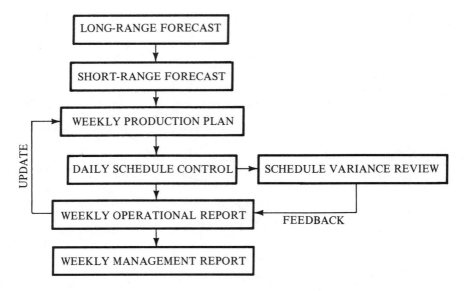

Figure 11–13. Short-interval scheduling system schematic

reporting cycle. Many companies review their performance on a daily basis in a "schedule variance review meeting." The purpose is not to finger-point, but to identify the causes of the problems and development of solutions. It is basically action planning on a day-by-day basis.

Some companies have had bitter experiences with short-interval scheduling because the implementers have gotten carried away with paperwork. Foremen wind up spending hours calculating numerous ratios in their offices instead of working on the floor dealing with the problems. A good SIS system does *not* need a lot of paper. Basically, the units expected, the units produced, and the reasons for the downtime are all that are needed. The rest of the information can be "rolled up" in the office the next day for summary reporting.

If an effective SIS system is installed, it provides many advantages:

☐ Allows for the effective planning of the work

☐ Shows the required manpower

☐ Schedules setups

☐ Provides fast feedback on both productivity and schedule attainment

☐ Recognizes individual employee contribution

☐ Identifies areas for improvement

☐ Pinpoints accountability for performance

This is a tool well worth investigating if schedule attainment on an individual or departmental basis is a serious problem.

VALUE ANALYSIS
Value Analysis vs. Value Engineering
Value Analysis Process

Up to now, we've talked about the productivity of our people, our equipment, and our facilities and how we can control and manage it. We have ignored one other aspect, the productivity inherent in our products (or outputs) themselves. This last area of improvement is addressed through the discipline of value analysis or value engineering.

VALUE ANALYSIS VS VALUE ENGINEERING

The two terms are almost synonymous, but there is a semantic difference:

Value engineering *is usually associated with examining the cost/function relationships* before *a product is designed.*

Value analysis *deals with improvements to cost/function after an item is designed and put into production.*

It is a very simple concept: It is an objective, engineering approach toward obtaining equal or *better performance* from our materials at the lowest cost. If we look at value as the following ratio and imagine that we can quantify "quality":

$$\text{PRODUCT VALUE} = \frac{\text{PRODUCT QUALITY}}{\text{PRODUCT COST}}$$

we can see that the objective of value analysis is to maximize that ratio.

VALUE ANALYSIS PROCESS

The process for value analysis follows somewhat the same thought processes as that for work simplification:

☐ Gather Information on the product:
  What is it?
  What does it do?
  What does it cost?

☐ Brainstorm alternatives

☐ Investigate each alternative

☐ Test the alternatives, if necessary, to be certain of the quality impact

☐ Implement the "best alternative"

Once again, this sounds deceptively simple, and it is. The importance of the value analysis approach as an entity is that it is *organized* and *systematic*. It is also somewhat unlimited in its areas of investigation.

Usually, value analysis is approached on a team basis, and once again, this makes it a natural activity for a Productivity Improvement Team. Ideally, if several functional disciplines are involved, there's a little more input. However, specialized expertise can always be called in to assist on individual projects.

Since value analysis is so all-encompassing, it is probably best illustrated through some examples:

A yacht-building company looked at many different aspects and came up with a number of cost savings:

☐ *Substituting some reinforced plastic parts for brass, reducing the cost of parts by 80 percent.*

☐ *Questioning its water bill and discovering that an air compressor was consuming an unnecessary amount of water (Controlling the water input saved $15,000/year)*

☐ *Reducing its annual casualty insurance bill by $50,000 by building a portable sprinkling system that can be put inside a boat after the deck is installed*

A snack-food company addressed its packaging costs and obtained significant cost reductions through lightweight glass, beaded tin cans, and substitution of packaging films in its bagged products.

A consumer-goods manufacturing company discovered that by a slight redesign of its product, it could nest the various parts more effectively, and package the product in a box half the size of the original. Not only were box costs reduced, but more units could be fitted on a truck.

A citrus company developed an animal-feed market for its fruit skins.

Architects for an x-ray lab building built a 14-foot earthen embankment around the new building instead of 7-foot-thick walls—for 10 percent of the construction cost.

As these examples demonstrate, the opportunities are only limited by human imagination. Value analysis merely organizes the efforts into an objective program.

SUMMARY

This chapter has covered a lot of ground. It is hoped that we have, among other things,

☐ Opened up the perspective of industrial engineering from strict time study and standards

☐ Generated a few ideas that can be applied in your environment.

However, there is one slight danger that we should discuss. While all of these techniques are proven and are successful in many different instances, they are *not* going to apply to or succeed in every environment.

The first step must be to assess what are the pressing problems, or better yet, the *most rewarding opportunities*, and choose the technique(s) that will best address that issue. Work simplification isn't going to do much in a processing plant with ten employees, but value analysis might provide some significant profit improvements. Looking at plant layout is probably not very pressing in a job shop that can't give a customer a reliable delivery date, but short-interval scheduling could help.

The caution is not to be a "kid in a candy store" about productivity improvement, but rather, to rationally set priorities and devote the full energies and resources of the organization to addressing the top priorities. There is always time to go after lesser opportunities. After all, managing a perfect organization wouldn't be any fun!

The second step is to apply the right technique to solve the identified problem. Table 11–1 shows a matrix of the techniques that were covered in the chapter and where they might be applied. This matrix is certainly not all-inclusive, and I am sure that all the techniques have been creatively applied to the various areas at one time or another. Yet the matrix provides some indication of common

TABLE 11-1. Techniques application matrix

FUNCTION	TOOLS							
	WORK SIMPLIFICATION	FLOWCHARTING	MACHINE PRODUCTIVITY	MATERIAL HANDLING	FACILITY LAYOUT	STANDARDS	SHORT-INTERVAL SCHEDULING	VALUE ANALYSIS
PRODUCTION	×	×	×	×	×	×	×	×
WAREHOUSING	×	×		×	×	×		×
SHIPPING/RECEIVING	×	×		×	×	×	×	×
MAINTENANCE	×	×	×			×	×	×
ACCOUNTING	×	×			×	×		×
SALES	×			×		×		×
CUSTOMER SERVICE	×	×	×	×	×	×		
ENGINEERING	×		×	×	×	×		×
DATA PROCESSING	×	×	×	×	×	×	×	
PERSONNEL	×				×	×		
ADMINISTRATION	×					×		×

uses of these techniques. Notice that standards and work simplification are universally applicable in all functions.

The third step—well, that is up to you and your team. The "toolbox" is now yours. It can either sit in the basement gathering dust or be used to build a sound structure of productivity improvement.

DECISION MAKING

CHAPTER 12

"You don't know how you do it; you just do it."

"I don't think businessmen know how they make decisions. I know I don't."

"It is like asking a pro baseball player to define the swing that has always come natural to him."
—Fortune *survey*

The art of management has been defined as making irrevocable decisions based on incomplete, inaccurate, obsolete information. This tongue-in-cheek definition is about as useful as the above comments that were reported in *Fortune* magazine by some of America's most successful corporate chief executives. Business managers are by profession decision-makers, yet for most of them the *process* of how they arrive at decisions is not clearly understood.

One reason for the indefinite explanations of how decisions are made is that the literature and teaching on the subject generally focus on the moment of decision rather than the whole lengthy, complex process of defining and exploring the many alternatives that precede the final act of deciding. The stereotype of the finger-snapping, coin-tossing manager fades as we examine three requirements for the process of rational decision making: (1) finding occasions for making a decision; (2) finding possible courses of action; and (3) choosing among alternative courses of action.

Decision making is a primary managerial skill. Many scholars and practicing managers believe that decision making and the processes leading up to it account for most of what managers do, at least in terms of their effectiveness as managers. Nothing helps or hinders the productivity of a manager more than the decisions that affect his or her area of responsibility.

Before proceeding to examine the decision making, it is useful to point out the difference between it and problem analysis. Problem analysis (Chapter 10) deals with the process of discovering the cause of a problem and therefore is concerned with the cause-and-effect relationship of past events. We didn't have to speculate because we had access to the facts and the discovery of the problem's cause consisted of analyzing past events.

Decision making, the subject of this chapter, is quite different. We are now dealing with an estimation of the future. The analysis therefore becomes more subjective, more dependent on value judgments, and more subject to qualitative choice. Nevertheless, it is a rational process.

DECISION MAKING:

THE CONCEPT OF RATIONAL CHOICE

Steps in Decision
Making

STEPS IN DECISION MAKING

Stated simply, decision making is the selection from among alternative possible courses of action that will achieve an objective. The process is at the core of management because no plan can be developed, and no controls established without a rational decision regarding a course of action.

If managers are to act rationally, they must first define or understand some goal, objective, or expected result that cannot be obtained without some positive action. Second, they must have a clear understanding of the alternative courses of action by which a goal could be reached under existing circumstances and limitations. Third, the rational decision-maker must also have the skills necessary to analyze and evaluate alternatives in light of the goal sought. A final condition in rational decision making is that the alternative selected must be the one that best satisfies or optimizes goal achievement. This last requirement, optimization of goal achievement, means that some criteria must be established by which alternatives can be measured.

The process of decision making that we will examine in this chapter is an imperfect one. It is imperfect because the factors affecting the decision cannot always be quantified. Value judgments are necessary. This is as it should be. Despite the recent growth of quantitative decision-making techniques (for instance, operations research, simulation), the overwhelming number of decisions faced by the ordinary manager are a combination of qualitative factors and are therefore probabilistic in nature. They must be made under conditions of uncertainty and with imperfect information. They must be made rapidly. There are no absolutely right answers, but the rational process will provide the best answer for you in accomplishing your expected results and overcoming the causes of your problems.

The techniques of decision analysis examined in this chapter will provide a method of analysis that is systematic, that will apply to almost any decision you are required to make, and will maximize your chances of making a right decision that can be implemented with confidence.

Like problem definition and analysis (Chapter 10), decision making is nothing new. It has been around a long time. Unlike problem analysis, however, decision making lacks an historical cause-and-effect relationship. It is basically choosing for the future. Nevertheless, both problem analysis and decision making have the same result in mind; achieving expected results. The role of both processes in managing work is shown in Figure 12–1. This figure also shows the steps in the decision-making process. These are listed below[1] and form the basis of discussion for this chapter.

STEP ONE: Define the Objective. *Restate the expected results sought, the cause of the problem to be solved, or the purpose of the decision.*

STEP TWO: Establish Decision Criteria. *Develop the factors or criteria, the yardsticks of measurement against which alternative courses of action can be weighed, one against the other.*

STEP THREE: Develop Alternatives. *State two or more courses of action that will achieve the objective.*

---

[1] Each of the steps in the decision-making process is illustrated by the continuation of the Office Systems, Inc. case at the end of this chapter.

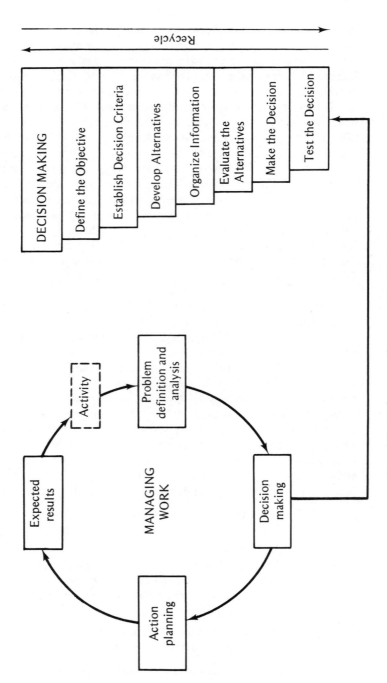

Figure 12–1. The role and process of decision making

STEP FOUR: Organize Information. *Establish the premises, the information, the "facts" surrounding the alternatives.*

STEP FIVE: Evaluate the Alternatives. *Judge each alternative against the decision criteria in order that the optimum choice can be made.*

STEP SIX: Make the Decision. *Choose the best alternative.*

STEP SEVEN: Test the Decision. *Evaluate the chosen alternative to see whether it is suitable, feasible, acceptable, and whether it is the best choice in view of potential problems.*

THE DECISION-MAKING PROCESS, I

Define the Objective
Establish Decision Criteria
Develop Alternatives
Organize Information
Evaluate the Alternatives

STEP ONE: DEFINE THE OBJECTIVE OF THE DECISION

This first step is similar to the problem definition phase in problem analysis. Here we review the purpose of making the decision. What is it that we must decide about? What is it that must be done?

In most cases, our definition of the objective of the decision will be concerned with the question: "How do I achieve the results expected?" or "What do I do about the cause of the problem that I have identified?"

In the chapter on problem definition and analysis I warned against the tendency to rush out and solve a problem that is not first defined. The same caution applies in decision making. Nothing is more futile than a decision that solves the wrong problem or the selection of a course of action before you decide where it is you want to go.

In most cases the objective of the decision will read: "The objective of this decision is to select the best alternative for...." For example:

The objective of this decision is to determine the following:

□ What is the best course of action to reduce costs?

□ Which individual should be selected for a vacancy?

□ Which vendor should be given the contract?

□ What is the best location for a new plant?

□ Should we approve a coffee break?

□ How can I reduce direct labor costs on line 1?

□ What should be our new credit policy?

and so on...

In the Office Systems, Inc. case at the end of this chapter, the objective of the decision might be stated: "The objective of this decision is to select the best data-processing system for the company's long-term future."

STEP TWO: ESTABLISH DECISION CRITERIA

If, as we have already agreed, decision making is selection from among alternatives, then it follows that criteria of selection are necessary. How is one to choose between alternatives A, B, and C unless the yardsticks of measurement are established beforehand? If there is a choice, there are two or more alternatives and there must be some measures to determine the relative values of each.

A typical decision that many of us face is the choice of a particular driving route from our homes to work each day. In choosing between two or more alternate routes we may consider such decision criteria as distance, elapsed time of travel, number of stoplights, amount of traffic, safety, comfort, gasoline consumptions, and so on. By identifying these criteria and assigning relative weights of importance to each, we can evaluate each alternative and choose the one that achieves the best overall balance.

The list of criteria for all decisions within the total organization is almost endless. Table 12–1 shows a few criteria for different problems.

Each decision has its own set of criteria. A good starting point is the checkoff list below. It will help ensure that major criteria have been considered.

Checkoff List for Major Decision Criteria

□ *Time:* How long will it take to implement the decision?

□ *Cost:* How much will this alternative cost?

□ *Equipment:* Do we have the equipment?

□ *Materials:* Are suitable materials available?

□ *Manpower:* Do we have the personnel skills available?

TABLE 12–1. Sample criteria

Decision	Decision Criteria
Introduce new product	Profitability
	Reputation
	Design costs
	Availability of sales training
Select new vendor	Delivery time
	Technical specifications
	Price
	Credit policy
Select plant site	Availability of labor
	Availability of transportation
	Union situation
	Willingness of personnel to move

□ *Customer:* Will the customer be satisfied?

□ *Competition:* Can we be hurt by the competition?

□ *Risk:* Is the payoff justified by the risk?

□ *Organizational Impact:* Will the decision be accepted? What will be the impact on morale? Are we organized to implement the decision?

□ *Return on Investment:* What is the return on investment?

□ *Sales:* What is impact of this decision on sales?

□ *Cash Flow:* Is cash flow positive? How much? When is payoff?

□ *Company Policy:* What is the company policy regarding this proposed alternative?

□ *Values of Management:* What are the values of management regarding risk, timing, conservativeness? How will these values affect the decision?

In the Office Systems, Inc. case at the end of the chapter, the decision criteria that Frank Jordon might develop for the data-processing decision are these:

□ Breakeven point (critical criteria)

□ Turnaround time (critical criteria)

□ Return on investment

□ Initial cost

□ Organizational impact, improved management

☐ Supports data-processing master plan
☐ Time to implement
☐ Design costs
☐ Operating costs

Critical Criteria

Perhaps the most important task in decision analysis is the identification of the critical criteria. This is a factor that is critical to the attainment of the objective. To put it another way, a critical criteria is one that rules out an alternative as a course of action unless it can be overcome. If a 10 percent profit is a requirement (critical criteria), all alternatives that do not achieve this rate of profit can be ruled out. There is no point in considering them. If the company is in a serious cash position and cannot raise cash for a plant expansion, then plant expansion is ruled out because of cash requirements.

It is important to identify critical criteria in the early stages of analysis so that the search for alternatives and related information can be confined to those that are realistic. Any alternative that doesn't measure up to the requirement of the critical criteria simply cannot be considered.

In the Office Systems, Inc. case, the general manager of the company has identified two critical criteria. First, he has said that no data-processing system should be considered that will cost the company more money than the money it saves. In other words, the system selected must not exceed the breakeven point. Second, he stated that the system selected must provide a capability for inquiry (by both customers and in-plant personnel) during the same day the inquiry is made. If a customer wants the status of an order or if the production manager wants the work-in-process status, the system must be able to provide the information on the same working day. This capability is known as turnaround time. So in this decision analysis, Frank Jordan has identified two *critical criteria:* These concern *breakeven point* and *turnaround time.* Any decision that is made must satisfy the requirements he has set for these two areas.

STEP THREE: DEVELOP ALTERNATIVES

Decision making is, by definition, making a choice between two or more alternatives. No alternatives means no decision. It should therefore be a universal rule that every problem to be solved, every decision to be made, should be accompanied by several alternatives. In management, as in science, we start not with the facts but with untested hypotheses; alternatives that can be tested against the decision criteria previously established.

Most of us fail to consider a full range of alternatives because we are conditioned by experience to jump to conclusions, to focus on a preconceived answer. We start out by assuming that our course of action is right and others are wrong.

Almost as bad as jumping to conclusions is the tendency to adopt an "either–or" approach that develops only two alternatives, one at both extremes of possible courses of action. Because we have been preconditioned to believe that profit is the difference between sales price and production costs, we develop only two extreme alternatives: (1) sell more, or (2) cut production costs. We don't consider the alternatives of product redesign, product mix changes, increasing prices, or subcontracting part of the manufacturing job. The old saying still applies: "There is more than one way to skin a cat."

For many decisions the alternatives are simply "go" versus "no-go" or "yes, we do" versus "no, we don't." In other cases the alternatives are fixed for us. Examples of this would include the choice between two candidates for promotion, the choice between three vendors, or the choice between a limited number of pieces of equipment to do a job.

Except for these yes–no situations, or when alternatives are fixed, the development of alternatives for decision making is a very innovative process and it requires creativity and imagination. Some people create alternatives by "brainstorming."

Creative decision-makers also welcome different opinions and even dissent. They know that the suppression of differing opinions is the quickest way to shut off a source of alternatives.

It should also be mentioned that one alternative course of action in most decisions can be to "do nothing." To "do something" is necessary when an opportunity will be missed or when a situation will degenerate unless something is done. On the other hand, "do nothing" might be the decision if the answer to the question "What will happen if nothing is done?" is "It will take care of itself."

In the Office Systems, Inc. case at the end of the chapter, Frank Jordon, at this stage in his decision-analysis process, was able to develop five alternatives that might possibly meet his objective of "selecting the best data processing system for the company's long-term future." He listed these:

- □ *Manual system.* This was essentially a "do-nothing" alternative because it involved maintaining the existing system.
- □ *Outside timesharing.* This alternative provides for all data-processing services to be accomplished by a timesharing service outside the company.
- □ *Minicomputer.* A small computer with limited applications and vendor application packages.
- □ *Large computer, vendor systems design.* Design of order processing, inventory, production control, and so on to be provided by computer manufacturer.
- □ *Large computer, systems design by in-company personnel.* Same computer as alternative 4 but with systems design by company trained personnel.

STEP FOUR: ORGANIZE INFORMATION

I have previously cautioned that the traditional advice in decision making to "first get the facts" is wrong. To start with fact gathering is a waste of time because we don't know what facts we are seeking. We can't answer the questions:

- □ What is the criteria of relevance of the facts?
- □ What would the facts have to be to make this alternative tenable?
- □ What do I have to know to test the validity of this alternative?

Of course it is impossible to ignore facts during steps 1 through 3 of the decision-making process, but if decision criteria and alternatives are first established, the information-gathering phase can proceed without detours and with a much greater economy of effort because the information that is gathered is much more likely to be relevant.

What Information Is Gathered?

There is no real answer to this question. To say that you gather all the information that is pertinent to the decision is obvious. To say that you gather all that is worth its cost is also obvious. To say that you reach a balance between cost and value is a truism. As a matter of practice, decision-makers can't wait for all the facts. They must decide on the basis of the facts at hand or on the facts that can be obtained within the time and cost limitations of the situation. You should therefore gather information to the point at which the cost of further investigation equals the benefit which can be obtained from the additional data.

Although the below list of information categories is not exhaustive, it does provide a convenient reminder, or checkoff list, to help you ensure that no major items have been overlooked. Four categories are listed:

- *External.* Data and information concerning considerations that are outside the organization.
- *Internal.* Data and information concerning considerations that are inside the organization.
- *Constraints.* Factors that limit the selection of alternatives.
- *Assumptions.* Unknown information and facts that cannot be obtained but that must be assumed or taken for granted.

EXTERNAL INFORMATION

Environmental	Political and governmental considerations
	Demographic and social trends
	Economic trends
	Technological environment
	Factors of production: labor, materials, capital
Competitive	Industry demand
	Firm demand
	The competition

INTERNAL INFORMATION

The sales forecast

The financial plan

Supply factors: manpower, plant and equipment, materials

Company organization: strategy, policies, program plans, organization

Resources: people, money, facilities, and so on.

CONSTRAINTS

Those external and internal factors that restrict the value of or the selection of an alternative. Typical constraints are the lack of resources (e.g., time, technology, personnel, money, and facilities) or those imposed by the nature of the organization such as policies and procedures.

ASSUMPTIONS

Assumptions include those items of information that bear upon the selection of an alternative but cannot be obtained for forecast with an adequate degree of certainty. Typical assumptions are those related to resource availability, sales, levels, economic conditions, weather, level of technology, competitive environment, interest rates, and so on. Remember: *Don't assume the problem away.*

The Information Matrix

For those decisions that have a number of alternatives and decision criteria it is frequently difficult to organize the information for study and evaluation. One way to do this is to construct some type of information matrix such as the one shown in Figure 12-2. This is a convenient way to summarize what might otherwise be an unmanageable amount of information.

Figure 12-2. Information matrix

Information Summary

Decision Criteria	Alternative #1	Alternative #2	Alternative #3	Alternative #4
Criteria #1	Information summary			
Criteria #2		Information summary		
Criteria #3			Information summary	
Criteria #4				Information summary
Criteria #5				

Note that in the Office Systems, Inc. case at the end of the chapter, Frank Jordan has constructed an information matrix to summarize the decision criteria surrounding the alternatives for meeting the objective of his data-processing decision.

STEP FIVE: EVALUATE THE ALTERNATIVES

At this point in the decision-making process, all the hard work has been completed. Criteria are established, alternatives developed, and information organized. It now remains to evaluate the alternatives against the criteria and information in light of the objective sought. One alternative may appear to be the most profitable but is ruled out because of the critical criteria of cash availability; another meets the return on investment criteria but involves a large degree of risk; still another better suits the customer's requirements. Which one should you choose?

The Decision Analysis Worksheet

The information needed to make a rational choice between alternatives is best organized on the Decision Analysis Worksheet (Figure 12-3). This is an excellent method for summarizing information and for bringing some quantification to what is otherwise a qualitative decision based on value judgments.

The technique is comprised of the four steps of *classifying*, *weighting*, and *rating* the decision criteria and then *ranking* the value of each alternative. These steps are summarized:

Step	How it is performed
1. *Classify* the decision criteria.	Separate into critical and regular.
2. *Weight* the decision criteria.	Assign a weight (on a scale of 1 to 10) to each criteria relative to its importance against other criteria.
3. *Rate* the alternatives.	Assign a rating (excellent, good, average, poor) to each alternative depending on how it fulfills the requirements of each criteria.

Weight criteria on scale of 1 to 10
Rate each alternative (Excellent = 4, Good = 3, Average = 2, Poor = 1)
Multiply rate by weight to get value

		Weight	#1 Manual	#2 Outside time sharing	#3 MINI computer	#4 Large computer, vendor design	#5 Large computer, in-company design
Critical Criteria	Breakeven point		(x) Yes ( ) No	(x) Yes ( ) No	(x) Yes ( ) No	( ) Yes (x) No	(x) Yes ( ) No
	Turnaround time		(x) Yes ( ) No	( ) Yes (x) No	(x) Yes ( ) No	(x) Yes ( ) No	(x) Yes ( ) No
Regular Criteria	Return on investment			ELIMINATE		ELIMINATE	
	Initial cost						
	Improved management						
	Supports master plan						
	Time to implement						
	Design costs						
	Operating costs						
	Totals						

Figure 12-3. Decision analysis worksheet

4. *Rank* the weighted and rated values of each alternative.

Extend the weighted and rated values as determined in steps 2 and 3 and arrive at a total value for each alternative.

Classify the Decision Criteria

Decision criteria have been classified as critical and regular, or noncritical. By distinguishing between these two classifications, we highlight the critical criteria, the one or more factors that must be satisfied before any alternative can be considered as a course of action. To say it another way, critical criteria represent mandatory requirements; these cannot be compromised and must be satisfied by a given alternative or it is eliminated as a viable course of action. Critical criteria must be satisfied by the alternative under consideration.

In the Office Systems, Inc. case, the critical criteria have been defined thus: (1) The breakeven point, and (2) the turnaround time must be one day. On the Decision Analysis Worksheet we enter these critical criteria. Then, for each alternative, we ask the question: "Are the criteria satisfied by the alternative?" If the answer is no, that alternative is eliminated from further consideration. Notice on the Decision Analysis Worksheet in Figure 12-3 that two alternatives have been eliminated by this process. Alternative 4 is eliminated because the extra cost of vendor systems design pushes the total cost beyond the breakeven point. Alternative 2 is eliminated because the time sharing service from outside the company cannot meet the turnaround time requirements because of the batch processing method of data processing.

Now that the critical criteria have "been taken care of," we can proceed to the regular decision criteria. These are also shown in Figure 12-3.

Weight the Regular Decision Criteria

After eliminating any alternatives that fail to pass the "critical criteria" test, we now proceed to evaluate the remaining alternatives.

The first step is to express some sort of preference for one criteria over the others by assigning differential numerical weights. By this process we will establish the relative importance of each criterion against all other criteria. A good way to do this is to pick the criterion that is considered the most important and give it a value of 10. The

Weight criteria on scale of 1 to 10

Rate each alternative (Excellent = 4, Good = 3, Average = 2, Poor = 1)

Multiply rate by weight to get value

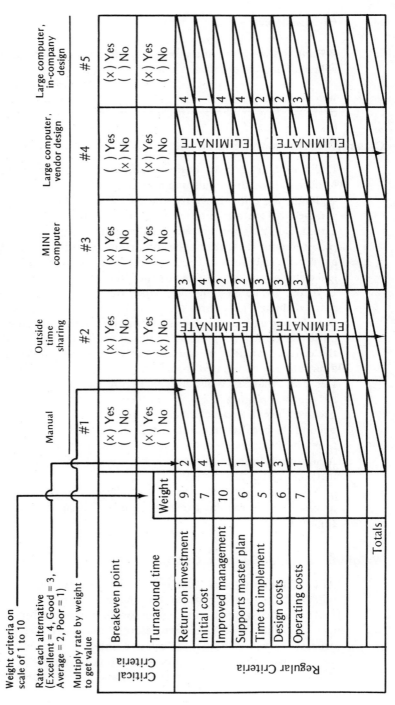

Figure 12–4. Decision analysis worksheet

remaining criteria can then be assigned weights that are relative to the "most important" criteria.

For the Office Systems, Inc. case, Frank Jordon has assigned the weights shown in Figure 12-4. Notice that he has assigned the highest or "most important" weight to improved management. He has given this a value of 10 and the remaining criteria are assigned values relative to this one.

Rate the Alternatives

The last step before ranking and selecting the best alternative is to rate them in accordance with their effectiveness in fulfilling the requirement of the decision criteria. For this purpose you can devise your own ranking scale (e.g., 1 to 10) or can use the one that I recommend. A good rating system is based on this scale: Excellent (4), good (3), average (2), poor (1).

In the Office Systems, Inc. case, Frank Jordon has assigned relative ratings to the remaining alternatives as indicated on the Decision Analysis Worksheet of Figure 12-4.

Rank the Alternatives

The evaluation process at this point is simply a matter of extending the weighted and rated values of each alternative to determine the best one. By integrating the relative weights that are assigned to each decision criterion with our judgment regarding how each alternative rates in fulfilling that criterion, we arrive at the total value of each alternative.

Figure 12-5 contains the completed Decision Analysis Worksheet for the decision regarding the selection of a data-processing system in the Office Systems, Inc. case. Notice that the total values for each alternative have been computed and entered on the worksheet.

THE DECISION-MAKING PROCESS, II

Make the Decision
Test the Decision
Suitability
Feasibility
Acceptability
Test for Potential Problems

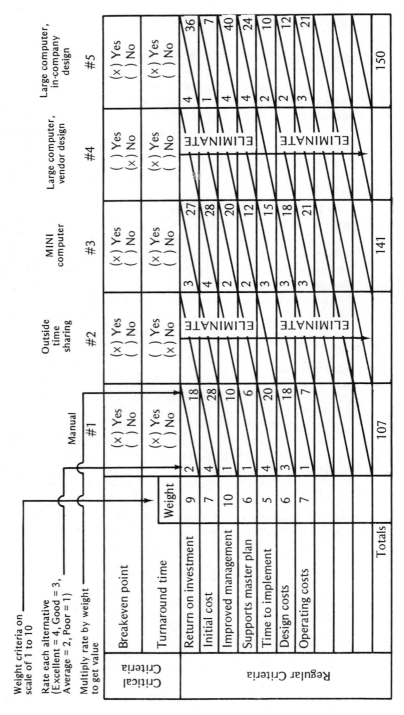

Weight criteria on scale of 1 to 10

Rate each alternative (Excellent = 4, Good = 3, Average = 2, Poor = 1)

Multiply rate by weight to get value

Figure 12–5. Decision analysis worksheet

remaining criteria can then be assigned weights that are relative to the "most important" criteria.

For the Office Systems, Inc. case, Frank Jordon has assigned the weights shown in Figure 12-4. Notice that he has assigned the highest or "most important" weight to improved management. He has given this a value of 10 and the remaining criteria are assigned values relative to this one.

Rate the Alternatives

The last step before ranking and selecting the best alternative is to rate them in accordance with their effectiveness in fulfilling the requirement of the decision criteria. For this purpose you can devise your own ranking scale (e.g., 1 to 10) or can use the one that I recommend. A good rating system is based on this scale: Excellent (4), good (3), average (2), poor (1).

In the Office Systems, Inc. case, Frank Jordon has assigned relative ratings to the remaining alternatives as indicated on the Decision Analysis Worksheet of Figure 12-4.

Rank the Alternatives

The evaluation process at this point is simply a matter of extending the weighted and rated values of each alternative to determine the best one. By integrating the relative weights that are assigned to each decision criterion with our judgment regarding how each alternative rates in fulfilling that criterion, we arrive at the total value of each alternative.

Figure 12-5 contains the completed Decision Analysis Worksheet for the decision regarding the selection of a data-processing system in the Office Systems, Inc. case. Notice that the total values for each alternative have been computed and entered on the worksheet.

THE DECISION-MAKING PROCESS, II

Make the Decision
Test the Decision
Suitability
Feasibility
Acceptability
Test for Potential Problems

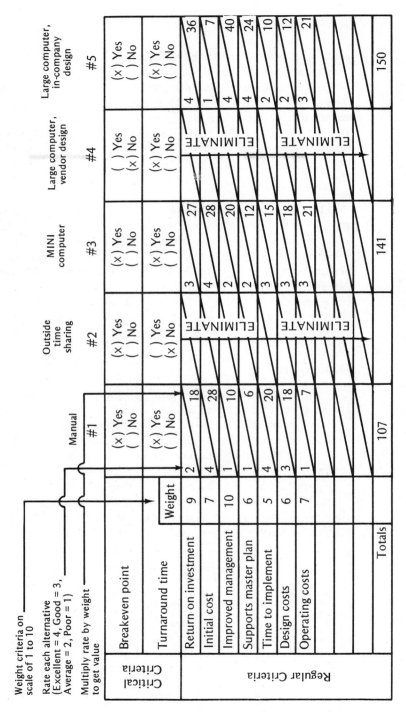

Figure 12–5. Decision analysis worksheet

STEP SIX: MAKE THE DECISION

The decision is now ready to be made. The objective has been stated, the criteria established, the information organized, and the alternatives evaluated. At this point the decision should "make itself." The course of action can now be chosen from the best of three remaining and in the Office Systems, Inc. case can be stated: "The best-data processing system for the company's long-term future is alternative 5: a large computer accompanied by systems design by in-company personnel."

STEP SEVEN: TEST THE DECISION

This is the last step in the decision-making process and it is performed as a final check to make sure that we haven't overlooked any potential problems and that the decision we have reached is the best one. The technique for performing the test is the Decision Testing Worksheet shown in Figure 12-6.

Test for Suitability, Feasibility, and Acceptability

The decision is *suitable* if, after implementation, the action taken will accomplish the objective to be attained. It must create an effect that is compatible in nature, completeness, and timeliness with the larger objective of which it is a part. Does it solve the problem? Does it achieve the results expected?

A decision is *feasible* if it can be carried out with the resources (money, manpower, equipment, materials, facilities) available in the face of any reasonable adverse circumstances. In order to declare that a decision is feasible, it is necessary to visualize the tasks necessary to carry it out and then determine the prospects of success.

The test for *acceptability* is really a double check on the cost–benefit analysis previously done when alternatives were weighed. It basically involves answering the question: "Are the probable results worth the costs?"

In the Office Systems, Inc. case, the three retained alternatives (alternatives 1, 3, and 5) are put to the test (Figure 12-6) and each of them is deemed to be suitable, feasible, and acceptable.

STEP EIGHT: TEST FOR POTENTIAL PROBLEMS

Most of us have had the experience of making a decision and having it go completely wrong during or after implementation. After the

	Manual system Alternative #1	MINI computer Alternative #2	Large computer, in-company design Alternative #3
Suitable: Does it achieve expected results?	(x) Yes ( ) No	(x) Yes ( ) No	(x) Yes ( ) No
Feasible: Do we have the necessary resources?	(x) Yes ( ) No	(x) Yes ( ) No	(x) Yes ( ) No
Acceptable: Are the results worth the cost?	(x) Yes ( ) No	(x) Yes ( ) No	(x) Yes ( ) No
Estimate the potential problems and the adverse consequences that might occur for each alternative Rank the *probability* (P) and *seriousness* (S) of each occurrence on a scale of 1 to 10.	Potential problems	P	S		P	S		P	S
Summary	Decision (Retained course of action)		

Figure 12–6. Decision testing worksheet

autopsy we ask: "What went wrong?" and when we discover the cause of failure we say: "I never thought of that!" The purpose of the test for potential problems is to "think of that" before it happens. We want to avoid disaster before it strikes by predicting what can go wrong. All problems can't be predicted, but we should do the best we can to foresee them.

This test involves the identification of potential problems and assigning some estimate of the probability of the event occurring and the seriousness if it does occur. Using a scale of 1 to 10, a value of 10 would mean a probability of practical certainty. Likewise, a scale of 1 to 10 for seriousness would mean that a value of 10 indicates a disastrous consequence if a potential problem should occur. We can readily see that if a potential problem has a value of 10 for both probability *and* seriousness it would absolutely occur and would likely rule out an alternative as a course of action.

The Decision Testing Worksheet (Figure 12-6) provides a technique for summarizing the impact of potential problems.

In the Office Systems, Inc. case, Frank Jordon wished to test his decision to "buy a large computer accompanied by systems design by in-company personnel." Figure 12-7 shows his computation and test. After further analysis and thought he began to worry about the potential problem of buying a very expensive large computer and letting it go substantially unused for a 12- to 36-month period during which time personnel were trained and systems designed. He predicted that the real payoffs from the computer would not be realized for at least two to three years and the completion of a master plan was probably five years away. These judgments caused him to identify a potential serious problem: "Computer is underutilized for next 3 to 5 years, causing very high expense." He assigned a seriousness of 9 to this problem and a probability of 8. This combination he estimated to be so negative in its impact that he ruled out "buy large computer" as a viable alternative and therefore as a decision.

Turning to the remaining alternatives, Jordon concluded that alternative 2, "minicomputer," would be a better decision. Although this was not the optimum decision as determined from the Decision Analysis Worksheet (Figure 12-5), he calculated that he could ultimately achieve the same result by "buying a minicomputer with vendor application packages and 'moving up' to a large computer at a later date."

DECISION MAKING
Programmed Decisions
and
Decision Rules
Case Study

THE PROGRAMMED DECISION

The discussion thus far in this chapter relates to the rational decision-making process—the *nonprogrammed* decision. This type of decision is nonprogrammed because it is unstructured, it is elusive or complex, or the choice of the best alternative is frequently a matter of value judgment. The programmed decision, on the other hand, is repetitive and lends itself to programming: make the decision once and derive a decision rule (e.g., calculation of payroll, economic order quantity).

	Manual system Alternative #1	MINI computer Alternative #2	Large computer, in-company design Alternative #3
Suitable: Does it achieve expected results?	(x) Yes ( ) No	(x) Yes ( ) No	(x) Yes ( ) No
Feasible: Do we have the necessary resources?	(x) Yes ( ) No	(x) Yes ( ) No	(x) Yes ( ) No
Acceptable: Are the results worth the cost?	(x) Yes ( ) No	(x) Yes ( ) No	(x) Yes ( ) No

Potential Problems

Estimate the potential problems and the adverse consequences that might occur for each alternative / Rank the *probability* (P) and *seriousness* (S) of each occurrence on a scale of 1 to 10.	P	S		P	S		P	S
	Continued human error in system — 7, 5	7	5	Not able to handle processing load in later phases of master plan — 8, 7	8	7	Underutilized for next 3–5 years causing very high expense — 8, 9	8	9
	Transaction speed unable to meet turnaround demands — 7, 4	7	4	Restricts ultimate implementation of master plan — 6, 6	6	6	Unable to train and retain proper personnel — 6, 8	6	8
				Incompatible with expansion of system in later phases — 3, 8	3	8	Unable to integrate with master plan — 3, 8	3	8

Summary
Selection of Alternative #3 delayed due to high probability of low utilization and high expense.

Decision (Retained course of action)
Buy MINI computer with vendor application packages and "move up" to large computer at later date.

Figure 12–7. Decision testing worksheet

Thereafter, the programmed decision is made by a clerk following a procedure or, better yet, a computer.

Decisions lend themselves to programming techniques if they are repetitive and routine and if a procedure can be worked out for handling them so that each is not an ad hoc decision or does not have to be treated as a new situation each time it arises. Naturally, the problems that lend themselves to programming are those that tend to be repetitive and occur frequently. Numerous examples of programmed decisions are available in almost any organization, the most familiar being the computation of pay in accordance with a union agreement, pricing orders, credit checks, shop-floor loading, purchasing, and those dozens of decisions made daily in accordance with company policy.

Decisions are nonprogrammed to the extent that they are unstructured, new, of high consequence, involve major commitments, or are elusive or complex and when two or more alternatives must be weighed in accordance with value judgments as criteria. These are the type that we apply the rational decision-making process to the solution.

DECISION RULES

There is tremendous potential in the typical organization for increased productivity through the programming (automating) of operations by *decision rule*. The great majority of business decisions are repetitive and routine. One survey found that routine decisions comprise about 90 percent of management decisions. If this is true, then there is a great need to automate or *program* these decisions so that the supervisor can get on about his or her true task, action planning for productivity improvement.

Each individual and Productivity Improvement Team (PIT) should consider the concept and application of programmed decision rules for the solution of problems and the improving of results. The use of programmed decision, decision rules, and management information systems offers a substantial opportunity for improving productivity in operating systems. The concept of these systems is shown in Figure 12–8.

SUMMARY

In Chapter 7 we argued that problem analysis should become a way of managerial life. The same argument can be made for the rational approach to decision making described in this chapter.

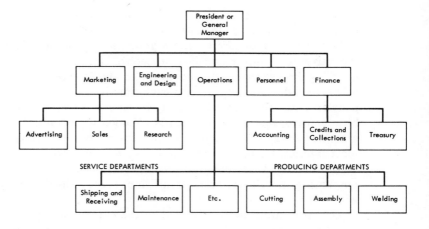

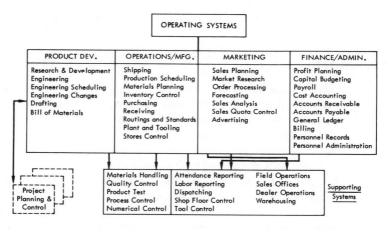

Figure 12-8. Operating systems that suggest programmed decision rules

Techniques, problem analysis, and decision making should all become second nature for you, your subordinates and your relations with your superiors.

If the rational problem-solving and decision-making methodologies outlined in these two chapters are followed they will provide these very important benefits:

□ People will take a rational approach to organizational problems rather than jumping to conclusions based on preconceived notions of what is right.

☐ There will be a common vocabulary and approach to planning staff work that will improve communication and reduce conflict.

☐ The approach will go a long way toward improving our systems approach to management which (a) focuses on results, and (b) achieves organizational integration.

CASE STUDY:
Office Systems, Inc., Part II

It was late May and Frank Jordon, the controller of Office Systems, Inc., was relaxed and confident as he entered the office of Greg Peterson, the general manager. Jordon's confidence was due to his success in reducing the level of accounts receivable to that amount required by the bank for renewal of the company's line of credit.

Reduction of the level of accounts receivable had been a simple matter once Jordon identified the cause of the problem. He recalled how overdue accounts had risen to a dangerous level because of serious errors in posting, billing, and inventory control. These errors in turn were caused by a change in posting and record-keeping procedures involving the movement of records from Warehousing to Order Entry. Jordon smiled as he recalled how the problem solution had involved a rather simple redesign of the paperwork system.

Partly as a result of the accounts-receivable problem, Jordon had decided to undertake a study that would lead to the redesign of all information systems in the company and the probable purchase of a computer for that purpose. He already had written a memorandum to Peterson regarding the study and it was this subject that accounted for his visit on this particular morning.

"Good morning, Frank," said Peterson. "First, let me congratulate you again on solving the receivables problem. It looks like our credit situation is fine now."

"Thanks again, Greg," replied Jordon. "As you know from my memorandum, this incident only serves to point up a larger problem of information systems design throughout the company. I would like to get your permission to proceed on a study that would lead to a decision regarding the long-term needs of the company. Also, If you have any particular guidelines or criteria, I would like to hear them."

"Well, Frank," Peterson began, "I certainly agree that our systems need an overhaul and it's probably time for us to get a computer. Lord knows, everyone else has one. And I agree that we shouldn't take a 'band-aid' approach. Let us think in terms of our long-term needs, our master plan. I've heard too many disaster stories of companies that took a patchwork approach to data processing and failed. I only have two requirements. First, we must be able to get fast response...turnaround time...from the system. When a customer calls about an order or when Production Control wants information, the system must be able to respond the same day that the information

Decision Criteria	Keep manual system Alternative #1	Outside time sharing Alternative #2	MINI computer Alternative #3	Large computer with systems design by manufacturer Alternative #4	Large computer with systems design by in-company personnel Alternative #5
Breakeven	No change	Vendor estimates positive	Yes	No. Probably take 5–6 years	Yes but may take 5 years
Turnaround time	OK	Cannot meet due to batch processing	Yes if located in company	Yes	Yes
Return on investment	No change	Positive due to clerical saving	Pays for itself	Can't estimate but probably negative	Positive. Best in long run
Initial cost	None	Low. Offset by clerical saving	Low	High. Bad strain on cash flow	Highest of all alternatives
Organizational impact Improved management	Poor. No improvement	Not good	Slow but long run effective	Good but takes time	Excellent. Improved management
Master plan	Nothing to advance	Does nothing	OK but requires more time	Takes too long	Excellent. Only way in long run
Time to implement	Immediate	Fast 6–12 months	Moderate 12–18 months	High 18–24 months	36–48 months for full implementation
Design costs	None	Included in total price	Low	Inclusive	Very high due to training and time involved
Operating costs	Same as existing	Included in total bid price	Moderate	High	Same as #4

Figure 12–9. Information matrix

inquiry is made. Second, the system has got to break even on costs. By that I mean you should be able to come up with cost savings in inventory, personnel, and other applications that will pay for the cost of the data-processing system that you install."

Peterson concluded: "Other than that, Frank, the decision is yours. Why don't you come back in a few days with your decision?"

After two weeks of fact gathering and study, Frank Jordon sat at his desk and began to review and summarize in his own mind the information he had gathered. He identified the two requirements laid down by Peterson as critical criteria and he labeled them: (1) fast turnaround time, and (2) break even on costs.

Jordon had identified a number of additional requirements of his own that he felt were useful in weighing one alternative against another. He listed these: return on investment, initial cost of the system, the organizational impact achieved by improved management, the requirement to ultimately achieve a master data-processing plan, the time to implement the system, the costs of design, and the costs of operating the system.

Jordon had also been thinking of a number of alternative ways to achieve his objective of "selecting the best data-processing system for the company's long-term future." These alternatives ranged from a "do-nothing" decision involving the retention of the existing manual systems to the other extreme of buying a large computer and training his own in-company personnel to design and operate the system.

As a last step in his analysis, Frank Jordon prepared the "information matrix" shown in Figure 12-9. He felt that this matrix summarized the pertinent information regarding his alternatives and he was now ready to make a decision.

□ It *focuses on objectives*. Without objectives we can't plan. Without a plan we cannot achieve objectives.

□ It provides a device for *control of operations*. Planning and control must be integrated; a well-designed plan provides built-in control through performance standards.

There are six basic questions that arise in planning: where you are, where you want to go, how you want to travel, when you wish to arrive, who is going to drive, and how much you will pay for the trip. Since we have already answered many of these questions through the process of decision analysis (Chapter 8), it only remains to determine the route and schedule through the process of action planning.

At this point in this book, we are familiar with all but one of the major steps in achieving productivity through results management. We have established, through the management by objectives (MBO) approach, the particular results expected (objectives) from our area of operations. We have analyzed the problem(s) surrounding the achievement of these results and completed the process of rational decision making, the selection of a specific course of action that will optimally satisfy the objective. The final, and payoff, step in this process is the design and implementation of a plan of action that will bridge the gap from where we are to where we want to go. This is the action plan.

ACTION PLANNING
Why Plan?
Why Document?

WHY PLAN?

There is an old adage in planning which says, "If you haven't written it out, you haven't thought it out." In practice this means that some practical approach is required in order to convert into system and method what has been done before by hunch and intuition. We need to substitute experience and "rule of thumb" with a logical pattern of organizing people and resources for achieving an objective.

The caution to "write it out" does not mean that a documented plan is necessarily a good one. On the contrary, we should not assume that the fruits of good planning are represented by documented, quantified, and detailed plans. It is the process that is important, not

ACTION PLANNING

"Planning is the most basic of all managerial functions."
"Decisions must be actionable."
"Unless objectives are converted into action, they are only dreams."
"One of the best ways to kill MBO is to have objectives but no follow-up plans." —Various

These quotations from prominent management writers and practitioners reflect the widespread conclusion that follow-up action planning is necessary if we are to get results.

The function of planning is probably the fastest-growing activity among the several jobs of the manager or the supervisor. Indeed, one can hardly read today's business literature without meeting frequent references to the growth of and the need for managerial planning.

The growth of this function is not surprising. Among the causes are the rapid rate of technological change, the growth of competition among firms and nations, the increasing complexity of the business environment, and the general difficulty of the management process.

The question also arises: why plan? The reasons are evident:

□ It helps *offset uncertainty* about the future. Although we cannot foretell the future, we can plan for uncertainty.

□ It improves the *economy of operations*. It saves money.

the prose, graphs, forms, or reports which it produces. Nevertheless, minimum documentation is desirable for these purposes:

☐ It helps clarify the thoughts and follow-up actions of the individual or the Productivity Improvement Team (PIT).

☐ It provides an excellent communication and coordination document between parties to the action plan.

☐ It serves as a blueprint or subsidiary action plan for subordinates or others involved in achieving the milestones or action steps contained in the plan.

DOCUMENTING THE ACTION PLAN

The documentation of a typical uncomplicated action plan might appear as in Figure 13-1. The top form, the *Action Plan Summary*, is supported by the additional forms shown. All these may not be essential or desirable in every case. The selection of the appropriate backup or supporting forms is a matter to be determined by the originator of the plan.

The remainder of this chapter will discuss the preparation of the action plan documentation. For illustration purposes I will use the Office systems, Inc. case study contained at the end of Chapters 10 (Problem Definition and Analysis) and 12 (Decision Making). You are advised to review that case study before continuing this chapter or preparing your own action plan.

You will remember that Frank Jordon, the controller of Office Systems, Inc., had a problem concerning the rising level of accounts receivable. He determined through problem analysis that the cause of this problem was customer dissatisfaction and confusion caused by erroneous order processing and invoicing. The cause of these errors was in turn attributed to the movement of inventory records from the warehouse to Order Entry. A simple redesign of the paperwork system for order processing solved this problem.

Following the return of accounts receivable to the desired level, Frank Jordon and the president of Office Systems, Inc. determined that further computer-designed information systems would be advantageous to the company. Jordon then undertook a study leading to a decision on how to achieve an objective that was stated as "selecting the best data processing system for the company's long-term future."

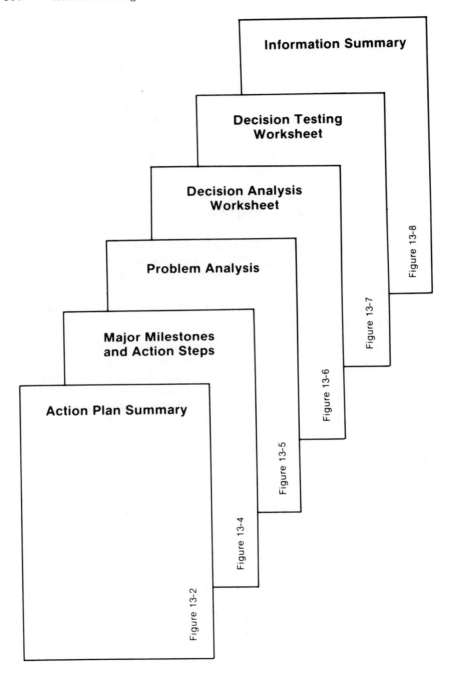

Figure 13-1. Documentation of the Action Plan

With this background in mind, consider the documentation of Frank Jordon's *action plan*. You can then make the transition to your own individual *productivity improvement objective* and the supporting *action plan*.

ACTION PLAN SUMMARY

THE PURPOSE

THE OBJECTIVE

THE PROBLEM(S)

THE DECISION

PRODUCTIVITY IMPROVEMENT

MAJOR MILESTONES

The Purpose

The purpose of the *Action Plan Summary* (see Figure 13-2) is to provide a succinct, one-page summary of the essential components of the plan for productivity improvement. This is where "it all comes together." The purpose of the remainder of the supporting documents in Figure 13-1 is to expand on or provide backup to the summary. The components are outlined below.

The Objective

The objective is what planning is all about. It is the reason for the planning process; the purpose of the action plan is to organize a course of action to achieve the objective.

A review of Chapter 2 provides us with an understanding of the objective in terms of results expected. In that chapter we learned how to define and express objectives by measurable yardsticks of performance. We also developed these acceptable criteria:

	Yes	No
Does the objective measure results and not activities?	( )	( )
Is it realistic?	( )	( )
Is it suitable?	( )	( )
Is it measurable and verifiable?	( )	( )
Is it controllable by feedback?	( )	( )
Is it acceptable?	( )	( )

Action Plan Summary

Name _____ Department _____

Objective

Action Verb	Results Expected	Time	Cost
To reduce	accounts-receivable level to 43 days	in 6 months	no increase in personnel or equipment
To select	best data-processing system for company's long-term future	reasonable	break even on costs

Problem(s)

1. Receivable up
2. Customer complaints up
3. Invoicing errors

4. Warehouse morale down
5. Backorder control

Cause(s):   1. Moving warehouse records to order processing
              2. Lack of data-processing system

Decision (Course(s) of action)

1. Redesign paperwork system for order processing
2. Install data processing system using minicomputer with ventor software applications and "move up" to a large computer at a later date

Productivity Improvement

Decision 1 will return accounts receivable to acceptable level and improve cash flow. Decision 2 will result in cost savings in inventory, production, and personnel and provide better customer service.

Major Milestones

	When	Measurement*
Select vendor	2/1	Purchase order issued
Acquire & test	3/15	Acceptance letter signed
Facilities & office	3/1	Work order released
Train personnel	3/15	Vendor course completed
Systems design	4/15	MIS committee signoff
Systems installed and tested	6/1	Up & running & vendor release

*How do I know when milestone is completed?

Figure 13-2. Action Plan Summary

The first step in planning, then, is to review the objective to determine to what extent it meets these criteria. The more closely it meets the criteria, the more easily it can be converted into an action plan.

There were two objectives in Frank Jordan's plan in the Office Systems, Inc. case. The first involved the immediate problem of "reducing accounts-receivable level to 43 days," and the second involves the longer-range objective associated with "selecting the best data-processing system for the company's long-term future."

The Problem(s)

This section summarizes the problem(s) surrounding the deviation or variance from expected results. It also lists the *cause* of the problem. In Frank Jordon's case the ultimate cause of the accounts-receivable problem is traced to the movement of the warehouse records to order processing. *Problem* and *cause* are determined after completion of the *Problem Analysis Worksheet* (Figure 13-5).

The Decision

In this section of the Action Plan Summary the decision is entered; the specific course(s) of action that will achieve the desired productivity improvement or the objective (results expected). The decision of Frank Jordon was made after the completion of the Decision Analysis Worksheet (Figure 13-6).

Productivity Improvement

This a precise statement, quantified if possible, of the productivity improvement that will result if the objective is achieved. This can be stated in terms of the $\dfrac{\text{Output}}{\text{Input}}$ ratio, time, cost, or other evidence of productivity.

Major Milestones

These are the *major* work packages or components of the work breakdown structure of the action plan that are to be achieved in sequential order. If, for example, the plan were to build a house, the major milestones would be construction/installation of foundation, walls, roof, electrical system, plumbing and so on. The work

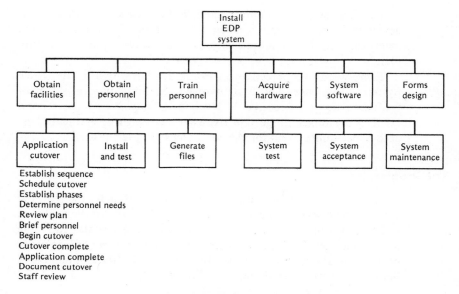

Establish sequence
Schedule cutover
Establish phases
Determine personnel needs
Review plan
Brief personnel
Begin cutover
Cutover complete
Application complete
Document cutover
Staff review

Figure 13–3. Work breakdown structure

breakdown structure (and major milestones) for installing a data-processing system is illustrated in Figure 13-3. The major milestones are accompanied by a date for completion (the "when" on the Action Plan Summary) and a measurement to determine when the milestone is complete.

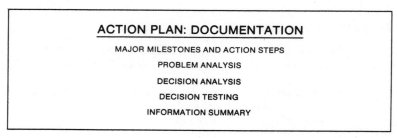

The backup documentation of the *Action Plan Summary* is illustrated in Figures 13–4 through 13–8 and discussed below.

Major Milestones and Action Steps (Figure 13–4)

This form provides a more detailed outline of the action steps necessary to achieve each major milestone. It is a decomposition or

Major Milestone   SYSTEMS DESIGN (Assigned to Accounting)

Action Steps	Start	Complete
Analysis of User Requirements	2/1	2/10
Select System Applications	2/28	3/5
Set System Objectives	3/5	3/10
Determine Information Needs	3/20	3/25
Determine Information Sources	3/22	3/25
Design System Concept	3/30	4/10

Major Milestone   FACILITIES AND OFFICE (Assigned to Plant Engineer)

Action Steps	Start	Complete
Finalize Equipment Configuration	1/10	1/10
Prepare Physical Plan	2/1	2/15
Review with Vendor	2/12	2/12
Equipment Room Modification	3/5	4/1
Equipment Delivered	3/25	3/25
Install and Test	4/1	4/1

Major Milestone   ETC., ETC.

Action Steps	Start	Complete
etc.		
etc.		

Figure 13–4. Major milestones and action steps

Problem Analysis

Description of variance

Accounts receivable are growing and are now averaging 67 days against industry average of 43 days.

	Variance Includes	*Variance Excludes*
Who	Primarily customers for resale items.	Few customers for company manufactured items.
What	Exceeds standard by 23 days.	Above standards before September.
Where	All customers and all territories.	Not isolated to specific customers or territories (except as described under *who*)
When	Started in September and increasing steadily since that time.	Not prior to September. Not isolated instances.
How Much	Majority of customers for resale items.	Not isolated complaints.

What is distinctive about the Includes and Excludes?	*What changes might explain the distinctions?*
Overdue customers are complaining about resale items, not company items. Level of receivables started to go up in September and has risen steadily since that time.	Moral of warehouse personnel went down in July & August. New customers added beginning in January, a year ago. Moved inventory records from warehouse to Order Entry in July.

Most probably cause of the problem:

Change in inventory recording and posting procedure in July when records were moved from the warehouse to Order Entry. Result was clerical errors & customer complaints.

How to verify the cause:

Interview warehouse supervisor, sales department, Order Entry, and Accounts Receivable. Check above cause.

Figure 13–5. Problem analysis

breakdown of the end result (major milestone) into the work elements necessary to achieve it.

Problem Analysis (Figure 13–5)

This form summarizes the logical progression of steps involved in the analysis of problem variance and its cause. This process of problem definition and analysis was described in Chapter 10.

Decision Analysis (Figure 13–6)

The Decision Analysis worksheet was decribed fully in Chapter 12. It documents the logical choices and the analysis that leads to the rational selection of the best course of action (alternative) to achieve the objective. Frank Jordon's Analysis Worksheet was illustrated in Figure 12–5 and is shown again in Figure 13–6.

Decision Testing Worksheet (Figure 13–7)

As a final check to ensure that a decision that has been made is a correct one, this worksheet provides a problem analysis of *potential problems* that might arise. Frank Jordon's worksheet was illustrated in Figure 12–7 and is shown again in Figure 13–7.

Information Summary (Figure 13–8)

This final form for documenting the action plan provides a brief, telegraphic summary of information related to each alternative considered in the decision analysis. It not only serves as backup information for the originator of the plan but provides any subsequent reader of the plan a summary of important related information leading to evaluation of alternatives and the resulting decision. It is useful for boss–subordinate or team or committee communications and discussion. Frank Jordon's information summary was illustrated in Figure 12–9 and is shown again in Figure 13–8.

THE COMPLEX PLAN

SCHEDULING

COORDINATION AND CONTROL

MILESTONE CHARTS

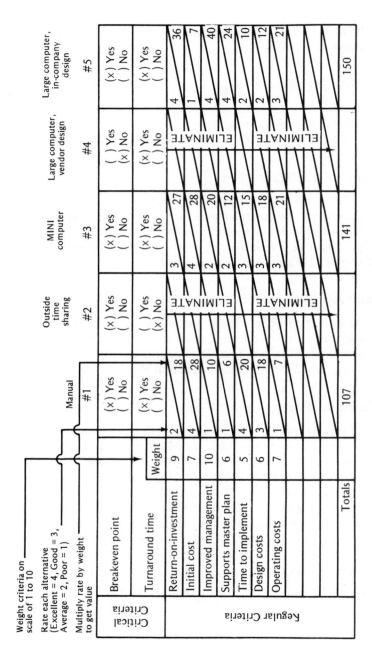

Weight criteria on scale of 1 to 10

Rate each alternative (Excellent = 4, Good = 3, Average = 2, Poor = 1)

Multiply rate by weight to get value

		Weight	Manual #1	Outside time sharing #2	MINI computer #3	Large computer, vendor design #4	Large computer, in-company design #5
Critical Criteria	Breakeven point		(x) Yes ( ) No	(x) Yes ( ) No	(x) Yes ( ) No	( ) Yes (x) No	(x) Yes ( ) No
	Turnaround time		(x) Yes ( ) No	( ) Yes (x) No	(x) Yes ( ) No	(x) Yes ( ) No	(x) Yes ( ) No
Regular Criteria	Return-on-investment	9	2 / 18	ELIMINATE	3 / 27	ELIMINATE	4 / 36
	Initial cost	7	4 / 28		4 / 28		1 / 7
	Improved management	10	1 / 10		2 / 20		4 / 40
	Supports master plan	6	1 / 6		2 / 12		4 / 24
	Time to implement	5	4 / 20		3 / 15		2 / 10
	Design costs	6	3 / 18	ELIMINATE	3 / 18	ELIMINATE	2 / 12
	Operating costs	7	1 / 7		3 / 21		3 / 21
	Totals		107		141		150

Figure 13–6. Decision analysis worksheet

	Manual system Alternative #1	MINI computer Alternative #2	Large computer, in-company design Alternative #3
Suitable: Does it achieve expected results?	(x) Yes ( ) No	(x) Yes ( ) No	(x) Yes ( ) No
Feasible: Do we have the necessary resources?	(x) Yes ( ) No	(x) Yes ( ) No	(x) Yes ( ) No
Acceptable: Are the results worth the cost?	(x) Yes ( ) No	(x) Yes ( ) No	(x) Yes ( ) No

Potential Problems

Estimate the potential problems and the adverse consequences that might occur for each alternative

Rank the *probability* (P) and *seriousness* (S) of each occurrence on a scale of 1 to 10.

Alternative #1	P	S
Continued human error in system	7	5
Transaction speed unable to meet turnaround demands	7	4

Alternative #2	P	S
Not able to handle processing load in later phases of master plan	8	7
Restricts ultimate implementation of master plan	6	6
Incompatible with expansion of system in later phases	3	8

Alternative #3	P	S
Underutilized for next 3–5 years causing very high expense	8	9
Unable to train and retain proper personnel	6	8
Unable to integrate with master plan	3	8

Summary

Selection of Alternative #3 delayed due to high probability of low utilization and high expense.

Decision (Retained course of action)

Buy MINI computer with vendor application packages and "move up" to large computer at later date.

Figure 13–7. Decision testing worksheet

Decision Criteria	Keep manual system Alternative #1	Outside time sharing Alternative #2	MINI computer Alternative #3	Large computer with systems design by manufacturer Alternative #4	Large computer with systems design by in-company personnel Alternative #5
Breakeven	No change	Vendor estimates positive	Yes	No. Probably take 5–6 years	Yes but may take 5 years
Turnaround time	OK ·	Cannot meet due to batch processing	Yes if located in company	Yes	Yes
Return on investment	No change	Positive due to clerical saving	Pays for itself	Can't estimate but probably negative	Positive. Best in long run
Initial cost	None	Low. Offset by clerical saving	Low	High. Bad strain on cash flow	Highest of all alternatives
Organizational impact Improved management	Poor. No improvement	Not good	Slow but long run effective	Good but takes time	Excellent. Improved management
Master plan	Nothing to advance	Does nothing	OK but requires more time	Takes too long	Excellent. Only way in long run
Time to implement	Immediate	Fast 6–12 months	Moderate 12–18 months	High 18–24 months	36–48 months for full implementation
Design costs	None	Included in total price	Low	Inclusive	Very high due to training and time involved
Operating costs	Same as existing	Included in total bid price	Moderate	High	Same as #4

Figure 13–8. Information summary

For more complex operations, the project or action plan can be supported by more detailed or sophisticated planning documents. Most of these have to do with planning or scheduling the action steps. In addition to the *work breakdown structure* (WBS), (see Figure 13–3), other techniques are available for scheduling, coordination, and control.

Scheduling

For the complex plan, it may be necessary or desirable to establish a network for scheduling the work breakdown structure. A network (PERT)[1] diagram provides a scheduling technique as well as an excellent visualization of the plan of action. It depicts the sequence of tasks as well as the relationship among them. Figure 13–9 demonstrates a diagram for illustrating the task relationships for the major categories of work shown in the work breakdown structure of Figure 13–3.

Coordination and Control

Plans must be coordinated and controlled, otherwise the objective will never be achieved or will be achieved at unnecessary cost of time delays.

Coordination is required both vertically and horizontally— vertically to the extent that each plan supports higher echelons and the upper-level plans of which it is a part. Horizontal coordination is needed to the extent that the plans of others (e.g., sales, engineering. personnel, finance, production) are integrated. Control is necessary to insure that performance, cost, and time targets are achieved.

If additional coordination and control are required, you can summarize the action steps onto a control timetable such as the one shown in Figure 13–10. Note that this control timetable also allows for obtaining appropriate approvals from outside the planner's own operational area, thus providing an additional measure of coordination.

---

[1] PERT or PERT/CPM stands for Program Evaluation Review Technique/Critical Path Method.

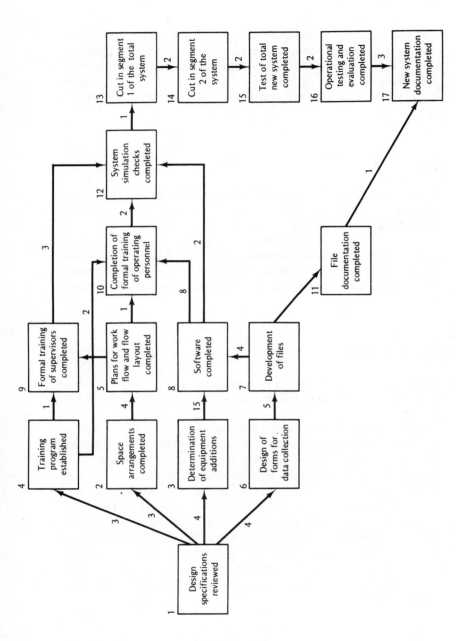

Figure 13–9. Network diagram

Objective: _____   Date _____

Action steps	Approval	Person responsible	Scheduled dates Planned start	Planned complete	Actual complete
1					
2					
3					
4					
5					
6					
7					
8					
9					
10					

Figure 13-10. Control timetable

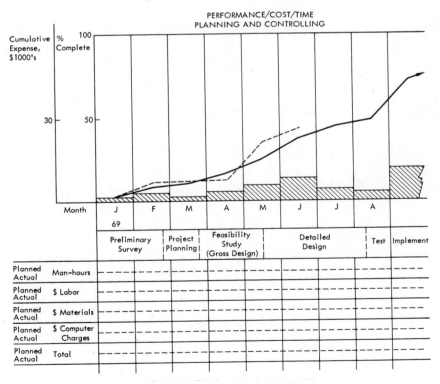

Figure 13–11. Integrated P/C/T Chart

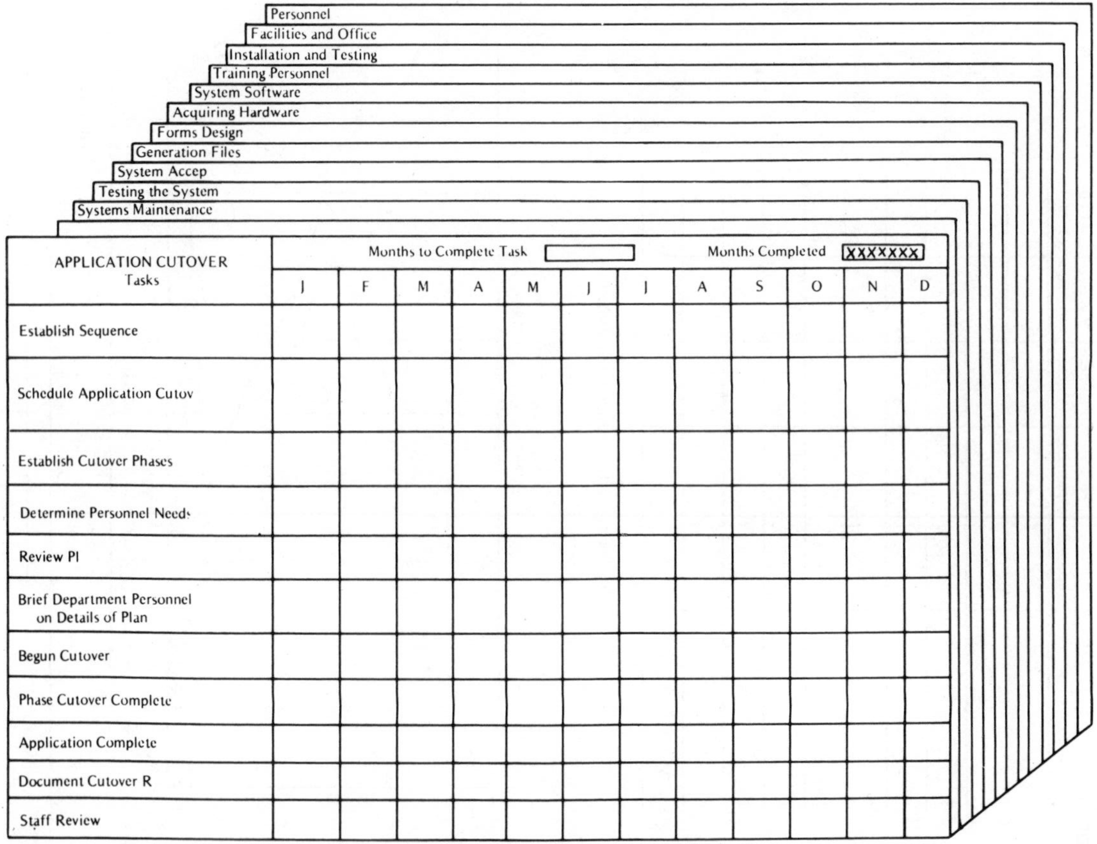

Personnel
Facilities and Office
Installation and Testing
Training Personnel
System Software
Acquiring Hardware
Forms Design
Generation Files
System Accep
Testing the System
Systems Maintenance

APPLICATION CUTOVER Tasks	Months to Complete Task						Months Completed					XXXXXX
	J	F	M	A	M	J	J	A	S	O	N	D
Establish Sequence												
Schedule Application Cutov												
Establish Cutover Phases												
Determine Personnel Needs												
Review Pl												
Brief Department Personnel on Details of Plan												
Begun Cutover												
Phase Cutover Complete												
Application Complete												
Document Cutover R												
Staff Review												

Figure 13–12. Milestone charts

Milestone Charts

For the more complex plan, the action may be coordinated and controlled by either an *Integrated Performance / Cost / Time Control Chart* (P/C/T Chart) or one or more *milestone* or Gannt chart. The P/C/T chart is illustrated in Figure 13–11 and the milestone charts in Figure 13–12. Both of these illustrate the Office Systems, Inc. case.

TIME MANAGEMENT

"Time is life. It is irreversible and irreplaceable. To waste your time is to waste your life."
— Alan Lakein, *Time-Management Consultant*

CHAPTER 14

"Remember that time is money," wrote Benjamin Franklin in his *Advice to a Young Tradesman* in 1748. This advice reflects what have always been the central concerns of the Western tradition; work and idleness. The American ethic demands that time not be wasted in idleness or nonproductive work.

When the Concorde supersonic plane began its twice-daily flights from Europe to the United States in 1976, the event capped a stream of time-saving technology that began in 1876 with the invention of the alarm clock. The working world hasn't been the same since. Saving time and running out of time have become two of the major concerns of the American worker.

Paradoxically, in our technological society, time becomes one of our scarcest commodities. Unlike the underdeveloped countries, we have a limited "supply" of time. The poorest societies are those in which individuals have the most time on their hands. The lack of concern for time in these societies is expressed in the widespread attitude of "mañana." Let's do it some time in the future. Contrast this with the United States, where the only manager who will admit to having sufficient time on the job is the manager who is unemployed.

Time remains the supervisor's scarcest resource. Unlike other resources, it can't be stored, put in the bank, or retrieved on demand. We can't stop the clock. Time moves on. It keeps on being used up no matter what we are doing or accomplishing. Our only hope for optimizing the use of time is to plan for it. This inexorable march reflects a paradox: no one has enough time—yet everyone has all there is. This paradox drives home the point that the problem is not lack of time. The problem is how we utilize the time we have.

The misuse and underutilization of time is a growing problem that results in part from the accelerating complexity of the manager's job. Most supervisors or managers frequently ask themselves, "Where did the time go?" or "How can I get more time to get my job done?" When they find themselves wishing for more of it, or wondering where it went, individual managers have a serious problem of time management. Long hours, firefighting, crisis management, frustration at working on unimportant matters, time-consuming interruptions by subordinates—all of these are evidence that they either can't solve problems or haven't the time to do so.

Alan Lakein, a consultant on time management, says that most people waste in excess of 50 percent of their time despite the fact that they give the impression of being perpetually busy. It is not known what percentage of the average manager's time is wasted, but it is a safe bet that it is a considerable amount.

NEEDED: A STRATEGY FOR TIME MANAGEMENT

What's the problem? We can plan and control other resources—why not time? The reason is that most people take a haphazard approach to managing their time. They try one technique or fad and drop it for a new one somewhat like the person who is always involved with the latest diet.

What is needed is a strategy, an organized approach to the problem. In the remainder of this chapter I will provide the outline for a strategy by identifying common time-wasters, suggesting solutions for overcoming them and recommending the framework for a personal time management plan.

TEN TOP TIME-WASTERS

A time-waster is anything that prevents you from achieving your work objectives. Since part of a time strategy is devoted to defeating time-wasters, it is important that each individual identify those that most often stand in the way of optimizing their time. Major time-wasters may vary for each manager, but generally the individual's problems can be traced to a combination of those discussed below. Although these top ten do not comprise an exhaustive list, you can relate most of them to your on-the-job situation.

People Interruptions

All of us have had the frequent experience of being interrupted by people. Our chain of thought is destroyed and valuable time is consumed. A return to the pre-interruption activity requires reorientation and occasionally abandonment of the task until a later time. Many of the visitors want to engage in unproductive socializing. Others involve minor service decisions or administrative trivia. Most involve subordinates who are "checking back" for instructions or getting clarification of a communication that is unclear.

Telephone Interruptions

This time-waster is near the top of everyone's list. The effect is the same as the people interruption. Despite the fact that the telephone is one of the greatest time-saving devices ever invented, it usually serves the opposite purpose. Most of us fail to ask, "Is this call necessary?" We make or receive the call anyway. We take incoming calls either because we don't want to offend the caller or we want to give the impression of being available. Many calls are not brought to a successful conclusion and require subsequent callbacks to provide or obtain additional information or to make a final decision. "Let me call you back on that" is a frequent termination of a telephone call.

Doing the Work of Subordinates

Many managers are running out of time while their subordinates are running out of work. This is because the boss either cannot "let go" or voluntarily or inadvertently agrees to take on the problems of a subordinate. Upon hearing the familiar greeting, "Boss, we've got a problem," the manager feels like a reply is necessary, even though he or she is rushed or lacks complete information. A common reply is, "Let me think about it and I will let you know later." What has happened in this familiar scene? The ball, formerly in the court of the subordinate, is now firmly in the court of the boss. The time of the boss is now being controlled by the subordinate rather than the other way around. The manager is doing the work of the subordinate rather than insisting that the subordinate submit recommendations, not problems.

Meetings

Too many meetings is not only a top time-waster but a sure sign of poor organization as well. When a manager spends one-quarter of his or her time in meetings, something is wrong. It means that decision and relations structures don't exist or aren't working. Even if meetings are justifiable, the human dynamics are so complex as to make them poor devices for getting any work done. This is especially true for the meeting that is poorly organized, that is allowed to drag on, and to which the participants come ill-prepared. Strange as it may sound, a significant percentage of meetings are held for the purpose of finding out whether there should be a meeting. The rule is to attend only important meetings and to go prepared. Reduce the number and make them more productive.

The Stacked Desk

The cluttered desk is a very common sight in today's corporate office. Unfortunately, many managers let their desk get piled high with papers because they believe it gives the impression that they are busy. People look in and say, "This person must really be busy." Other managers justify the clutter based on the argument that it represents a method of organizing and assigning priorities, putting their work into neat piles. While there may be some justification for this particular filing method, consider the disadvantages to the stacked desk: (a) It allows you to delay action indefinitely by building up a backlog of pending items; (b) it's hard to find the specific material required at any given time; (c) you lose control of your priorities and action items; (d) the omnipresent desk arrangement constantly takes your attention away from doing anything else; and (e) the discouraging sight of the desk each morning is anything but conducive to getting down to work.

The take-home briefcase is an adjunct. It is the portable cluttered desk. For many managers it becomes a security blanket. Others take home two briefcases in an effort to appear twice as important.

To some managers the briefcase becomes a fine tool of procrastination and time wasting. One survey estimated that 80 percent of managers take briefcases home at night but only 15 percent open them. These people need time management, not more time.

Firefighting

This is the principle known as the "tyranny of the urgent," frequently called the busy-busy syndrome. We engage in firefighting rather than fire prevention. Optimizing time requires that we distinguish between the *urgent* and the *important*. The urgent tasks, although not significant, call for instant action and tend to make us forget the important ones. We respond unwittingly to the endless pressures of the moment, the procedural requirements of the system and the administrative minutiae, never getting around to what really counts. I have made the point again and again that productivity requires a focus on results rather than activity. We need to think of doing the right thing rather than doing things right. To do otherwise is to permit firefighting to become our objective. The conclusion is that unless the urgent task is important, delegate it or put it on the back burner in favor of the important job.

Spending Too Much Time on Unimportant Tasks

This time-waster is similar to firefighting but different in that we fail to distinguish the important job from the unimportant. We don't assign priorities and hence do not allocate time to where it will do the most good. Even though our efforts may be efficient, they are not effective because they are directed to the wrong tasks, at the wrong time, or without the desired results. These activities are somewhat like impulse buying in the supermarket. If we allow our impulses and spur-of-the-moment decisions to rule, we run out of money and time before the real purpose of shopping is achieved. Effectiveness means doing the right job right.

Procrastination

Webster's Dictionary defines procrastination: "To put off doing something until a future time." Most of us exhibit this tendency at one time or another. With some of us, it's an occupational hazard.

To procrastinate is human. We postpone the unpleasant and this means doing first what we like to do rather than what we find to be difficult. Research has shown that action on 80 percent of the items in the typical manager's in basket could be completed without further delay upon first examination. Yet we usually will find a considerable backlog of action items in the *pending* basket or on a *stacked desk* because of the occupant's tendency to postpone the unpleasant. It is much easier to read the paper, take a coffee break, or socialize with a colleague.

Waiting for Others

Most of us spend entirely too much time waiting for other people; for the boss, for colleagues, for a secretary, for subordinates, for a customer. We wait for the boss to ask what to do rather than taking the initiative ourselves. We make periodic trips to the offices of colleagues in order to "coordinate" a decision and find them out of the office, on vacation, or unavailable. We wait for subordinates in order to "check this" or "follow up" on that—efforts that could have been avoided by simple planning and control. We wait for the secretary to find a file, place a call, address an envelope, or perform some other service that could be performed more quickly by ourselves. It seems that we are always waiting for others.

Lack of Objectives, Priorities, and Deadlines

This is the biggest time-waster of all and one that must be overcome if time is to be managed properly. There's an old saying in planning: "If you don't know where you're going, all roads lead there." By failing to establish objectives and plans, you are planning to fail. Activity becomes random and misdirected. Unless priorities are established you run the risk of firefighting and spending your time in efforts that are unrelated to the real objective of the job. Deadlines are necessary to insure that tasks are completed.

The establishment of objectives, priorities, and deadlines is what time management is all about.

TIME MANAGEMENT: SOLUTIONS

Ten Solutions

DELEGATE

STOP DOING SUBORDINATES' WORK

80/20 RULE

PRIORITIZE

PROGRAM IT

RUN ON TIME

UNPLEASANT THINGS FIRST

DO IT NOW

HIDEAWAY

MAINTAIN PERSPECTIVE

TEN SOLUTIONS FOR TIME-WASTERS

Ten basic approaches to the problem of avoiding time-wasters are discussed below. These are not techniques or gimmicks but fundamental approaches to the way you perform your job. Time management should become a philosophy, a way of managerial life.

Learn to Delegate

One well-known executive complained, "Ninety-five percent of the stuff on my desk is problems that others haven't solved." This comment reflects a classic difficulty of managers everywhere and yet, of all the solutions to time wasting and wheelspinning, delegation heads the list as an effective, immediately available means of gaining more time.

Notwithstanding the critical importance of delegating and the immediacy with which it can be implemented, managers find it psychologically difficult to practice it. Most failures occur not because the manager doesn't understand the benefits but because of inability or unwillingness to apply it in practice. The manager just doesn't want to "let go." Personal attitudes need to be changed to realize that delegation is an art. The art of delegation requires

- ☐ *Receptiveness* to other people's ideas.
- ☐ *Willingness* to let others make small mistakes as the price of personal development.
- ☐ *Willingness* to trust subordinates. They will repay this trust many times.
- ☐ *Willingness* to delegate by results expected.
- ☐ *Willingness* to let go and release the right to make decisions to subordinates.

Incidentally, for the typical manager, the most productive "delegatee" is usually the secretary. It's amazing how these paragons of efficiency can, if encouraged, perform a significant number of tasks that otherwise keep the boss involved in busy-busy work.

Stop Doing the Work of Subordinates

The effective manager insists that subordinates do their own work and solve their own problems. Before a manager can delegate and develop initiative in subordinates, he or she must give them an opportunity to display initiative. But they can't if the manager takes the opportunity away by performing the subordinate's job.

Some managers never recover from their first promotion to a supervisory job. Upon being promoted they find the new job somewhat more difficult and demanding than performing the technical tasks to which they are accustomed. They are familiar with the old job so they spend time at the technical aspects of the old job doing the work of the subordinate rather than the managerial tasks of the new job.

All managers are familiar with the greeting, "Boss, we've got a problem." Indeed, the behavior of most managers encourages their subordinates to buck pass the problem up the line. To the complaint of subordinates that "We've got a problem," he usually replies, "OK, send me a memo," or "Let's get together and talk about it," or "Let me know how I can help." In each case the manager has taken the problem from the subordinate. The subordinate is now *supervising the boss*. The manager wonders who is working for whom.

Instead of voluntarily or inadvertently accepting problems, managers should explain that they are willing to work jointly on a solution (by appointment) but the next move is up to the subordinate. They should explain to the subordinate: "If I accept your problem, then you no longer have one and I cannot help a person who hasn't got a problem."

Doing the work of others not only results in wheelspinning for you, it deprives them of the opportunity to grow by taking on tough tasks and learning how to perform them successfully.

Delegate! Give subordinates an assignment that is measured in terms of results. Give them the tools and the authority to do the job in their own way and get periodic feedback. This approach will allow you dig out from under *operating* work and do more *creative* work.

Identify What's Important: The 80/20 Rule

Surveys on how supervisors spend their time have shown that much of it is wasted on the unimportant, the trivia, the activities and procedures related to the system, rather than results. This reflects a human tendency to respond to the urgent (however unimportant) rather than take care of the important. Yet we can't focus on the important items unless they are identified.

There is an old rule of management called the "80/20 rule." It applies to almost anything we do. Eighty percent of sales are made by 20 percent of the salespeople; 80 percent of telephone calls are made by 20 percent of the callers; 80 percent of the TV time is devoted to watching 20 percent of the programs most popular with the family. And so on.

What the rule says is: *If all the things you need to do on the job are weighted according to importance, 80 percent of the results will come from only 20 percent of the items.*

The message is clear. Identify those few items (20 percent) that provide 80 percent of the importance of your job. Focus on them and not the many urgent distractions that don't yield results. Give them your attention and work on them first. Chances are you would do no real harm if you skip the remaining 80 percent of the items that give you 20 percent of your results.

Assign Priorities and Set Deadlines

Now that the 80/20 rule has helped you focus on the important part of the job, you are on your way to working smarter, not harder. The next step is to assign priorities to what needs to be done and set deadlines. Both short-run and longer-range tasks should be assigned priorities: A for the most important, B for less important, and C for the lowest priority. The A items demand your full attention. The chances are good that the B items can wait or be delegated to subordinates. The C items will frequently solve themselves or be forgotten if no action is taken. This is in accordance with the "principle of calculated neglect" which says that some problems will go away if left alone.

Unless you can establish criteria of your own (e.g., what the boss wants done), you might want to try these suggested criteria for assigning priorities to your work:

☐ Does it relate directly to my job objectives?

☐ What is the immediacy?

☐ Who has a claim on completion of the job?

☐ What is the nature of the work?

☐ Can it be combined with another job?

☐ Can it be delegated?

Deadlines for completion need to be set or the job will invariably involve a time overrun. Not only should deadlines be set but they must be realistic. Setting unrealistic deadlines gets us into the habit of ignoring them or constantly failing to meet them.

Program Recurring Operations and Decisions

One of the most overlooked opportunities for saving time is the potential for programming or routinization of simple or repetitive operations and decisions.

In one large company, well over 90 percent of the decisions that managers had to make over a five-year period were found to be "typical" and fell into a small number of categories. Despite the potential for programming these decisions, the majority of them either "went looking for a home" or were bucked up to a much higher level than was necessary.

We have achieved amazing productivity increases from automating mechanical operations, but we have hardly begun to apply the notion of automating or programming decisions and repetitive administrative operations. The challenge is to move the frontiers from the simple operation (payroll, account payable, inventory reporting) to the more complex. The more a repetitive operation can be procedurized, the more it can be accomplished by a clerk, or better yet, a computer.

The work of the manager can be classified as either routine or creative. Let's give ourselves more time for the creative job by programming the routine decisions and operations.

Run on Time

Benjamin Franklin's admonition that "time is money" was nowhere more evident than among the railroads of the nineteenth century. Indeed, the railroad gets the credit (or blame, depending on your view) for transforming time in America. The heart of the railway system was the timetable, the matrix of system cordination. Even a one minute delay would mean that one of two trains would be a mile away from a siding or a passing track when they were scheduled to pass. Time was exact. Everyone had to carry a fine timepiece that would not gain or lose more than 40 seconds in two weeks. Watches were inspected by a railroad watch inspector.

Have you noticed the odd times on a railroad or airline timetable— 10:03; 12:18; 6:37? These timetables contain two lessons. First, we must learn to block out our schedule in more precise time allocations. Avoid the tendency to assign 15-minute or 30-minute blocks just because these are round numbers. Of course, it goes without saying that we should adhere to the schedule or everyone else in the system (boss, subordinate, colleague, visitor, client) is off schedule owing to the "multiplier" effect of our own actions.

A second lesson from the timetable is that we should set "odd" times for appointments. Don't say, "I'll see you at 10 o'clock." This is interpreted as meaning anytime from 9:45 to 10:15. However, if you set the time at 10:05, who would dare be late or overstay the appointment time?

Do Unpleasant Things First

Einstein's theory says that time is relative. Two minutes sitting on a hot stove is relatively longer than the same two minutes spent in an activity that we enjoy. This theory explains why we do the pleasant things first.

Research has shown that the most successful sales representatives cultivate the habit of doing the unpleasant things. Once they become habit, they no longer are perceived as unpleasant.

Most of us begin the day by working on petty chores with the idea of working up to bigger projects as the day progresses. It never happens. The outboard motor catalogue or trade magazine becomes more interesting than the unpleasant items in the in basket. As the day moves on, things get worse instead of better as we realize that time is getting shorter and the priority "A" projects remain undone.

How much better it is to start with the difficult tasks. This not only has the advantage of directing efforts to where they count but we are building in a reward for having completed the important tasks. When the task is finished, we can give ourselves some time off or relax with the pleasant items of work.

Don't Procrastinate: Do It Now

Let's face it. Decision making is hard work. It gives us mental fatigue. We tend to put it off.

Most of us, having been pressed for a decision at home or on the job, have replied, "I'll let you know later," or "Check back with me on Thursday." The chances are good that you will be no smarter or have no better facts on Thursday than you do today. The shortest route between two points is a straight line, so don't take a detour. Do it now!

It isn't hard to rationalize delaying a decision. We need more detail. It should be referred to a committee. We need to look it up in a book. Some managers take refuge in the bottle or simply put on their hat and go home.

The conclusion: Do it now! Do it now and save the time of agonizing over not having made the decision. Moreover, if the decision is wrong, you have earned yourself extra healing time or time to correct the damage.

Have a Hideaway

A growing custom is the hideaway or the "quiet hour." Managers are discovering that the only way to avoid interruptions is to get away for a reasonable predetermined amount of time each day or week. This can be at home, at another "secret" office, or behind the locked doors of your own office. The idea is to avoid disturbances or interruptions by people or the telephone.

Some companies provide these "hideaway" offices either on or off the company premises. It is increasingly realized that an hour of concentrated, uninterrupted work can result in as much output as four or five hours of a normal workday.

Maintain Perspective

A manager must relate today's actions to tomorrow's goals, otherwise the future will be neglected in favor of today's crisis. Today's urgent activity may be tomorrow's "nothing."

The manager should constantly ask, "How does today's task relate to tomorrow's objective or the long run objectives of my job? If it doesn't relate, forget it or relegate it to the pile of priority "C" work.

TIME MANAGEMENT: STRATEGY

Identify Time-Wasters
Get a Plan
TIME DAIRY
TIME PLAN

IDENTIFY TIME-WASTERS

Before developing a plan for time management it is first necessary to analyze the use of your time; to find out where your time is going, whether you are spending it on high-priority activity, and the frequency and type of interruptions. For this purpose it is essential that some form of detailed time log or diary be kept for a minimum of eight to ten working days.

Figure 14–1 demonstrates a suggested format for keeping a time diary that will form the basis for further analysis. Each activity and interruption should be noted along with the time involved. It should be noted whether the activity was planned or whether it arose as a result of an interruption. This will allow an analysis of "planned vs. interruptions" and will permit a subsequent plan for interruption control. Priority of each activity can also be checked to see whether too much time is being spent on priority "B" or "C" type jobs. An analysis of the "involved with" column will tell you whether your activities are under your control or if they are initiated by other sources. If you find that you frequently work on tasks that are initiated by interruptions or the arrival of correspondence, or that you are spending most of your time with one or two people, you may have isolated one or more important time wasters.

At the bottom of the Daily Time Diary in Figure 14–1 is space for summarizing the major time-wasters for the day and for writing in a possible solution.

After analyzing eight or ten working days, a pattern of time wasting should emerge that will form the basis of a time management plan.

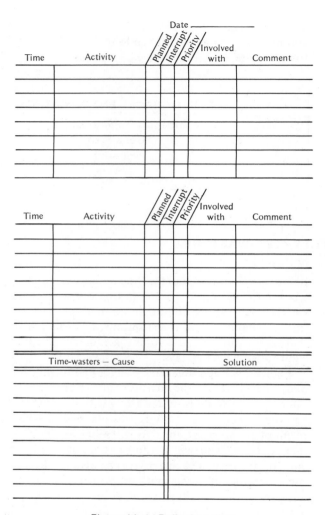

Figure 14-1. Daily time diary

TIME MANAGEMENT STRATEGY: A PLAN

The problem is never the lack of time—nobody is going to get more than what is available. The problem is putting time where it counts. This requires self-discipline that results in a plan.

The "principle of visibility" says that you can't remember what you can't see. Nor have you thought out a plan until you have written it out. Most of us are aware of these truisms so at various times we resolve to "get organized." We make a list of things to do. The trouble is that we rarely get around to completing the jobs on the list because we work on the easy items first and never get to the hard ones. Moreover, the list seems to grow longer and faster than we can complete the items. So we usually abandon the list or throw it away and start over.

In order for the "principle of visibility" to work for time management, we need a plan that relates to our job objectives, that sets priorities for the action involved, and that establishes deadlines for completion.

Following the time-waster analysis of Figure 14–1, we should now take a broad view of time by planning total time requirements for about a month ahead. Figure 14–2 is a suggested approach to accomplish this. The top part of this form provides the breakdown of what, in your opinion, constitutes an ideal work day. This will vary from day to day, of course, but the purpose here is to provide a

Figure 14–2. Daily/monthly time breakdown

Normal Activity
(Ideal work day)

Category	Percent of time	Amount of time

Monthly Time Plan

Major projects	Priority	Deadline	Amount of time allocated

Date _____

Objectives: (1) _____   (2) _____

(3) _____   (4) _____

Time	Project/Action	Priority deadline	Comment[1]

[1] This space can be used for further description of action items and periodic analysis of such comments as: Delegate to secretary, Get interdepartmental approval, Don't accept responsibility in the future, Consolidate with other jobs, and so on.

Figure 14–3. Daily time plan

general guide to productive daily activity and avoid slipping back into old time-wasting habits.

The bottom half of Figure 14–2 is designed to set out total time requirements for a month ahead.

After establishing the broad picture, you can now prepare a daily time plan that is based on objectives, priority of action, and deadlines. This daily plan can be maintained in a desk diary or other convenient format. Figure 14–3 is a suggested daily time plan. It not only provides for planning the action necessary to achieve results; it also permits a continuing analysis of time-wasters as well.

The best time to construct the daily time plan is the last 5 to 10 minutes of the work day preceding. This is the most knowledgeable time to plan your schedule for the following morning and to set your priorities for the forthcoming day.

TIME MANAGEMENT: CONCEPTS!

Some key concepts of time management are summarized below. Many of these have been discussed in this chapter. This summary will provide a convenient checkoff list or reminder for the manager who is serious about managing time.

Formulate *Alternatives*. Decisions can be reached more quickly and time saved if viable alternative courses of action can be developed in the early stage of the decision-making process.

Do an *Analysis*. The determination of significant time-wasters is necessary to form the basis of a time management plan. For this purpose it is desirable to analyze the existing use of time by means of some form of daily time diary.

Allocate Time for *Big Problems*. Major problems and decisions should be allocated sufficient blocks of time to bring the job to a successful conclusion. Interruptions should be avoided.

Be Brief. Economize on words in speaking and writing. It saves time and promotes better communication.

Say No. Managers who can't say no to the boss, to subordinates, to colleagues, will find themselves working for others more than for themselves.

Communicate. Lack of communication is a top time-waster. Learn to communicate on the basis of results expected.

Consolidate. Activities that are similar should be grouped for economy of handling. Group phone calls, letter writing, and discussions with the boss are examples.

Make *Deadlines*. These must be realistically set or we will form the habit of ignoring them.

Delegate. The first principle of time saving and good management. Overcome the reluctance to "let go."

Do It Now. Indecision and procrastination will not improve the quality of the decision or the effectiveness of the action.

Know the Difference between *Effectiveness* and *Efficiency*. Stop worrying about doing the job right (efficiency) and concentrate on doing the right thing (effectiveness).

Follow the *(80/20) Rule*. If all the things you need to do on the job are weighted according to importance, 80 percent of the results will come from only 20 percent of the items.

Practice *Exception Management*. Don't worry about the details of normal operations. Put your attention on the exception and design control reports to highlight the exception.

Provide *Feedback*. Periodic feedback on progress against planned results is necessary both for action planning and control and for the revision of plans as required.

Avoid *Firefighting*. Manage crises. Avoid firefighting and concentrate on fire prevention. Remember that the urgent activity is not usually the important activity.

Be Flexible. Some events are beyond your ability to forecast and plan so be prepared to be flexible in the scheduling and execution of your time.

Focus on Results. A basic tenet of the systems approach and management by results. Don't be a bureaucrat and get bogged down in activity without asking what results the activity is supposed to achieve.

Use *Foresight.* "An ounce of prevention is worth a pound of cure." Try to anticipate problems before they occur. This will save a lot of time in problem solving.

Do *Important Things First.* Work on the important results-producing activities first before the lower-priority jobs. Avoid the natural inclination to do the pleasant task and leave the unpleasant for later.

Control *Interruptions.* Interruptions are the number one time-waster. It is essential that we get control of them or they will control us.

Know the Principle of *Limited Response.* Sometimes called "the principle of calculated neglect." If items of minor importance are neglected, the need for activity concerning them frequently goes away.

Avoid Too Many *Meetings.* If one-fourth of your time is being spent in meetings you need to get organized. Avoid meetings unless they are important and prepare for those that you do attend.

Formulate *Objectives.* In order for time management to be meaningful it is essential that you understand and reconcile your own personal objectives, your job objectives, and the objectives of the organization.

Do *One Thing at a Time.* Concentrate your efforts on one thing at a time.

Cut *Paperwork.* Handle paperwork only once and generate as little as possible. Throw away nonessential papers as soon as you've read them. Cut the flow to your in basket.

Know *Parkinson's Law.* Work expands to fill the time available.

Set *Personal Goals.* Set goals and priorities in your personal life. Go after them.

Keep *Perspective.* Keep the perspective on your daily activities by asking how they support long-range objectives.

Utilize *Prime Time.* Find out when you do your best work and concentrate best. Take care of important matters during this time and less important matters outside of prime time when your efficiency is not as high.

Assign Priorities. Assign priorities to your jobs, otherwise you will find yourself working on the easy or the unimportant.

Do *Problem Analysis*. Don't waste a lot of time attacking the symptom of a problem. Go after the cause.

Program. Routinize or procedurize repetitive operations and decisions.

Cut Down on *Reports*. Eliminate the unused and the unnecessary.

Run on Time. Make a timetable and stick to it. Make appointments at odd times to emphasize the need for adhering to a schedule.

Delegate to Your *Secretary*. Delegate to your secretary, probably your number-one time-saver.

Form a *Team*. Form your subordinates into a team with specific goals. Allow them the freedom of problem solving and method improvement. This will get a lot more done in a lot less time.

Make *Time Estimates*. Impose accurate time estimates on jobs and adhere to them. Otherwise procrastination and indecision will result.

Don't Shirk *Unpleasant Tasks*. Do them first or you will never get around to them. Make a habit of doing the unpleasant. Work on the difficult jobs during prime time.

Maintain a *Visible Time Plan*. We forget what we can't see. Make your time plan visible. If you haven't written it out, you haven't thought it out.

Cut *Waiting Time*. Cut down on the amount of time you spend waiting on others. If unavoidable, put the waiting time to use.

Write Less. Use phone calls or memos rather than letters. Reply to letters with a handwritten note on the original.

MANAGING THE PRODUCTIVITY IMPROVEMENT PROGRAM

"Managers have to manage separately the productivity of all four key resources: capital, crucial physical resources, time, and knowledge. But what matters in the end is the total, overall productivity of a specific institution in using its resources."

—Peter Drucker

The Strategic Planning Institute of Cambridge, Massachusetts, after extensive research on productivity and investment, concluded: "We seem to have developed a serious problem in the way we go about trying to improve productivity. We concentrate too much on expensive plant and equipment, and not nearly enough on reducing the labor content of value added. Apparently, we are increasingly using capital equipment to cover up the bad habits of labor and management."

As we suggested in earlier chapters, the answer to improved productivity lies in *better management*. We can put it to work immediately at no cost and the potential payoff is enormous. But productivity through better management needs to be institutionalized—made a way of organizational life.

There is no quick or magic solution to instant success in improving productivity or installing a program. It takes time, and *good management.* There is a right way and a wrong way to undertake this opportunity. The wrong way is to approach it as just another special program. Every supervisor is familiar with ad hoc, short-lived programs, such as cost reduction, EEO, health and safety, preventive maintenance, value analysis, and so on. These programs are usually viewed as an intrusion upon an individual's time and a diversion from the primary responsibilities of the job.

Productivity is not a special program. There is no "quick and easy" route to achieving ongoing success. It involves a managerial way of life and as a substantial potential resource it has to be managed. It requires *preparation, planning, organization, and control.*

MANAGING THE PROGRAM: APPRAISAL

Are You Ready?
Problems and Opportunities
SURVEY PHASE
EVALUATION PHASE

The first step in undertaking a productivity improvement program is to conduct an appraisal of where you are, where you want to go, and how you plan to get there. The objective is to identify opportunities and problems within the organizational environment and to lay the groundwork for action planning to follow. It could be termed "strategic productivity planning." More specifically, the appraisal process surveys and evaluates both *operating* and *management* systems for the purpose of identifying the potential for improving productivity and implementing a program.

IS YOUR COMPANY READY FOR PRODUCTIVITY?

Two questions arise: "Are you sure you want to increase productivity?" and "Are you ready to start a program?"

Managers will frequently reply "yes" to the first question without realizing what is involved. They pay lip service to the notion but are unwilling to spend the necessary time. They believe that productivity involves a package of techniques that can easily be put in place. This, of course, is not the case. *Productivity means change.* New methods and systems may be required, an appraisal of current practices is needed, and, most of all, a reorientation of beliefs about relationships with people may be necessary. The major dimension is the human-resource environment and philosophy—the values held by top management.

Regarding the second question, "Are you ready to start a program?" a certain managerial environment should exist, or be established, before the chances of success can be estimated as good. The American Productivity Center in Houston, Texas lists eight thought-provoking questions that should be answered as an indication of whether or not you need preliminary groundwork to ensure that your program has the best chance of being successful. These are:

☐ Are management/employee/union relations in the company such that these parties would not view negatively an expressed desire to tackle head-on the pressing issue of productivity improvement?

Comment: Confidence is needed for everyone to give the program a try.

☐ Does the company have a positive rating on working conditions, pay levels, company personnel policy and administration, and job security?

Comment: If these ingredients are out of line, the climate might not be right to begin.

☐ Is top management willing to share with employees at all levels the economic benefits that can be derived from improvements in productivity?

Comment: Unwillingness to share benefits reduces credibility and increases the feeling of exploitation on the part of employees.

☐ Is the company's accounting system "healthy" and flexible enough to accept changes required to effectively portray productivity data?

Comment: Some integration between productivity measurement and accounting system may be desirable.

☐ Is top management willing to listen to the employees?

Comment: Impetus for the program comes from the top down, but most improvement ideas will come from the bottom up.

☐ Is the technology employed by the company flexible so that improvements in the organization of work can be made?

Comment: Inflexible technology or production systems may reduce the potential for productivity improvement.

☐ Does top management believe that the company's performance depends substantially on the efforts of its human resources?

Comment: Only people can get you increased productivity.

◻ Is the company serious about improving its economic performance?

Comment: If the company is content with its progress or if "managerial menopause" has set in, forget it.

APPRAISAL: IDENTIFYING PROBLEMS AND OPPORTUNITIES[1]

The approach to an organization productivity appraisal is not too different from that involved in a traditional management audit. This is to be expected, because productivity improvement is really a function of how well the management process is performed.

The objective for appraisal is to *survey* and *evaluate* both operating and management systems in order to identify areas, techniques, and plans for improvement.

The Survey Phase

In the *survey* phase of an appraisal, the systems are reviewed to identify existing practices in order to later seek out unproductive or improper methods. The hundreds of items that could be surveyed depend upon the nature of the organization and the scope of the appraisal. Some factors that might cause trouble are shown in Table 15–1. Although the factors listed there were developed for a research and development organization, the same list would be appropriate for any type of company or operation.

The range of *operating systems* that might be included in the survey are as follows:

Operating Systems	Support Systems	Administrative Systems
Sales	Personnel	General Accounting
Manufacturing	Design	Data Processing
Purchasing	Quality Control	Production Control
Shipping	Maintenance	Marketing Services
Warehousing	Plant Engineering	Inventory Control
etc.	etc.	etc.

[1] A more detailed approach to appraisal has been prepared by the American Productivity Center in Houston. That organization has prepared a comprehensive manual for this purpose.

TABLE 15–1. Twenty-five Factors Most Likely To Cause Serious Counter-Productivity Within R&D Organizations

1. Ineffective planning, direction, and control

2. Overinflated organization structures

3. Overstaffing

4. Insufficient management attention to productivity, and to the identification and elimination of counter-productive factors within the organization

5. Poor internal communication

6. Inadequate technology exchange

7. Insufficient or ineffective investment in independent research and development (IR&D) efforts

8. Poor psychological work environment

9. Lack of people orientation in management—insufficient attention to employee motivation

10. Poor employment practices

11. Ineffective structuring of assignments

12. Lack of effective performance appraisal and feedback

13. Insufficient attention to low producers

14. Technological obsolescence

15. Ineffective reward systems which inadequately correlate individual productivity and compensation

16. Lack of equitable parallel managerial and technical promotion ladders

17. Lack of equity in operations

18. Ineffective customer interface

19. Ineffective engineering/production interface

20. Ineffective subcontractor/supplier interface and control

21. Operational overcomplexity—constrictive procedures and red tape.

22. Excessive organizational politics and gamesmanship

23. Excessive provincialism

24. Ineffective management development

25. Inadequate investment in and lack of proper maintenance of capital facilities

Source: Hughes Aircraft Company, *R&D Productivity*, 1978

Management systems might include an inventory of good and bad management practices and productivity improvement techniques in the following illustrative areas:

Planning	Organization	Control
Strategic planning (including major objectives and policies)	Structure, responsibility, and resources	Accounting system and reports
	Human-resource organization & records	Productivity measures
The planning system (developmental, operational, financial, functional, etc.)	Extra layers of organization and overlapping duties.	Performance measurement analysis
		Project & program control
etc.	Management values	
	Employee relations climate	etc.
	Productivity incentives	
	Training and development	
	etc.	

As a part of the survey phase, the appraisal might include an *attitude survey*. Since productivity is the result of the behavior of people and this behavior is largely a result of attitudes, the best way to change behavior is to change attitudes. This cannot be done unless existing attitudes are determined. Opinion and supposition are not dependable means for making this determination. We tend to perceive attitudes as we would like them to be or present glowing reports because to do otherwise might reflect on our competency. Surveys also represent a report card for management and tells it how well or poorly it's doing its job in the eyes of the employees.

Evaluation Phase

The *evaluation* phase of a productivity appraisal program attempts to evaluate the unproductive methods and techniques and the performance of units, departments, and individuals for the purpose of identifying opportunities for improvement. Wherever possible, productivity measures should be used for that purpose. These measures may be macro (companywide) or micro (functional or departmental). Figure 15-1 illustrates one approach to documenting and evaluating these measures.

The evaluation will provide the basis upon which company, unit, and departmental action plans will subsequently be developed. It will also provide the vehicle for participation, communications, and implementation.

MANAGING THE PROGRAM: SYSTEMS

Planning
Organizing
Controlling

To repeat what was said earlier, managing a productivity improvement program is no different than managing any other program, function, or activity. It requires that *objectives* be set, *plans* developed, and *organization* structured and progress *controlled*. However, the management of productivity cannot be applied like a Band-aid over an existing management system that has serious shortcomings. If good plans and controls do not exist within the framework of a good organizational structure, and if all the other manifestations of good organization and management are not present, then a productivity improvement system becomes a crutch to overcome bad practice. With good management systems, we can *plan, organize,* and *control* a productivity improvement program.

PLANNING

Planning is the most basic of managerial functions because it involves the determination of organizational strategies, objectives, and the means to achieve them. It is no different in planning for productivity. Because major objectives, of which productivity is one, are a part of company strategy, it follows that productivity should become a part of organizational strategy and objectives in support of it should be developed.

Hershey Foods, of Hershey, Pennsylvania, is among the growing number of companies that conduct comprehensive and continuing strategic planning. Among the major considerations resulting from

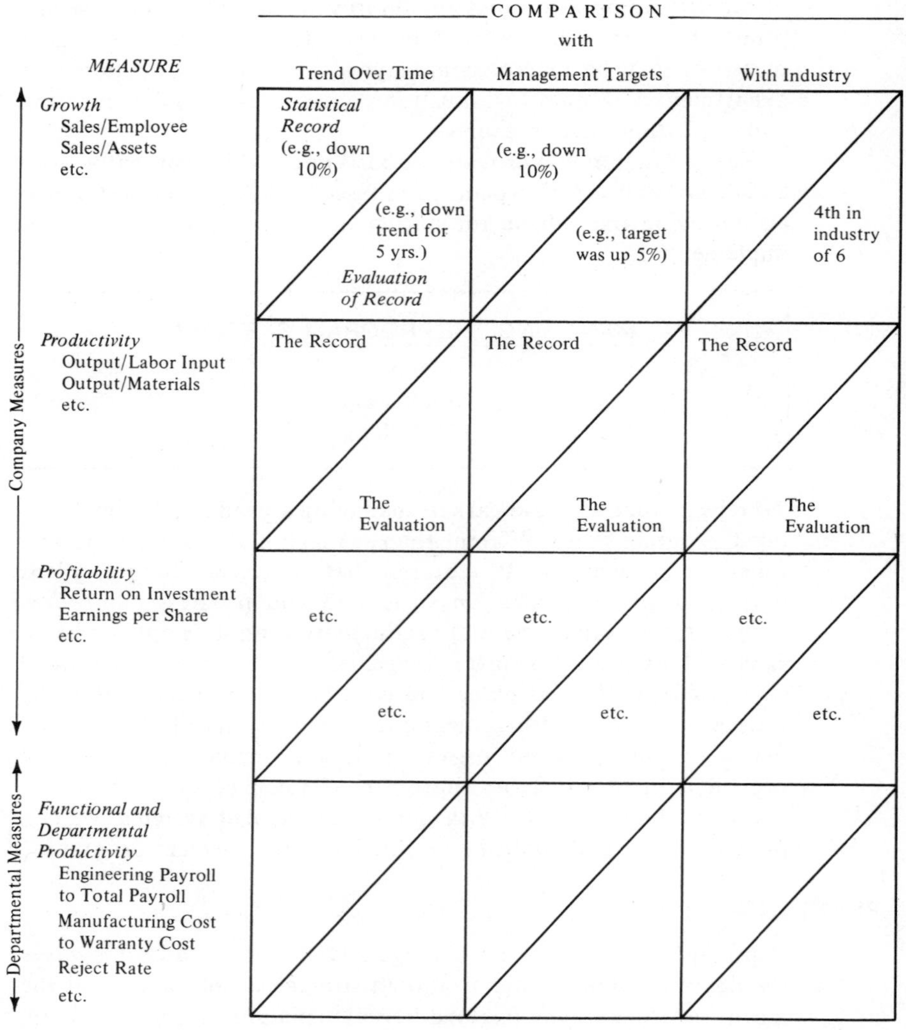

MEASURE	Trend Over Time	Management Targets	With Industry
Growth Sales/Employee Sales/Assets etc.	*Statistical Record* (e.g., down 10%) (e.g., down trend for 5 yrs.) *Evaluation of Record*	(e.g., down 10%) (e.g., target was up 5%)	4th in industry of 6
Productivity Output/Labor Input Output/Materials etc.	The Record The Evaluation	The Record The Evaluation	The Record The Evaluation
Profitability Return on Investment Earnings per Share etc.	etc. etc.	etc. etc.	etc. etc.
Functional and Departmental Productivity Engineering Payroll to Total Payroll Manufacturing Cost to Warranty Cost Reject Rate etc.			

Company Measures

Departmental Measures

Figure 15–1. Evaluation of past productivity performance

this process at Hershey are objectives and follow-up programs related to productivity.

The ultimate objective, of course, is to make human, physical, and financial resources more productive. A variety of subgoals could be developed in support of this objective. For example:

☐ Develop, disseminate, and implement the use of productivity improvement techniques.

☐ Establish an information base to support the program.

☐ Conduct a management audit and appraisal to determine readiness for a productivity program.

☐ Originate plans to bring awareness of productivity throughout the organization.

☐ Establishment a measurement system.

☐ Install a work design and quality of worklife program.

The question is frequently asked: "Should we develop a separate or a parallel planning and control system for productivity or integrate it into the existing managerial, financial, or operating systems?" The answer is that the existing systems should be used or modified where appropriate. You will recall the previous caution about the shortcomings of financial ratios and accounting systems that contain data that include the effects of inflation, tax depreciation, and arbitrary fixed-cost allocations—information unrelated to the productive process under study. These may be entirely appropriate for some purposes (e.g., total factor productivity when deflated) but not for others where absolute or unit measures are more important than financial ones.

Whatever management system is used or developed, it should be integrated with *operational* and *business* plans. In this way responsible people are required to "buy in" on operational improvements and productivity becomes an integral part of business planning.

The linear organization chart described in Chapter 7 can be used as a tool for organizing, recording, and tracking objectives. The plans in support of these objectives can be developed along the lines of the action plans contained in Chapter 13, Chapter 16, or in the traditional approach to project work breakdown structure.

Organizing

Productivity improvement isn't just going to happen. It needs to be *organized*. This implies a program structure, assignment of tasks and responsibilities, and involvement of people.

In a multidivisional company or one with several profit centers, the organization structure might appear conceptually as shown in Figure 15–2. The makeup and suggested duties of the structure might appear thus:

Title	*Duties*
Chief Executive Officer and Top Management	Gives full and active support to the program. The CEO's support is critical for initiating and follow-up. The executive committee and other top management must stand behind the efforts, demand progress reports, and recognize success when it occurs.
Steering Committee	Comprised of a cross-section of line and staff top executives, the committee will guide the implementation of the program after they determine major goals, policies, and procedures. They are the "board of directors" for the program. Targets should be determined for all major sectors of the organization and records kept on progress. Individual committee members may head teams for solving problems in specific areas. The committee also serves as a forum for exchanging ideas and monitoring company policy.
Productivity Manager or Coordinator or Administrator	Reports to steering committee and is the primary individual concerned with implementing and monitoring the program. Coordinates all activities and prepares reports on progress. Audits, monitors, and evaluates all programs. Communicates with unit/division/profit center managers on productivity questions. Acts as consultant, trainer, researcher, and disseminator of materials and ideas.
Productivity Council	The council is comprised of one representative (productivity manager, coordinator, administrator) from each operating division or unit having a separate program. The chairperson is the company productivity manager or coordinator. Each council member

has the same duties within his or her division or unit that the productivity coordinator has for the entire company. In addition to the duties of the individual members, the council develops and disseminates good ideas, goals, plans, programs, and practices to promote productivity improvement. Additionally, members serve as the recommending and monitoring group for company and division practices.

The Union-Management Committee

It is unlikely that a productivity improvement effort will be successful without union involvement. Since improvement will eventually involve these employees it makes sense to draw them into the effort in the early stages.

Figure 15–2. The productivity improvement organization

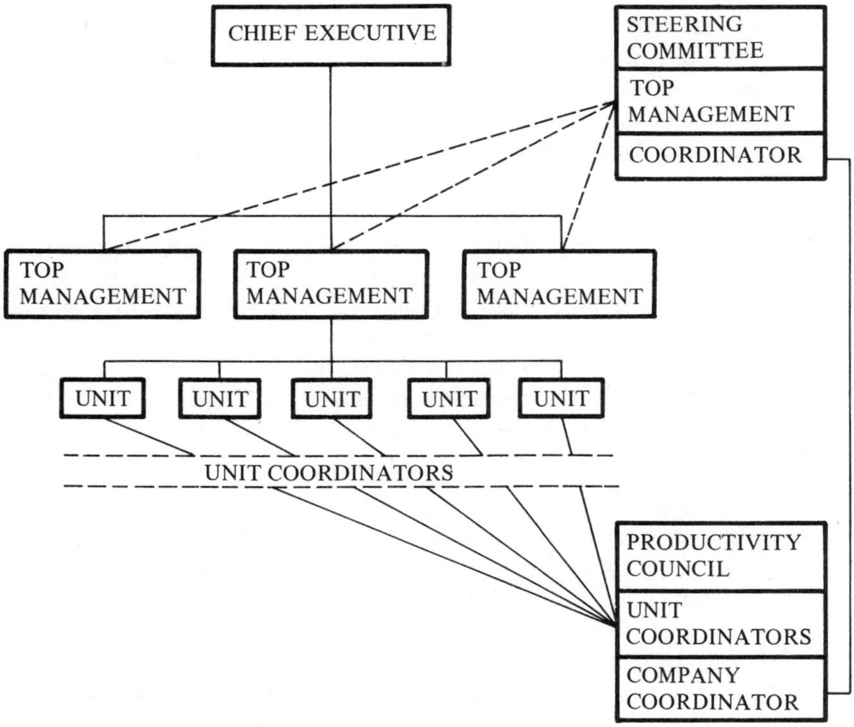

Many managers are reluctant, even fearful, of getting the union involved but are hard-put to give one good reason why it shouldn't happen. Labor can contribute important know-how, innovation, and ingenuity in such areas as increasing output, bringing about gains in preventative maintenance, reducing waste, increasing cost awareness, and improving the several ways to make the human resource more effective.

The *Joint Labor-Management Committee* is one vehicle to achieving more involvement. Such committees can interface with the company organizational components described above. Informational meetings of 25 to 50 people can be held and both the company top operating executive and the union president should address the committees on the urgency for increasing productivity and service. The committees can also function as recruiting reservoir from which Productivity Improvement Teams (PIT) or quality circles (QCs) can be organized.

CONTROL

Productivity, as is the case with other programs, must be controlled. The control process consists of these steps: (1) set standards; (2) report on progress; and (3) correct deviations.

Where planning is integrated with controls, the goals or standards are established during the planning process. If, for example, objectives or measures are established for total factor, partial factor, and departmental productivity, these measures become the standard against which feedback is obtained on performance. Where programs and/or measures are not integrated into existing reporting systems, some provision is needed to report on that progress. If new systems are designed—*keep them simple! Keep them simple!*

Goals and measures established by individuals, teams, or departments can be set and tracked at the workplace. The results should be displayed so that involved persons can watch progress and correct any deviations from *results expected.*

Westinghouse Electric Corporation has initiated a major corporate-wide productivity program, strongly supported by senior management, and designed to enlist the participation and support of company personnel at all levels. A corporate productivity committee is made up of key executives in the operating companies. Productivity improvement plans have been made a formal part of the strategic planning and business planning processes. The chairperson of the productivity committee says: "Westinghouse has established productivity improvement as a critical objective for all business units. As part of our near-term productivity improvement effort, we plan to concentrate attention on improving communications and people management."

```
┌─────────────────────────────────────────────────────┐
│                                                       │
│          MANAGING THE PROGRAM: AWARENESS              │
│          ─────────────────────────────────           │
│             The Message of Productivity               │
│                 Getting Organized                     │
│               Communication Media                     │
│                                                       │
└─────────────────────────────────────────────────────┘
```

Achieving optimum productivity improvement is not just a matter for top management alone. It is an "all-hands" evolution and requires the participation of people at all levels. In order to achieve this participation, organizations need to make employees and managers aware of the importance of productivity and the need for involvement.

As I have already mentioned, productivity is frequently perceived by management simply as cost-cutting or across-the-board reductions and by employees as speed-up, layoffs, and time studies. Others think that it is only applicable on the shop floor or in manufacturing industries. All these notions are, of course, wrong. But we need an approach to bring *awareness* to both management and labor about the importance of productivity and the benefits it can bring. *Awareness* is the first step in achieving *participation* and *commitment*. Employees want to know what's going on in their company and they can't very well help the improvement program if they don't know or don't understand what's going on.

Awareness is simply a matter of communications: originating the appropriate message in terms the recipient can understand; getting organized; and choosing the correct media and programs to complete the process. Common sense and the experience of others indicate that an awareness program can be designed by selecting the appropriate action from these:

☐ The message of productivity

☐ Getting organized

☐ Communication media: meetings

☐ Communication media: printed

☐ Programs

☐ Training

THE MESSAGE OF PRODUCTIVITY

Gaining acceptance of productivity improvement is largely a matter of understanding its importance to the national economy, to the viability of the company, and to the future job security and style of living of the individual. Most people will accept the need for productivity if the argument, "sales pitch," or message is phrased in terms that demonstrate how their needs may be met. Some reasons to answer the question "Why productivity?" are the following:

NATIONAL

☐ Maintain the American economic system at a level that improves or even sustains our current standard of living.

☐ Ensure the survival of the private enterprise system.

☐ Provide a lasting solution to inflation and unemployment.

COMPANY

☐ Strengthen our competitive position in domestic and world markets.

☐ Generate funds for capital investment and expansion.

☐ Meet the pressures of rising costs.

☐ Enhance customer satisfaction.

☐ Improve our competitive edge.

☐ Make higher return on investment.

☐ Provide more job and advancement opportunities.

INDIVIDUAL

☐ Reduce waste and conserve resources.

☐ Maintain job security.

☐ Increase leisure time.

☐ Improve job satisfaction and working conditions.

☐ Improve communications by means of worker involvement.

☐ Maintain wages at fair levels in real terms.

Getting Organized

In this chapter I have described the typical or the ideal organization structure for a productivity improvement program. The mere act or process of organizing will bring substantial attention to the topic.

People will want to know "What's happening upstairs?" To avoid rumors and irresponsible statements, it is advisable to begin the "Why productivity?" message simultaneously with a number of related organizational actions. These might include the following:

☐ Establish *labor-management committee* to achieve endorsement and commitment from the union.

☐ Make productivity improvement an integral part of the regular organization *management process*. Responsibility for improvement should follow the line organization from top management to the first-line supervisors.

☐ Establish a *system for measuring, evaluating, and reporting results*. This action not only sets up the method for setting goals and objectives but evaluates performance and improvement efforts.

☐ Integrate with *executive compensation*. Nothing will get greater attention and participation.

☐ Get *level-to-level commitment* through the organization structure from top to bottom. At the top is the Steering Committee and Productivity Council. At the front-line level get commitment from Productivity Improvement Teams (PITs), quality circles (QCs), task forces, and other groups that are organized for productivity.

COMMUNICATIONS MEDIA

Meetings

In addition to the meetings conducted by groups specifically organized for the purpose of productivity improvement (e.g., Council, PITs, QCs), the topic can be included on the agenda of a wide variety of other regular company meetings. Conferences, discussion programs, round-tables, and association meetings provide a sample of opportunities to raise the topic.

Don't overlook *customers and suppliers*. These two groups are part of the effort and can lend valuable assistance when they are part of the "team."

Special Media Vehicles

Most companies have a number of standard vehicles for communicating to a variety of audiences. These range from annual reports to bulletin boards and generally are not adequate to bring awareness to a program as important as productivity improvement. Although these standard communciations channels can and should be used to promote the idea, consideration should be given to designing *special* media vehicles for this special purpose. Consider these:

☐ Employee *attitudinal surveys* to determine receptivity to and misunderstandings about productivity. Such surveys can also serve the additional purposes of indicating training needs, promoting involvement, and serving the purpose for follow-up action.

☐ *Brochures and newsletters* help to keep interest alive and bring understanding and awareness. These media can include such items as publicity and photographs of team or quality-circle improvement efforts and achievements, rewards and recognition, industry news, and a variety of information articles, cases, and techniques.

☐ *External media* such as local newspapers, trade journals, and association magazines give publicity to the company and its people and promote a feeling of pride in achievement.

☐ *Videotapes* are being produced by some companies. These tapes can serve the dual purpose of providing awareness and training. The content can range from informative to substantive; uses can range from introductory to basic training in skills related to teams and individuals.

☐ The *personal letter* from the top operating officer to the employees at their homes can be effective. It can give the reasons for the effort ("Why productivity?") and include a rundown of company actions. The letter can help to allay the fears of employees concerning job security. It might also include a few words from the union president, reiterating a stand for collective bargaining and productivity.

☐ In addition to the awareness effort itself, supplementary and/or related *programs* can serve the additional purpose of promoting awareness. A good title for such an approach could be "The Productivity Incentive Program." It could be both for individuals and teams or circles. This effort is broader in scope than the traditional "cost-reduction" program and incentives could include such actions as:

Recognition of each incentive submission with gift certificate
Monthly or quarterly luncheons with plant management for functional winners
Publication of winners by function in newsletter or digest
Publicity photographs of winners posted on announcement boards

☐ *Training* is perhaps the best way to bring awareness of productivity.

It not only contains the essential messages of "Why productivity?" but it serves the additional purpose of *developing productivity improvement skills.* Some effort at training and development is almost essential. In addition to training that is developed by in-company resources, there are many different external sources such as seminars and consultants.

MANAGING THE PROGRAM: TRAINING

Technical Skills
Productivity Improvement Skills

PROBLEM ANALYSIS

DECISION MAKING

WORK ANALYSIS TOOLS

Supervisory Skills: Management Process
Supervisory Skills: People Skills

Training is the key to everything. To make any new idea, program, or system work, managers and first-line supervisors have to be trained in order to become part of the program. In most cases they were selected for *technical,* not *supervisory,* skills and in very few cases have they been trained in those topics and skills related to productivity improvement. Because middle-management people and supervisors are keys to implementing the plan, their training and development is crucial.

It is frequently said that productivity improvement is achieved by the practice of good management principles; this is true. What are good management principles, techniques, and skills? I believe these can be categorized as follows:

☐ *Technical knowledge and skills.* These comprise the functional knowledge and work skills that are peculiar to a particular job, such as computer programming, accounting, production control, test, assembly, and so on. These many technical areas, in turn, vary with the individual company and the industries within which they operate.

☐ *Knowledge and skills peculiar to productivity improvement.* Every individual, in trying to improve productivity on his or her job or in his/her team or group, needs exposure to and practice in the basic methods of analyzing work and discovering opportunities for improvement. Following the establishment of objectives (results expected), problem definition and analysis can be undertaken. As an essential part of developing problem analysis and identifying improvement opportunities, skills development in the *tools* of work analysis (e.g., work simplification, asset productivity, standards, value analysis, scheduling, etc.) is necessary. Only then can *decision making and action planning* provide the essential disciplines for documenting and implementing improvements. It isn't going to happen unless the effort ultimately results in an individual action plan. That in turn cannot be developed without the logical reasoning process that precedes it.

☐ *Supervisory drills in practicing the management process.* In the case of supervisors and managers, it is important to learn the wide differences between technical knowledge and ability on the one hand and managerial or supervisory ability on the other. An exposure to the basic principles of management (plan, organize, staff, control, communicate, etc.) is highly desirable to those who use the management process to improve operations.

☐ *People skills.* Nothing gets done except by and through people, and it is the specific and essential role of the supervisor to develop, lead, and communicate with people for the purpose of greater productivity and job satisfaction.

TRAINING
Technical vs. Supervisory Skills
A Training Program

TECHNICAL VS SUPERVISORY SKILLS

Technical skills comprise a special problem, owing to the extremely large number of topics and the techniques and body of knowledge surrounding each. The magnitude of the scope of technical training can be appreciated by considering that the Labor Department's *Dictionary of Occupational Titles*, running more than 1,300 pages, codifies more than 20,000 job definitions. A sampling of "techniques" that might be offered in the production-oriented function alone gives some idea of the potential scope of a training program:

Function	Work Skills	Work Techniques	Resources	Management Techniques
Receiving	Welding	Standards	Personnel	PERT-CPM
Material Flow	Cutting	Methods	Equipment	Forecasting
Production Control	Painting	Flowcharting	Materials	Project Management
Shipping	Assembly	Scheduling	Tools	Records Management
Maintenance	Test	Work Measurement	Space	Management Information Systems (MIS)
etc.		Value Analysis	etc.	etc.
		etc.		

The purpose of elaborating on "technical" versus supervisory skills is not to suggest that this type of training is not needed. Rather, I am suggesting that the scope of this book does not permit even a cursory treatment. Moreover, the techniques involved are too limited in application to be appropriate for a general training/development program for productivity improvement. I do, however, include a chapter (11) on the *tools* of work analysis that are common to all companies and functions.

A SUGGESTED TRAINING/DEVELOPMENT PROGRAM

Figure 15-3 provides the framework and topical *flow* for a program that I have found very successful with hundreds of middle-level managers and supervisors. The approach is summarized as follows:

OBJECTIVE: *Participants achieve improved productivity as both individuals and team members through the application of better knowledge and skill.*

ACHIEVED BY: *Awareness of importance of productivity and the commitment for individual improvement by the application of new knowledge and skills.*

The output of the training program is the development and implementation of an individual and/or a team ACTION PLAN for achieving a specific productivity improvement (result expected).

TRAINING METHOD: *(1) Presentation of principle, technique, or skill*
(2) Reinforcement by individual and group discussion of illustrative cases or incidents
(3) Development and practice of applied skill by individual and group application to the job situation

Table 15-2 illustrates a session-by-session summary of a suggested program. Individual training directors, facilitators, productivity coordinators, and others concerned with training and development will wish to modify the outline to meet specific needs of the company or to include one or more "techniques" as appropriate. Sessions generally run for four hours. Homework (cases, outside readings, projects, etc.) can be assigned as desired. Textual material may include this book, company materials, selected readings, or a combination of these sources. All necessary textual material is contained in appropriate chapters of this book.

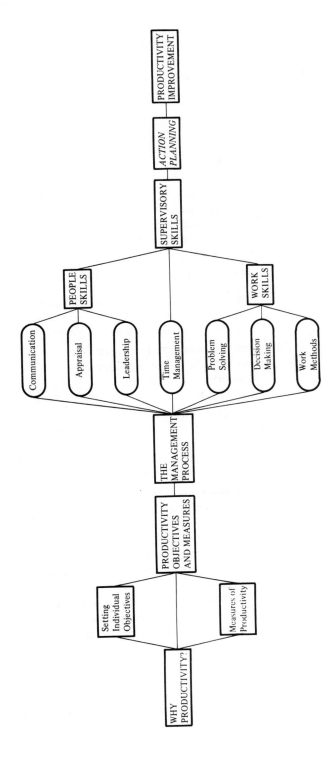

Figure 15–3. The framework for productivity training and development

TABLE 15–2. Outline of A Suggested Training/Development Program

	Outline

Session	Topic

1. (a) *Introduction to Productivity*
   Why productivity?
   The decline of productivity in the U.S.
   Why the decline?
   Why have a productivity improvement program?
   The bottom-line leverage
   The productivity concept: $\dfrac{\text{Output}}{\text{Input}}$
   Objective: (1) Develop argument for a productivity program.
   (2) Demonstrate the bottom-line leverage in the company and in your operation.

1. (b) *Improving Productivity in Your Job*
   Five ways to increase productivity
   Measuring productivity
   Setting team and department objectives
   Setting individual objectives
   Objective: (1) List five ways to improve productivity in your job.
   (2) Establish a specific individual and/or team objective for productivity improvement.

2. *People and Productivity*
   Principles of motivation
   Motivation and productivity
   Job Satisfaction vs. job development
   The quality of work life
   Motivation through results management
   Productivity Improvement Teams (PIT)
   MBO: The approach and the practice
   Objective: (1) Distinguish between motivating and hygiene actions. Identify actions leading to productivity.
   (2) Demonstrate how job-development principles lead to motivation in your job and group. Show how you can develop the job of a subordinate.
   (3) Organize a Productivity Improvement Team (PIT).

Session	Topic

(4) Integrate productivity and MBO.

3.   ***Supervisory Skills: People Skills***
   Communication
   Appraisal
   Coaching and counseling
   Leadership style
   Time management
   Objective: (1) Utilize principles of communication and appraisal to improve productivity and supervisory effectiveness.
   (2) Identify and improve your own leadership style.
   (3) Identify time-wasters and develop a time-management plan.

4.   ***Supervisory Skills: Tools of Work Analysis and Improvement***
   Techniques of methods analysis and work improvement for the purpose of identifying productivity improvement opportunities
   Objective: Utilize these techniques on the job to identify opportunities and as a tool for problem solving.

5.   ***Supervisory Skills: Problem Definition and Analysis***
   Problem definition
   Problem analysis
   Identifying, testing, and verifying the problem cause
   Objective: Use problem analysis discipline for both individual and group use for identifying and explaining the causes of variances from standard or expected results. Use the technique to define the problem associated with achieving the productivity objective.

6.   ***Supervisory Skills: Decision Making***
   Overcoming the cause of the problem
   Decision statement and decision criteria
   Developing alternative courses of action
   How to evaluate alternatives
   How to test the decision
   Objective: Objectively utilize rational decision-making process to determine best alternative means for

Session	Topic

achieving productivity improvements. Document
the process for subsequent action planning.

7.   ***Supervisory Skills: Action Planning***
Stating the improvement target
Documenting the problem and decision analysis
The information summary
The work breakdown structure
Major milestones and action steps
Scheduling the activities
Coordinating the plan
Implementation and follow-up
Objective: Develop a documented, approved, coordinated
action plan for achieving the previously
determined productivity improvement objective.
Using the plan as an action document to see that
the results happen.

IMPLEMENTING A PRODUCTIVITY IMPROVEMENT PROGRAM
The Action Plan

CHAPTER 16

The action plan is where it all comes together.
—Joel Ross

In many respects, the first fifteen chapters of this book are a prelude to developing an action plan for starting a company productivity improvement program. Such a suggested plan makes up the remainder of this chapter.

For those companies already involved in a program, this plan will serve as a checkoff list for further refinement and modification. For those companies deciding to begin a program, the plan will provide a roadmap of actions to be taken. In either case, the content of the plan is not cast in bronze. It is and should be flexible and changed to meet the particular needs of the organization.

Finally, I remind you that each major milestone and action step (subtopic) is discussed in the related chapter of the book. You may wish to refer to the appropriate description as an aid in developing and implementing your own plan.

PRODUCTIVITY IMPROVEMENT PROGRAM

action plan ⟶

Department _____

Name _____

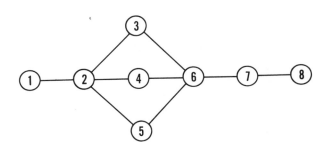

an action plan

MAJOR MILESTONES

1. Getting Organized
2. Appraisal
3. Awareness
4. Productivity Management
5. Measurement
6. Quality of Work Life
7. Management by Objectives
8. Training

	Start	Complete	Assigned To

Getting Organized

1.1 GET TOP-LEVEL ACCEPTANCE AND INVOLVEMENT

    1.11 Set goals and objectives for the program _____ _____ _____

    1.12 Develop a selling plan and a presentation _____ _____ _____

    1.13 Prepare a proposal for presentation and acceptance (Who, What, Why, When, Where, How) _____ _____ _____

1.2 DEVELOP PROGRAM STRUCTURE AND ORGANIZATION

    1.21 Establish composition and duties of: _____ _____ _____
STEERING COMMITTEE
PRODUCTIVITY COUNCIL
PRODUCTIVITY COORDINATOR
UNION–MANAGEMENT
   COMMITTEE
JOINT LABOR–MANAGEMENT
   COMMITTEE

    1.23 Identify personnel _____ _____ _____

    1.24 Establish meeting & agenda _____ _____ _____

    1.25 Identify funding, budget & resource allocation _____ _____ _____

    1.26 Establish composition & duties of additional teams or groups having

**administrative and/or
implementation
responsibility:**
MEASUREMENT TEAMS
MOTIVATIONAL TEAMS
ANALYSIS TEAMS
SPECIAL ASSIGNMENT TEAMS

Appraisal

**2.1   CHECK YOUR READINESS
TO BEGIN**

**2.11 Are you sure you want to
increase productivity? It
means change in
methods, systems, and
managerial climate
regarding people.** ☐

**2.12   Are you ready to start? Do
you have:**
GOOD EMPLOYEE & UNION
   RELATIONS? ☐
WORKING ENVIRONMENT? ☐
WILLINGNESS TO SHARE
   BENEFITS? ☐
POTENTIAL FOR
   MEASUREMENT? ☐
WILLINGNESS TO LISTEN TO
   PEOPLE? ☐
FLEXIBLE TECHNOLOGY & WORK
   ORGANIZATION? ☐
SERIOUSNESS ABOUT
   IMPROVING
   PRODUCTIVITY? ☐
A BELIEF THAT PERFORMANCE
   DEPENDS SUBSTANTIALLY
   ON HUMAN RESOURCES ☐

**2.2   IDENTIFY AREAS FOR
APPRAISAL AND
IMPROVEMENT**

2.21 Overall control. Is there a
system in place (ROI,
Management Audit,
Strategic Planning, etc.)
so the board or CEO can
maintain overall control?   _____ _____ _____

2.22 Operating systems Sales,
Manufacturing,
Purchasing, etc.   _____ _____ _____

2.23 Support systems. Design,
Personnel, Maintenance,
etc.).   _____ _____ _____

2.24 Administrative systems.
Data Processing,
Accounting, Marketing,
etc.   _____ _____ _____

2.25 Organization climate   _____ _____ _____
regarding human
resources, results
management, bureaucratic
vs. participative style,
upward communications,
etc.

2.26 Personnel system. Do job   _____ _____ _____
descriptions focus on
activity or results?
Appraisal system directed
to results or personal
traits? Compensation
system support
productivity improvement?
Adequate resources
available for training and
development in technical
skills, general management
skills supervisory skills?

2.27 Management systems. Do   _____ _____ _____
good management
practices and productivity
improvement techniques
exist for planning,
organizing, control?

2.28 Company operations. Do   _____   _____   _____
unproductive practices
exist in operations?

2.3 CONDUCT APPRAISAL:
Identify problems and
opportunities

2.31 Conduct survey phase.   _____   _____   _____
Review operating, support,
and administrative
systems and other areas
identified above in 2.2 to
identifying existing
practices in order to seek
out unproductive or
improper methods. This
phase may include an
attitude survey to
determine employee
attitudes regarding
productivity or company
practices and its
management.

2.32 Conduct evaluation   _____   _____   _____
phase. Evaluate the
unproductive methods &
techniques and the
performance of units and
departments for the
purpose of identifying
opportunities for
improvement.

**2.33 Conduct evaluation of the
company's productivity**
record. Compare past   _____   _____   _____
productivity and
performance of the
company using these
comparisons and
measures (or others that
may be more meaningful):

COMPARISON
  Trend over time
  Against management targets
  Against competition & industry

MEASURES—COMPANY
  Growth (sales/employee, sales/
    assets, etc.)

Productivty (output/labor input,
output/material input)
Profitability (ROI, earnings per
share, etc.)

MEASURES—FUNCTION &
DEPARTMENTAL

Selected $\dfrac{\text{Output}}{\text{Input}}$ ratios
appropriate to company such
as engineering payroll/total
payroll manufacturing cost/
warranty cost, etc.

Awareness

3.1 DEVELOP THE MESSAGE OF PRODUCTIVITY

3.11 The *philosophy* is to open the door to innovative ideas and constructive change for improvement.

_____   _____   _____

3.12 The *definition* of productivity as improving (a) the effectiveness of resource utilization, and

(b) the ratio $\dfrac{\text{Output}}{\text{Input}}$

_____   _____   _____

3.13 The *focus* is on results, not activity.

_____   _____   _____

3.14 Why productivity?:

_____   _____   _____

NATIONAL LEVEL
  Decline in U.S. (statistics)
  Reasons for decline
  Benefits (stop inflation, improve
    real income, growth, survival of
    free enterprise, decrease
    unemployment, etc.).

COMPANY LEVEL
  Develop statistics for company
    relative to industry
  Reasons for individual company
    decline
  Benefits (ROI, more job
    advancement opportunities,
    more capital for investment
    in technology, job security,
    competitive position, customer
    satisfaction, meet cost
    pressures, etc.).

INDIVIDUAL LEVEL (WHAT'S IN IT
  FOR ME?)

Recognition, reward, personal
  success & growth, job factors
  incuding responsibility &
  independence, better job
  content and satisfaction,
  reduction of waste and
  conservation of resources, job
  security, improvement of
  communications, etc.

**3.15 The *objectives* of
company program:**   _____ _____ _____

ACHIEVE MEASURABLE
  IMPROVEMENTS

RECOGNIZE EMPLOYEES FOR
  CONTRIBUTION

IMPROVE THE QUALITY OF
  WORKING LIFE AND JOB
  SATISFACTION

DEVELOP PROGRAMS THAT WILL
  ENHANCE PRODUCTIVITY
  IMPROVEMENT

**3.16 Demonstrate the leverage
of productivity.**

DEVELOP FIGURES TO SHOW
  HOW MINOR PRODUCTIVITY
  IMPROVEMENTS IMPACT THE
  BOTTOM LINE.

**3.17 Five ways to increase
productivity:**   _____ _____ _____

COST REDUCTION	$\dfrac{\text{OUTPUT STABLE}}{\text{INPUT DOWN}}$
MANAGING GROWTH	$\dfrac{\text{OUTPUT UP}}{\text{INPUT UP BY LESSER AMOUNT}}$
WORKING SMARTER	$\dfrac{\text{OUTPUT UP}}{\text{INPUT STABLE}}$
PARING DOWN	$\dfrac{\text{OUTPUT DOWN}}{\text{INPUT DOWN BY GREATER AMOUNT}}$
WORKING EFFECTIVELY	$\dfrac{\text{OUTPUT UP}}{\text{INPUT DOWN}}$

**3.2 TAKE RELATED
ORGANIZATIONAL ACTIONS
TO GET AWARENESS**

3.21 **Establish Labor– Management Committee and get endorsement & commitment from the union.** ———— ———— ————

3.22 **Integrate responsibility for productivity improvement with regular line organization.** ———— ———— ————

3.23 **Establish a system for measuring, evaluating, and reporting results.** ———— ———— ————

3.24 **Integrate with executive compensation.** ———— ———— ————

3.25 **Get level-to-level commitment from top management to work teams.** ———— ———— ————

3.3 **GET AWARENESS THROUGH COMMUNMICATIONS**

3.31 ***Meetings*, conferences, discussion programs, association meetings, and with customers and suppliers.** ———— ———— ————

3.32 **Media:** ———— ———— ————
BROCHURES AND NEWSLETTERS
    TO INCLUDE PUBLICITY OF
    TEAM ACHIEVEMENTS,
    REWARDS & RECOGNITION,
    INDUSTRY NEWS.
EXTERNAL MEDIA SUCH AS
    NEWSPAPERS, TRADE
    JOURNALS, ASSOCIATION
    NEWS.
VIDEOTAPES FOR AWARENESS
    & TRAINING.
A PERSONAL LETTER FROM TOP
    OPERATING OFFICER GIVING

REASONS FOR EFFORT &
RUNDOWN OF COMPANY
ACTIONS. INCLUDE A FEW
WORDS FROM UNION
PRESIDENT.

3.33 Programs:

"PRODUCTIVITY INCENTIVE
PROGRAM"
RECOGNITION OF SUBMISSION
WITH GIFT CERTIFICATE OR
AWARD
LUNCHEONS WITH PLANT
MANAGEMENT FOR WINNERS
PUBLICITY FOR WINNERS

3.4 NEW OR MODIFIED PROGRAMS TO FOCUS ON PRODUCTIVITY AND AWARENESS

3.41 These may include measurement, idea suggestion, incentives for group and/or individuals, job development, appraisal system, recognition & reward, training, work and procedures analysis, MOB, etc.

Productivity Management

4.1 DEVELOP AN INFORMATION BASE

4.11 The productivity information library:

BIBLIOGRAPHY OF BOOKS,
ARTICLES, FILMS
GOVERNMENT & INDUSTRY
SOURCES (BUREAU OF LABOR
STATISTICS, AMERICAN
PRODUCTIVITY CENTER,
TRADE ASSOCIATION, ETC.)
LIST AREAS WHERE MORE
INFORMATION IS REQUIRED.

4.12 Company information: _____ _____ _____
DIRECT VS. INDIRECT COSTS
OFFICE COSTS
COMPANY MEASURES

4.13 Industry information: _____ _____ _____
TECHNOLOGY IN THE INDUSTRY
LABOR SAVINGS IN
   TECHNOLOGY
INDUSTRY PRODUCTIVITY
   MEASURES

4.2 PLANNING PRODUCTIVITY

**4.21 Incorporate productivity
into corporate strategy
and major objectives.**   _____ _____ _____

**4.22 Establish goals and
objectives and quantitative
targets for productivity
improvement.**   _____ _____ _____

**4.23 Integrate productivity
planning into regular
business planning.
Require managers to "buy
into" productivity
improvement.**   _____ _____ _____

**4.24 Develop action-planning
format for:**   _____ _____ _____
OVERALL PRODUCTIVITY
   PROGRAM
UNITS, FUNCTIONS,
   DEPARTMENTS
GROUPS AND INDIVIDUALS

4.3 ORGANIZING FOR PRODUCTIVITY

**4.31 Complete action in
section 1.0 above (getting
organized).**   _____ _____ _____

**4.32 Identify supporters of the
program.**   _____ _____ _____

4.33   Review Japanese experience with quality circles.   _____ _____ _____

4.34   Organize Productivity Improvement Teams (PIT) and establish their duties and functions.   _____ _____ _____

4.35   Establish work skills training for work teams (PIT).   _____ _____ _____

4.4   CONTROL THE PROGRAM

4.41   Select standards—those total-factor, partial-factor & departmental measures that suggest monitoring by the Productivity Council.   _____ _____ _____

4.42   Integrate reporting into existing system or design new system. *Keep it simple!*   _____ _____ _____

4.43   Track and display results so that involved persons can watch progress and correct deviations from *expected results.*   _____ _____ _____

Measurement

5.1   GET SUPPORT FOR THE MEASUREMENT SYSTEM

5.11   Develop proposal and "sales pitch" to include: _____ _____ _____
"WHY HAVE MEASURES?" (TO

BETTER MANAGE WORK,
WORKERS, AND YOURSELF)
COMPANY MEASURES AND
TRENDS SALES/EMPLOYEE,
UNITS/MAN-HOUR, ETC.)

5.2 REVIEW THE LITERATURE AND EXPERIENCE OF OTHERS ON THE USE OF FINANCIAL AND ACCOUNTING SYSTEMS FOR MEASURING PRODUCTIVITY

———————   ———————   ———————

5.3 SELECT PERSONNEL FOR MEASUREMENT TEAMS

———————   ———————   ———————

5.4 SELECT CONCEPTS AND UNITS OF MEASUREMENT

5.41 Develop overall measures

———————   ———————   ———————

TOTAL FACTOR PRODUCTIVITY

$$\frac{\text{TOTAL OUTPUT}}{\text{LABOR + MATERIALS + ENERGY + CAPITAL}}$$

PARTIAL FACTOR PRODUCTIVITY

$$\frac{\text{TOTAL OUTPUT}}{\text{LABOR INPUT}}, \frac{\text{TOTAL OUTPUT}}{\text{MATERIAL INPUT}}, \text{ETC.}$$

5.42 Develop measures for each key function and/or department.

———————   ———————   ———————

Examples

QUALITY ASSURANCE   UNITS
RETURNED FOR WARRANTY
REPAIR AS A % OF UNITS
SHIPPED.
MATERIALS STORAGE   PARTS
PICKING TIME, STORAGE PER
SQUARE FOOT, STOCKOUT
RATE.

5.43 Establish industry measures:

———————   ———————   ———————

REVIEW SOURCES FOR INDUSTRY
MEASURES (BUREAU OF
LABOR STATISTICS, TRADE
ASSOCIATION, ETC.).

ANALYZE AND COMPARE YOUR
MEASURES WITH THOSE IN
THE INDUSTRY (COMPANY
DATA, INDUSTRY DATA,
NATIONAL DATA).

**5.44   Individual and team
measures:**
ESTABLISH A **RESULTS-ORIENTED** FORMAT
FOR SETTING INDIVIDUAL AND
TEAM MEASURES AND
PRODUCTIVITY
IMPROVEMENT OBJECTIVES.
REQUIRE SPECIFIC
STATEMENTS OF **RESULTS
EXPECTED** (NOT ACTIVITY),
TIME TO COMPLETE, AND
COST.

**5.45   Establish an organization-
wide system for measuring
"indirect" or "white-collar"
or "service" employees.**
DEFINE HOMOGENEOUS
GROUPS OF ACTIVITIES THAT
COMPRISE BASIC
ORGANIZATIONAL
FUNCTIONS (PERSONNEL,
PURCHASING, ETC.).
DEFINE OUTPUT INDICATORS
THAT "DRIVE" THE ACTIVITIES
(SEE CHAPTER 3).
RELATE OUTPUT INDICATORS AS
A DETERMINANT OF
RESOURCES ASSIGNED TO
AND AS A MEASURE OF
PRODUCTIVITY FOR THE
ACTIVITIES IN THE FIRST
STEP.

**5.46   Integrate measurement
system with existing
management information/
control system(s). *Keep it
simple!***

**5.5   CONSIDER INDUSTRIAL
ENGINEERING AND WORK
METHODS TECHNIQUES FOR**

SETTING MEASURES AND
STANDARDS BUT
ENCOURAGE PARTICIPATION
BY THE INDIVIDUALS
INVOLVED   _____ _____ _____

5.6 **GET COMMITMENT FROM   _____ _____ _____
     TARGET GROUPS** (Get them
     involved and obtain their
     endorsement in the early stages.)

5.7 **PERFORM COST-BENEFIT
     ANALYSIS TO DETERMINE IF
     MEASUREMENT IS WORTH
     THE COST**   _____ _____ _____

5.8 **IMPLEMENT AND FOLLOW   _____ _____ _____
     UP** (Determine the need for
     modification or redesign.)

Quality of Work Life

6.1 **ESTABLISH UNION–
     MANAGEMENT OR EMPLOYEE-
     MANAGEMENT QWL AND
     PRODUCTIVITY COMMITTEE**

     6.11 **Appraise QWL   _____ _____ _____
           environment in company.**

     6.12 **Research what others _____ _____ _____
           have done.**

     6.13 **Establish topical agenda _____ _____ _____
           for committee meeting.**

     6.14 **Set up organizational _____ _____ _____
           relations.**

6.2 **ESTABLISH AND
     DISSEMINATE PARTICIPATIVE
     MANAGEMENT CLIMATE IN
     COMPANY** (Use policies,

performance appraisals,
supervisory development,
incentives, etc.)   _____ _____ _____

**6.3 ORGANIZE PRODUCTIVITY
IMPROVEMENT TEAMS (PIT),
QUALITY CIRCLES (QCS) OR
OTHER PARTICIPATIVE,
PROBLEM-SOLVING TEAMS**
(Train in techniques of problem
solving and work methods.)   _____ _____ _____

**6.4 ESTABLISH JOB-
DEVELOPMENT SYSTEM**
(Allows employees to have
discretion concerning how a
job is to be done.)   _____ _____ _____

**6.5 ESTABLISH INCENTIVES AND
FEEDBACK** (Promote setting of
realistic objectives and receiving
of feedback concerning progress.
Use such techniques as MBO,
team and individual goal
setting, self-control, recognition
and appraisal.)   _____ _____ _____

Management by Objectives

**7.1 INTEGRATE MBO WITH
PRODUCTIVITY
IMPROVEMENT PROGRAM**

7.11 Each supervisor develops: _____ _____ _____
AN OBJECTIVE FOR ONGOING
  OPERATIONS
A PRODUCTIVITY IMPROVEMENT
  OBJECTIVE

**7.12 Establish organization   _____ _____ _____
"hierarchy of productivity
improvement objectives,"
integrating these with
productivity measurement
system and business
planning system.**

7.13 Set up linear organization chart to track progress toward objectives established for:
KEY RESULT AREAS
ONGOING FUNCTIONAL
     DEPARTMENTS
PRODUCTIVITY IMPROVEMENT
     OBJECTIVES

7.2 INSTITUTIONAL MBO   _____   _____   _____

7.21 Document and integrate with job definition by expected results and job description. Relate performance appraisal to productivity and results.

Training

8.1 ORGANIZE FOR TRAINING

8.11 Research what others have done.   _____   _____   _____

8.12 Establish duties of council, committees, teams, coordinators, training department, etc.   _____   _____   _____

8.13 Determine in-house resources and capabilities.   _____   _____   _____

8.14 Take an inventory of human resources—skills on hand and skills required. Forecast training needs.   _____   _____   _____

8.2 STRUCTURE THE PROGRAM

8.21 Awareness and introductory survey of   _____   _____   _____

productivity. (Why? Measurement, etc. per section 3.1.)

8.23 Fundamentals of management. (Plan, organize, control, etc.)   _____   _____   _____

8.24 Supervisory skills— technical. (Functional techniques and productivity methods applicable to particular jobs).   _____   _____   _____

8.25 Supervisory skills— work improvement. (Work methods, I/E techniques, problem solving, decision making, action planning, etc.)   _____   _____   _____

8.26 Supervisory skills— people. (Motivation, communications, coaching & counseling, appraisal, leadership style, etc.)   _____   _____   _____

8.3 DEVELOP PROGRAM

8.31 Training methods & learning materials. (Text, cases, exercises, visuals, etc.)   _____   _____   _____

8.32 Instructors and facilities   _____   _____   _____

8.33 Action plan and schedule   _____   _____   _____

8.34 Implement, follow up, and determine effectiveness.   _____   _____   _____

Index